WELSH
HISTORY

A CHRONOLOGICAL OUTLINE

WELSH HISTORY

A CHRONOLOGICAL OUTLINE

Glyn E. German

y Lolfa

First impression: 2015

© Glyn E. German & Y Lolfa Cyf., 2015

Photographs courtesy of the author unless noted otherwise

Cover design: Y Lolfa

ISBN: 978 1 84771 822 8

Published, printed and bound in Wales by
Y Lolfa Cyf., Talybont, Ceredigion SY24 5HE
e-mail ylolfa@ylolfa.com
website www.ylolfa.com
tel 01970 832 304
fax 832 782

Foreword

The scope of this book is huge, as Glyn German notes all the major events of Welsh history from prehistoric times to the present day. There is no doubt that it will be of immense use and interest not only to students, but also to all those who wish to acquaint themselves with any aspects of the history of the Welsh nation. Glyn clearly demonstrates that that history is extremely rich. Indeed, not only does the book cover historical and political events, it also delves into the history of Welsh religious life throughout the ages as well as the literary, artistic and technological achievements of the Welsh people.

Glyn deserves our immense gratitude and sincere respect for the diligence and attention to detail which he has shown in the creation of this invaluable volume. It is a book which can be digested at leisure by browsing through the various periods, as well as serving as a tool for those who need to access concise and precise historical information. It is perhaps ironic that the work should be published in the year in which Wales lost its arguably most talented historian, namely Dr John Davies, or John Bwlch-llan as he was affectionately known by most people. I am convinced that John would have been genuinely excited by the contribution of Glyn German.

I am confident that Glyn's book will be consulted regularly by school pupils of all ages, as well as university staff and students, and, of course, those of us who have a passionate interest in the events of our country's history. Further, in addition to this expertly produced hard copy, I am convinced that social and other electronic media will ensure that the work is accessed on a worldwide basis.

I commend this work and thank Glyn for the enormous effort required to produce it, as well as Gwasg Y Lolfa for agreeing to publish it.

Derec Stockley
Former Director of Examinations and Assessment
CBAC / WJEC

Introduction

When I first began writing this book at the end of 2009, my ambition was to present the early history of Wales and the common culture that binds it with Brittany and Cornwall. As I delved more deeply into the subject, and as my work advanced, it became obvious that Wales shares historical, linguistic and cultural connections not only with the Celtic countries, as one would expect, but also with the nations of continental Europe. My initial objective thus gave way to a more ambitious and comprehensive one, which was to present a chronological outline of Welsh history from the origins of Celtic Britain to modern, present-day Wales.

Another reason that prompted the writing of this book was the relative lack of easily accessible historical tools for students and non-specialists. Indeed the span of time covered here is mind-boggling and one cannot avoid being impressed by the extraordinary heritage of the Welsh nation, a heritage having its roots in the European Iron Age and beyond. In order for the reader to have a coherent and comprehensive overview of the past of this remarkable nation, only the most significant events are recorded for each year. It seemed to me that this method was a simple, straightforward way of presenting the most noteworthy episodes which have marked Welsh history throughout the ages. The method adopted here is thus similar to that found in the early Welsh histories, such as the *Annales Cambriae* and the *Historia Brittonum*. The emulation of the early historians is thus intentional and is designed to provide a broad overview and sense of historical and cultural continuity.

My hope is that this approach will stimulate all those who read this book to dig more deeply into the historical and cultural developments that have made Wales and its people what they are today. In this regard, I found John Davies's *History of Wales*

(1993) and Geraint Jenkins's *Concise History of Wales* (2007) to be particularly rich and useful sources. Many others are indicated in the bibliography. Of course, because of the nature of this work, there will be numerous *lacunae* and it is hoped that the reader will be indulgent in this regard.

Finally, this book focuses not only on the historical background of Wales, but also the artistic, religious, social, economic and political aspects that have contributed to the development of the extraordinarily resilient culture of the Welsh people. In this sense, the book highlights the various metamorphoses that Wales has undergone as a nation and the impressive contributions of Welsh men and women, not only in Wales and Great Britain, but also in all those places of the world where the Welsh have settled over the centuries, from Brittany to the United States, Canada, Patagonia, and Australia.

* * *

I would not have been able to write this book without the work of many specialists of Welsh and Celtic studies. In particular, I would like to thank Professor Dafydd Johnston, the head of the Centre for Advanced Welsh and Celtic Studies, Aberystwyth, and his predecessor, Professor Geraint H. Jenkins, as well as Dr Wynne Hellegouarc'h (born Thomas, from Port Talbot), professor at Caen University (France), for having reread my work, for their corrections and many valuable suggestions. Without their assistance, this book would not have been possible. All remaining errors are my own.

I am also grateful to my parents and sister, Morwenna, for their encouragement and especially my brother, Ronan, for having taken the time to prepare the maps.

Finally, I would like to thank the editors of Y Lolfa for their support and for believing in my idea of a chronological presentation of Welsh history.

Contents

List of maps and illustrations

illuminated manuscript by Jean Froissart, Bibliothèque Nationale de France)

Figure 16: Photograph of the abbey of Nouaillé, the Black Prince's headquarters

Figure 17: Illustration of Owain Glyndŵr (*c.*1404)

Figure 18: Map of Wales after the 1536 Acts of Union (inspired by G. Jenkins, 2007)

Figure 19: Cover of the 1588 Welsh Bible (National Library of Wales)

Figure 20: Photograph of Raglan castle (*c.*1646)

Figure 21: Cover of Edward Lhuyd's *Archeologica Britannica* (*c.*1707)

Figure 22: Photograph of Sarah Jane Rees (Cranogwen), by John Thomas (*c.*1879–1889)

Figure 23: Photograph of David Lloyd George, by John Thomas (*c.*1890)

Figure 24: Maps comparing the number of Welsh speakers in 1891 and in 2011 (inspired by G. Jenkins, 2007)

Figure 25: Photograph of Saunders Lewis (*c.*1962)

Figure 26: Photograph of Gwynfor Evans (*c.*1966)

Figure 27: Map of Wales in 1974 (inspired by G. Jenkins, 2007)

Figure 28: Photograph of the miners' strike in the 1980s (*c.*1984–5)

Figure 29: A Cymdeithas yr Iaith demonstration for a Welsh Language Act in Central London (*c.*1993)

Figure 30: Map of Wales in 1996 (inspired by G. Jenkins, 2007)

Chapter 1

Prehistoric Wales, Britain and Western Europe

This chapter explores the first signs of human habitation in Wales. Significantly, Oxford geneticists Sykes (2006) and Oppenheimer (2007) have shown that the oldest human fossils found in Britain (going as far back as 350,000 BC) are unrelated to any living human beings living in the United Kingdom and Ireland today. The majority of modern Britons and Irishmen are directly descended from hunter gatherers who began arriving in these islands around 9,000 BC.

500,000 BC – 350,000 BC: Lower Palaeolithic

First signs of human habitation in Britain are found at Eartham Pit, Boxgrove, near Chichester, West Sussex. Acheulean[2] flint tools and remains of animals are found on the site during an excavation led by Mark Roberts (Institute of Archaeology, University College London) between 1983 and 1996. In 1994, a partial tibia and a tooth from the body of an individual related to the Heidelberg man (600,000 BC – 200,000 BC) are discovered. He probably weighed 80 kilos and was around 6 feet tall.

400,000 BC: Man masters the use of fire in Europe. One of the earliest sites proving this is at Menez-Dregan, Plouhinec (south-western Brittany) where a 400,000-year-old cave-dwelling was excavated in 1985 by the Breton archaeologist, Bernard Hallegouet, and his team. They believe the site was in continuous use for several generations.

250,000 BC – 40,000 BC: Middle Palaeolithic

250,000 BC: Pontnewydd Cave, in the Elwy Valley, Denbighshire. In 1981, one human tooth and part of a jawbone, dating back 230,000 years, are found in this cave, belonging to an 11-year-old Neanderthal boy. It is thought that he belonged to a group of hunters who dwelt in the Elwy Valley during the interglacial period.

125,000–70,000 BC: The caves of Coygan and Laugharne in Dyfed show signs of human habitation during this period.

70,000 BC: Another ice-age (last glacial period or *Devensian*) begins. Northernmost populations move southward into present-day southern France where the weather is more clement.

59,000–37,000 BC: These periods are marked by global warming. Parts of Wales are reoccupied by people of the Mousterian[3] culture who are skilled in the fabrication of flint tools (examples: axes, scrapers and arrow and spear points). The caves of Pontnewydd and Ffynnon Beuno in Clwyd show signs of human habitation during this period.

40,000 BC: *Homo sapiens* reach Europe where they replace the *Homo neanderthalis*.

35,000 BC – 15,000 BC: Upper Palaeolithic

Ten of the 40 Lower Palaeolithic archaeological sites and ten out of the 60 Upper Paleolithic sites in Britain are located in Wales (examples: Paviland and Ffynnon Beuno).

29,000–26,000 BC: The Red Lady of Paviland is discovered by Rev. William Buckland in 1823 in a limestone cave in the Gower Peninsula. More recent research has shown that the 'lady' was in fact a 21-year-old man who, at the time of his death, was covered with red ochre, hence the nickname of 'red lady'. Buckland details this find in his book *Reliquae Diluvianae* (Remains / Relics of the Flood).

o Around this time, the Neanderthals become extinct. The reasons for this are unclear and remain the subject of fierce scientific debate.

24,000–12,000 BC: The temperature in northern Europe drops drastically, ushering in the last major ice age known as the Würm glaciation (cf. Younger Dryas below).

18,000–15,000 BC: On account of the intense cold, what is today Wales is uninhabitable. Low sea levels allow hunter-gathering populations living in Britain to follow the migrating herds of animals towards warmer, more southerly regions of Europe in areas such as the Dordogne valley in southern France.

Chapter 2

Prehistoric Population Movements and the Roots of proto-Celtic Culture

As the title indicates, this section explores the early movements of human populations in prehistoric Europe. The complex cultural and linguistic genesis of the Indo-European language and culture are also examined. Various theories concerning the possible origins and spread of Celtic culture across Europe are presented.

11,000 BC – 5,500 BC: Mesolithic ('Middle Stone Age')

10,800–9,500 BC: The Younger Dryas (or Big Freeze) marks the end of the last ice age. By 9,500 BC – 8,300 BC, Wales is free of glaciers. As mentioned above, the sea-level is far lower than it is today and the English Channel is dry land. Human beings begin returning to Britain on foot from areas in France. This is supported by archaeological and genetic evidence. Oxford geneticist Bryan Sykes (2001) argues that over 80 per cent of the European mitochondrial DNA (traced through the mother) goes back to seven matrilineal clans that lived in Europe at periods ranging between 17,000 and 50,000 years ago. Very recently, University of Turin geneticist, Cavalli-Sforza (et al., 2000), also concludes that around 80 per cent of Y-Chromosomes (traced through the father's line) originate from ten patrilineal clans living in Europe during the same periods. The conclusion is that the vast majority of native Europeans are descendants of the survivors of this last ice age (cf. Bibliography: Bryan Sykes, Stephen Oppenheimer, and Mario Alinei). This discovery marks a revolutionary break with Colin Renfrew's hypothesis (cf. below).

Most geneticists believe that Britain and Ireland have been continuously inhabited since at least 9,000 BC. It is generally estimated that 60–80 per cent of the modern British population's genetic heritage (90 per cent for the Irish) comes from these original inhabitants, a large portion of whom may have originated in the Iberian Peninsula. According to this view, successive waves of Celts, Romans, Anglo-Saxons, Vikings and Normans would have contributed relatively little to the overall genetic makeup of the island's original hunter-gatherer inhabitants.

o The major Welsh archaeological sites of the Mesolithic period are: Burry Holms (Gower, south Wales), Trwyn Du (Anglesey), and Nab Head (Pembrokeshire). Many stone/flint tools and objects (for instance microliths, points, scrapers and shale beads) were discovered on these sites.

8,300–3,000 BC: The global temperature is 2.5° centigrade warmer than today. Glaciers melt and the seas rise. Britain and Ireland both become islands. The Severn Sea[1] also comes into existence. Some believe that the Welsh legend of the flooding of *Cantre'r Gwaelod* (literally: township of the sea bottom) may be a popular memory of this historical event.[2]

7,600 BC: Human occupation of Star Carr (near Scarborough, in North Yorkshire). It is occupied by approximately 250 people, mainly hunter-gatherers, who live on the meat of red deer, elk, aurochs and wild boar that they hunt with the assistance of dogs.

7,150 BC: Bryan Sykes (2001) extracts mitochondrial DNA

from the Cheddar Man (Gough's Cave, Somerset). His research demonstrates that the Cheddar Man has many direct descendants in Britain (including the history teacher in the local elementary school). Once again, this reinforces the argument that a dominant proportion of the modern British and Irish population has always lived on the islands and directly contradicts the 19th-century 'clean sweep theory' (cf. **AD 602**).

6,500–5,500 BC: New discoveries in genetics and archaeology appear to challenge the view proposed by Colin Renfrew (Professor of Archaeology at Cambridge University). In 1987 he proposed a model known as the Indo-European dispersal theory. According to him, peaceful Indo-European-speaking agriculturalists would have entered Europe from the Middle East at the end of the Mesolithic Period and introduced both farming and the Indo-European languages into Europe, perhaps as early as the 7th millennium BC. This theory rejected the 19th-century idea of an Indo-European invasion by blond-haired, blue-eyed Aryans who would have conquered Europe and subjugated the native populations.

> **Commentary**: Studies in genetics and archaeology presented by Sykes, Oppenheimer and others would thus offer a strong counter-argument in favour of population continuity in Europe since the earliest periods of human habitation. On the surface at least, this would appear to lend some credence to the Palaeolithic Continuity Theory, first proposed by the Italian archaeologist and linguist, Mario Alinei (formerly of the University of Utrecht).
>
> In 1996 he presented a radically new alternative to Renfrew's theory (which is, as yet, marginally accepted in the academic world) and which argues that the Indo-European languages have been spoken in Europe since the

Upper Palaeolithic when the first settlers began arriving from Africa, a far earlier date that has ever been suspected. He bases his conclusions on the lack of archaeological evidence for a massive population movement from the Middle East. His theory is founded on a dating method which compares the Indo-European words for Upper Palaeolithic and Mesolithic implements linked to hunting, fishing and agriculture (i.e. fish hooks, bait, spades, axes, etc.) which he claims demonstrates harmony between the linguistic data and the early archaeological record.

He concludes by saying: 'Any thorough and unbiased analysis of the rich Indo-European record points to a Palaeolithic depth for the earliest layers of Proto-Indo-European vocabulary, and to a very early, Upper Palaeolithic and Mesolithic linguistic differentiation of Proto-Indo-Europeans.' (Alinei, 2003)

As mentioned above, this might be supported by Sykes's 2001 research showing that over 80 per cent of the European genetic stock has been native to the region since the Paleolithic period. The question is thus whether there is necessarily a link between the genetic origins of the ancient European population and the languages they may have spoken. The answer is that there probably can be no definitive association between the two. (NB: Despite the obvious importance of genetic research, it is vital to bear in mind that biological origins are not the essential criterion for determining human identity. Language and culture are far more significant indicators.)

4,800–3,000 BC: Construction of megaliths in Brittany (Barnenez, Carnac). Alinei also believes that western civilization has its roots in Brittany from which its Neolithic culture radiated out along the western fringe of Europe.

4,500 BC – 2,300 BC: Neolithic Period

H. J. Fleure[3] measures the heads and faces of the Welsh people in Plynlimon (Pumlumon, in the Cambrian Mountains, in Ceredigion) and determines that the modern Welsh are descendants of the original inhabitants of the island, skulls being of the same type as those belonging to the earliest skeletal remains. Beginning of agriculture in Europe (the term 'Neolithic Revolution' is first used by Australian archaeologist Gordon Childe[4] in the 1920s to qualify this phenomenon).

3,700 BC: Cattle are domesticated and are plentiful all over Britain suggesting that animal husbandry was mastered. Sheep are also domesticated during this period.

3,500 BC: A megalithic Severn-Cotswold tomb (chamber tomb) and a portal dolmen located next to each other are discovered in Dyffryn Ardudwy, in Gwynedd. Other examples are the *Parc Cwm* long cairn, Swansea; Windmill Hill near Avebury, in Wiltshire; Tinkinswood and St Lythans (both in Glamorgan). The builders of these monuments have clear cultural links with Brittany, which appears to be at the origin of the spread of this megalithic culture.

o   There are 150 dolmen (a Breton word meaning 'table stones', a chambered tomb). They are numerous in north Wales (Anglesey, Gwynedd), and also in south Wales (Vale of Glamorgan and Pembrokeshire), but not in the other counties of central Wales, where stone circles and megaliths are found. Examples: Pentre Ifan (Pembrokeshire) and Bryn Celli Ddu (Anglesey). John Koch[5] and Barry Cunliffe (2008) show there were active links between Wales and the continent via sea routes at this time.

2,900 BC: Appearance of corded ware pottery and stone

Figure 1: The Cromlech of Pentre Ifan, Pembrokeshire (*c.*3,500 BC)

skills. It also suggests that the inhabitants of what are today England and Wales may have shared a common culture and language.

The axe hammer of Preseli (Pembrokeshire), made of dolerite, shows similarities with dolerite axe hammers found at Stonehenge. The Wessex culture[6] (2,600–1,600 BC) is associated with the building of Stonehenge.

2,700–2,200 BC: This is the traditional date for the arrival of the Beaker Folk in Britain. The term Beaker Folk was coined by the Scottish archaeologist John Abercromby (1904) to qualify a type of drinking vessel which was shaped in the form of a beaker (a kind of cup or goblet). This pottery is also found in central Europe (Czechoslovakia, Austria) and Western Europe (Iberia, Jutland and Ireland), and appears to have its origins in an area between southern Russia and the estuaries of the Rhine.

o   Cunliffe believes the Beaker Folk may have spoken an early form of Celtic related to those varieties of Celtic that were spoken in southern France and Iberia. If so, this could reinforce John Koch's recent conclusions about Tartessos inscriptions.

2,600–1,600 BC: Britain's main export during this period is tin, exploited in Cornwall, Devon, Wales and Brittany. It is used to transform copper into bronze. From around 2,200 BC a thriving trade develops throughout Britain and Ireland with population centres in the Iberian Peninsula and the eastern Mediterranean.

2,500 BC: The first towns are built in southern Europe, notably in Spain on the south-eastern coast (example: Almeria in Andalusia).

2,400 BC – 1,400 BC: Early Bronze Age

Most prevalent lifestyle is nomadic pastoralism which survived into recent times in certain parts of Britain: warmer termperatures of the period permitted more extensive exploitation of highland zones.

2,000–1,400 BC: During Bronze Age, the Wessex Culture (example: Breach farm, near Cowbridge) is defined by British archaeologist Stuart Piggott[7] in 1938. Britain has commercial links with the Baltic Sea (from which it obtains amber) but also with Gaul, Germany (jewellery) and Mycenaean Greece (which takes its name from the town of Mycenae, 1,600–1,100 BC). Standardized tin-bronze appears (2,200–2,000 BC), such as the Gold Lunula ('lunula' meaning 'moon crescent' according to Alinei), found near Llanllyfni (Gwynedd) in 1869, a type of necklace made during this era also found mainly in Ireland, but also in Brittany (Kerivoa and Saint-Pôtan, in the Côtes d'Armor), Cornwall (Harlyn Bay), and Scotland (Orbliston, Moray).

o Geneticist Stephen Oppenheimer, supported by Barry Cunliffe, proposes a revolutionary new idea arguing that the Celtic homeland is not in central Europe, as claimed by most 19th- and 20th-century historians, but rather in southern France and the Iberian Peninsula. According to this view, Celtic civilization had its sources in the Atlantic Bronze Age. In recent years, Professor John T. Koch and others have provided evidence that the Tartessos[8] inscriptions of southern Spain may in fact be an ancient variety of Celtic. The earliest textual, archaeological and genetic sources point to an early Iberian and southern French origin for the Celtic homeland as opposed to central Europe (cf. Hallstatt and La Tène cultures). (For another view, cf. Graham Isaac, 2010). Koch's hypothesis could be supported by old insular Celtic legends about the Iberian origins of the Irish and ancient Britons. The suggestion is founded on the supposition that these traditions reflect traces of an ancient popular memory (J. Koch, 2010; Oppenheimer, 2007).

o Cultural and economic bonds would have led to close contacts between cultures from Portugal, Andalusia, Galicia, coastal France and Brittany, the British Isles and Ireland. Koch demonstrates that the Atlantic Bronze Age is maintained by regular maritime exchanges, the major trading centres being Cornwall, Devon, Ireland, Brittany, Galicia, Portugal, and as far as Denmark and the Mediterranean. If true, Celtic culture spread from south to north and then, later, west to east into central Europe.

1,400 BC: End of Neolithic

Metal bronze tools are now used by most people from about 2,500 BC onwards. The temperature is 1° centigrade warmer than today. Oxen are now harnessed and used for ploughing fields.

- o The climate deteriorates after 1,400 BC. On account of dropping temperatures, agriculture is abandoned in the highland zones of Wales, northern England and Scotland.

- o Life in the lowland zones (south and east of the British Isles) is relatively easier. Small fishing vessels made out of leather and wood, called coracles, are already in use during this time. Julius Caesar describes them in his *Commentaries on the Gallic Wars*.

1,400 BC: After this period, the Brythonic tribal groups begin to form. They occupy the same general territories they control when the Romans arrive in 55 BC.

*c.***1,000 BC:** Copper mining expands. Gold objects dating from this period are discovered during the early 19th century. The increase in the number of coin hoards discovered indicates sophisticated economic development. The fact that the hoards were actually buried shows that the inhabitants were probably subjected to more warlike conditions. Examples:

- o Shields made of bronze were found at Moel Siabod (Capel Curig, in Conwy), and at Llanychaearn and Lampeter, both in Ceredigion.

- o The Nannau bucket was found around 1826 near Arthog (Gwynedd). It is made of sheet bronze and is 20 inches high. It is possibly an import or a copy of a central European (Hungarian or Romanian) container.

It may have been a drinking set belonging to an aristocratic family. It has been dated to about 1,100 BC by archaeologists E. G. Bowen and C. A. Gresham in 1967.

1,000–50 BC: Dillon and Chadwick (1979), argue in favour of the traditionally accepted view that the Celtic language was introduced into Britain during the Hallstatt and La Tène periods from central Europe. According to this account, the Celts became culturally and linguistically dominant all over Britain and Ireland around this time. A clearly defined Celtic civilization would have appeared in two phases:

o **1,200–450 BC:** The Bronze Age Hallstatt[9] culture. These dates correspond closely to those given for later Bronze Age, or Atlantic Bronze Age (1,400–600 BC).

o **450 BC – AD 50:** In contrast to the view just expressed, the traditional line is that the La Tène[10] culture, showing a combination of Hallstatt and Scythian influences, originates in southern Russia. The cradle of Celtic civilization would thus be in central Europe from which successive waves of Celts moved westward into Britain and Ireland. They are called *Keltoi* or *Galatae* by the Greeks and *Celtae* or *Galli* by the Romans. Graham Isaac (2010) argues that the linguistic evidence leans in favour of this traditional interpretation.

o **400 BC:** In his 2006 book, *The Origins of the British*, Stephen Oppenheimer argues that the traditional theory of a central-European Celtic homeland was based on a misreading of the Greek historian Herodotus (*c.*484–*c.*425) who stated that the *Keltoi* (Celts) originated from the mouth of the River Danube. Herodotus believed this source to be in the Pyrenees and he clearly states this. According to this view, it is from there that the Celts would have migrated to northern Italy and central and Eastern Europe, not the reverse.

The Golden Age of Celtic Europe

390 BC: P-Celtic speaking Gaulish Celts sack Rome under their chief Brennus.[11]

350–320 BC: Pytheas of Massilia, a Greek explorer, describes his journey in Gaul and Britain. He provides a precise description of Britain (which he calls the *Prettanic Isles*). [12]

o   The inhabitants of Britain during this period speak a form of P-Celtic called Brythonic that is intimately related to Gaulish (spoken across modern Belgium, France, western Germany, Switzerland, northern Spain and northern Italy. Brythonic is the ancestor of Breton, Welsh, Cornish but also Cumbric, a variety of Brythonic once spoken in western and northern England and the lowlands of Scotland as late as the 10th and 11th centuries.

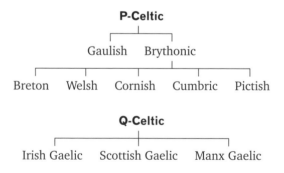

Figure 2: Branches of the Celtic language family

o Nearly 600 hill forts are built in Wales during the period between 300 and 100 BC and at the beginning of the Roman occupation. Twenty-two of the hill forts are more than six hectares and are located near the border with England or in mid-Wales (Llanymynech, Powys, 57 hectares; Y Breiddin, Powys, 28 hectares; Dinas Powys, Glamorgan[13]), probably to defend the territory of the *Cornovii*, the *Deceangli*, and *Ordovices*,[14] whereas 200 hill forts between one and six hectares were built along the coasts: Pen Dinas (Aberystwyth, Ceredigion); Y Bwlwarcau and Mynydd Margam (both near Port Talbot, south Wales); Tre'r Ceiri (Llŷn Peninsula, Gwynedd), presumably to prevent attacks by seaborne invaders from Ireland.

279–278 BC: A large army of Celts, led by another leader named Brennus, fight and lose large numbers of men against a coalition of Greeks. Later, they cross the straits of Thermopylae and ransack Delphi. A legend says that the gold of Delphi was taken by the *Tectosages* to the town of Tolosa (Toulouse), where they later settle.

232 BC: The Celtic-speaking kingdom of Galatia, situated in modern Turkey, is conquered by the kingdom of Pergamon, which is allied with Rome. In the 5th century, Saint Jerome claims the form of Celtic spoken by the Galatians (i.e. the same Galatians addressed by St Paul in his new New Testament letters) is the same as that spoken by the Gauls of France. Note that the name for Wales in modern French is Pays de Galles.

222 BC: The Celts of northern Italy submit to Roman rule.

179 BC: The Celtiberians in northern Spain are overcome by the Romans.

100 BC: The *Belgae* arrive in south-eastern England (Sussex and Kent). Hill fort defences are strengthened. Belgium takes its name from this same tribe. According to Julius Caesar, their capital is called *Venta Belgarum* (modern Winchester). The name is mentioned by Ptolemy (c. 90–168) in his *Geography*.

o Celticists such as Karl Horst Schmidt and Léon Fleuriot, etc. argue that Gaulish and Brythonic were dialects of the same P-Celtic language. Classical writers, such as Caesar and Tacitus, confirm that the Gauls on either side of the channel spoke the same language. As we have seen, modern Welsh is descended from P-Celtic.

58–50 BC: The Gallic Wars – Julius Caesar leads his Roman legions into Gaul (modern France and south-western Germany) to quash a rebellion. He obviously considers the Gauls and Britons to be one people and explains in his 'Gallic Wars' that his invasion of Britain is intended to stop support of the Britons for their continental kinsmen. He claims that Brythonic tribes, such as *Atrebates* and *Belgae* (originally from Belgium) or the *Parisi* (who gave their name to Paris) and *Catuvellauni* originally from northern Gaul, persist in helping their Gaulish brethren against the Romans.

55 BC (summer): Caesar[15] sails from what is today Boulogne-sur-Mer and lands on the south-east coast of Britain with two legions. Extant Brythonic sources imply that he is defeated (cf. Rachel Bromwich, 1978). He returns in 54 BC with four legions, and fights his way along the River Thames. He defeats Cassivellaunus (Welsh: *Caswallawn fab Beli*), King of the *Catuvellauni*[16] (a tribe from the south-east of Britain; meaning 'valorous in battle' and which is directly related to the personal name *Cadwallon*, 7th-century King of Gwynedd).

52 BC: Julius Caesar defeats the Gaulish chieftain, Vercingetorix (chief of the *Arvernes*[17] tribe) at the Battle of Alesia (in Burgundy), thus ending the Gaulish rebellion.

27 BC: Octavius, Julius Caesar's great-nephew, proclaims himself emperor as Augustus marking the beginning of the Roman Empire.

Chapter 3

Celtic Britain and the Roman Empire (AD 30 – AD 405)

The conflict between Britons and Romans eventually gives way to a fusion in areas where the Romans are most densely settled, namely in the lowlands of England (especially in the south-east). In these areas, the Latin language and Roman culture are assimilated by the Brythonic ruling classes, following a process of Romanization that also occurred in Gaul.

If the Romans had not abandoned Britain in the 5th century, Latin, and not Old English, might have become the dominant language of the island, just as in France. Nevertheless, the Britons of the south-west, Wales, and the north-west, clung tenaciously to their Celtic language and culture in spite of the long Roman occupation.

AD 30: Cunobelinus (Welsh: *Cynfelyn*, d. 40),[1] King of the tribe of the *Catuvellauni*[2] (capital: Camulodunum[3], now Colchester) conquers the area from Sussex to Surrey from the *Regnenses* and the *Atrebates*.

40: Caratacus (Welsh *Caradog;* Breton: *Caradec*) and Togodumnus succeed Cunobelinus. Their brother, Amminius, is dispossessed and seeks the assistance of Rome.

43: Aulus Plautius, who later becomes the first governor of Britannia, crosses the channel with 40,000 Roman troops and defeats the *Catuvellauni*. The *Iceni*, living in modern Norfolk and the *Regni* of Sussex are delighted. They see the Romans as their liberators, not conquerors.

The Chronological stages
of the Brythonic language(s)

Brythonic (also called 'Brittonic' or 'British'):
the Celtic language spoken throughout Britain (south of the Forth and the Clyde) until the middle of the 6th century

Late Brythonic:
the latest stage of this language – mid-5th to 6th century

Primitive Welsh:
mid-6th to mid-9th century

Old Welsh:
mid-9th to 11th century (according to Kenneth Jackson, 1953)
8th to 11th century (according to David Willis, 2009)

Middle Welsh:
12th to 14th century

Early Modern Welsh:
early 15th to late 16th century

Modern Welsh:
1588 (the first edition of the Welsh Bible) to the present

The Brythonic roots of the Welsh language

Although the modern Welsh language descends from Brythonic, it is important to remember that, because of linguistic evolution, it no longer bears much resemblance to it. This explains, for instance, the great differences between Brythonic and Middle Welsh names such as Maglocunos-Maelgwn, Vortigern-Gwrtheyrn, Voteporix-Gwrthefyr, Votadini-Gododdin, etc.

47–52: Caractacus mobilizes the Silures, the inhabitants of south Wales. The *Brigantes* (who rule over an area corresponding to Lancashire and Yorkshire) are nominal allies of the Romans and waver in their support of their fellow Britons. The Romans decide to drive a wedge between the *Brigantes* and the *Cornovii*, the *Ordovices* and *Deceangli*.

48: Ostorius Scapula, the new governor of Britannia (AD 47–52), reaches the Dee and defeats the *Deceangli*.[4]

48–79: The Romans wage 13 campaigns in Wales and its borders. Not a single fort is built in the south and east of the British Isles known as the 'lowland zone'.[5]

49: The 20th Roman legion builds a fort in Gloucester providing it with a base from which to attack Wales. Camulodunum, the capital of the *Catuvellauni*, becomes a Roman colony.

51: The *Ordovices* of north-west Wales are defeated and Caractacus seeks the protection of Cartimandua, Queen of the *Brigantes* (43–69). She turns him over to the Romans.

52: The *Silures*[6] defeat a Roman legion, probably the 20th.

60: In order to break the spirit of the Britons, the Romans destroy the druidic sanctuaries on Anglesey (*Ynys Môn*) which is where the druidic priests of Gaul and Britain go for their religious training. Nora Chadwick (1966) describes them as the 'native intellectual class of the early Celtic peoples of Gaul [...] There can be no doubt that the druids were the most enlightened and civilizing spiritual influence in Prehistoric Europe.'

61: Suetonius Paulinus, the Roman governor of Britannia (under Emperor Nero), crushes a revolt led by Boudicca, Queen of the *Iceni*. Henceforth the Britons of eastern England are forbidden to carry weapons.

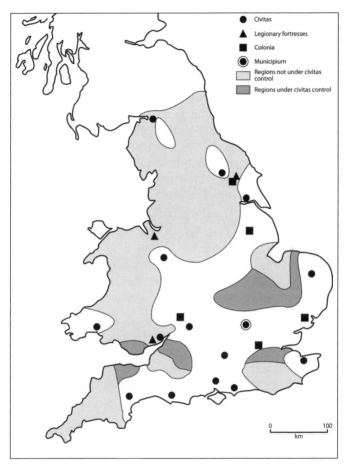

Figure 3: Map of Roman Britain (inspired by David Mattingly, 2007)

67: The 20th *Valeria Victrix* legion establishes a camp at Viroconium (Wroxeter), near Shrewsbury in order to counter hostile natives of the region.

68–69: The 'year of the four Emperors': After Nero commits suicide in AD 68, Galba, Otho, Vitellius, and Vespasian succeed each other as Roman Emperors. In Britannia, Marcus Trebellius Maximus (63–69) resigns from the governorship under pressure from the commander of the 20th legion, Marcus Roscius Coelius, who becomes the new governor. He sends 8,000 men to fight alongside General Vitellius. In AD 69, the next governor, Marcus Vettius Bolanus, arrives in Britain. Meanwhile, Cartimandua is overthrown by her husband, Venutius, and she asks for help from the Romans. The latter are powerless because most of the legions stationed in Britain are fighting in Gaul and Germania.

71: Before being appointed governor of Britannia in the same year by Emperor Vespasian, Petilius Cerealis, then at the head of the 9th *Hispana* legion, builds Eboracum (York, in Yorkshire; *Efrawg* in Welsh[7]), a fort where the 9th legion is based until 117. He uses it as his headquarters to conquer the neighbouring Brigantes.

74: Julius Frontinus,[8] the governor of Britannia, makes an alliance with the Silures and the Ordovices. The headquarters of three of the four legions campaigning in Britain are located on the borderlands of Wales. He may also have built the forts of Isca (Caerleon, south Wales) and Deva Victrix[9] (Chester, also known in Welsh as *Caerlegion*).

75: The 2nd *Augusta* legion (5,500 men) is based in Deva Victrix (Chester), then later in Isca (Caerleon) in south Wales. Under the leadership of Julius Agricola, it pacifies the Silures by romanizing towns such as Venta Silurum (Caerwent) and giving them more autonomy.

78–84: Julius Agricola, the governor of Britannia, finally defeats the *Ordovices*. He is the father-in-law of Tacitus, one of the major Roman historians of the first century and author of *Agricola* and *Germania*.

80: *Lindum Colonia* (*Lincoln: Lindon > *llyn* 'lake' and '[legionary] Colonia'), built around AD 60, becomes a colony after the 9th *Hispana* legion leaves for Eboracum (York).

83: Agricola leads a Roman army against the warlike Caledonians[10] (Caledonia, modern Scotland) and defeats them at the Battle of Mons Graupius.

87: The 20th legion replaces the 2nd *Augusta* legion at Chester (known as Adiutrix).

97: Gloucester (Glevum) becomes a Roman colony under Emperor Nerva bringing Roman power closer to Wales.

117: The 2nd *Augusta* legion has only partial garrisons at Caerleon (which numbers 2,000 inhabitants at this time) suggesting that the relations between the Romans and the local population are becoming more stable. During the same time, the 6th *Victrix* legion replaces the 9th *Hispana* legion in York until 400.

Figure 4: Roman amphitheatre at Caerleon

122: Hadrian's Wall is built during the reign of Emperor Hadrian (117–138), between the River Tyne and the Solway Firth. It has been a UNESCO World Heritage Site since 1987.

127–148: In his *Geography* (Book II), the Greek geographer Ptolemy gives us information (although incomplete on many points) about the organization of the cities in Britain and more particularly the Brythonic tribes of Wales: the *Silures* (south-east Wales), the *Demetae* (south-west Wales), the *Ordovices* (north-west Wales), and the *Deceangli* (north-east Wales).

142: The Antonine Wall (named after Emperor Antoninus Pius, 138–161), 100 kilometres to the north of Hadrian's Wall, is constructed to contain the Picts (north-eastern Scotland) and the Britons, namely, the *Maeatae, Selgovae, Novantae, Damnii,* and *Votadini*, who lived in the lowlands of what is today Scotland.

162: The Romans abandon the Antonine Wall to the Picts, mainly because the supply lines necessary for its defence are stretched to the limit. The Roman legions retreat to Hadrian's Wall.

170: After this date, the forts to the south of the River Usk (near Newport, Monmouthshire) are garrisoned by fewer Roman troops. This suggests improved relations between the Romans and the Silures since 75 (cf. above). Nevertheless, the *Ordovices* continue to resist the Roman occupation and do not seem to be attracted by Roman culture or the high standard of living it offers.

193–197: The Roman army of Britain supports Clodius Albinus, governor of Britain, and names him emperor of Rome. He attempts to seize power from Septimus Severus, the

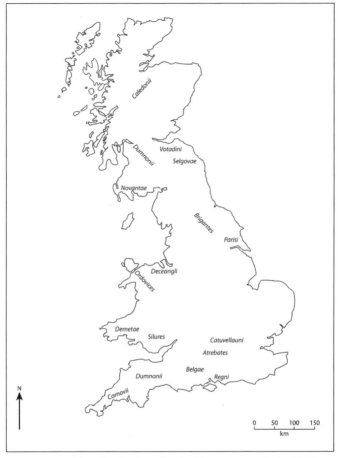

Figure 5: Map of Brythonic tribes (inspired by David Mattingly, 2007)

legitimate Roman emperor. Albinus crosses the channel with his Romano-British troops in 196, but is defeated the next year at *Lugdunum* (the original name of Lyon, in France).

200: *Viroconium* (Wroxeter, Shropshire), *civitas*[11] of Cornovii, is now the fourth largest one in Britain, covering 190 acres. Only *Londinium* (London, 316 acres), *Corinium Dobunnorum* (Cirencester, 217 acres) and *Verulamium* (St Albans, 195 acres) are bigger.

200–230: *Maridunum* (Carmarthen) is the *civitas* of the *Demetae* tribe.

211: Emperor Septimus Severus dies in *Eboracum* (York). The *Votadini* tribe (*Gododdin* in Middle Welsh, cf. **541**) has friendly relations with Rome. Its capital is *Caer Eidyn*, modern Edinburgh, an important kingdom in early Welsh literature.

214: Emperor Caracalla extends citizenship to all freemen throughout the Roman Empire. This has a profound effect on the Romanization of the Britons, especially in what is today England. The Britons of Wales and the north-west of Britain are far less affected by the process of Romanization.

216: Britain is divided into two provinces: *Britannia Superior*, the capital of which is *Londinium*, and *Britannia Inferior*, whose capital is *Eboracum* (York).

237: *Eboracum* (York) becomes a colony under the reign of Philippus II Severus (237–49).

244–284: This is a period of considerable political instability. The Roman legions posted throughout the Roman Empire nominate 55 of their commanders as Emperors of Rome. Gaul is invaded by the Alamanni and the Franks.

250–350: Despite this political instability, Roman Britain prospers, but there is a considerable contrast between the standard of living of the inhabitants in the outlying regions, such as Wales, and those living in the cities.

260: A seven-metre-high stone wall is constructed around

Caerwent, the *civitas* of the *Silures*. It is inhabited by approximately 3,000 to 4,000 people.

- o **286–293:** Carausius (*Carawn*[12] in Welsh), the commander of the Roman fleet (*Classica Britannica*, based in Boulogne), claims independence from Rome. He belongs to the Belgic *Menapii* tribe (whose *civitas* is Cassel in the north of France). In 293, he is assassinated.

293–311: Diocletian divides the Roman Empire into four regions ruled by an *Augustus*, a senior emperor, assisted by a *Caesar* (junior emperor). Gaul, Spain and Britain (capital: Trier) are controlled by Constantius Chlorus (293–305), then Constantine (307–337).

296–305: Constantius Chlorus (the father of the future Emperor Constantine) reunites Britain and Rome, which is now divided into four parts. Wales may have been part of *Flavia Caesariensis* with its capital at Lincoln.

300: Emperor Diocletian reforms the cavalry and a mobile force is created under the command of a new officer called the *Dux Britanniarum* (the duke or leader of Britain). This new unit is based in York. By this time, large numbers of Germanic tribesmen are serving in Britain as part of the Roman army. *Saxons* (from Lower Saxony, near Hanover, in modern-day Germany) and *Frisians*[13] are allowed to settle eastern Britain as *foederatii* (mercenaries). By this time, a Romano-Brythonic and Germanic culture is evolving in eastern England.

306–324: Because of the difficulty of ruling and defending such an enormous political entity, the Roman Empire is divided in two parts. The Western Roman Empire is ruled by Constantine and the Eastern Empire is ruled by Licinius.

310: Individual monks begin to spread Christianity throughout the Western Roman Empire. Those who evangelize in Britain and Gaul have monastic traditions with origins in Egypt.

312: Constantine becomes Emperor of the Western Empire.

313: The Edict of Milan is signed both by Emperors Constantine (Western Empire) and Licinius (Eastern Empire). It marks the official end of persecutions against the Christians.[14] Christianity spreads very quickly thereafter and becomes the official religion of the empire in 380 when Emperor Theodosius I signs the edict of Thessalonica.

314: Three bishops from Britain are present at the council of Arles in southern Gaul (Eborius of York; Restitus of London; and Adelfius of Lincoln).

324: Emperor Constantine (*Custennin* in Welsh), ruler of the Western Roman Empire, defeats and kills Licinius, emperor of the Eastern Empire, thus becoming the only emperor.

o The 5th century *Notitia Dignitatum* provides the names of the forts built along the coast of Britain. The most important forts constructed during this time in Wales are in Cardiff and Caer Gybi, modern-day Holyhead in Anglesey, probably to defend against Irish assaults.

350–360: The Roman *limes* line of fortifications in northern Gaul are overwhelmed by Germanic tribes (Angles, Saxons, Franks, Alemanni, etc.) setting the stage for Germanic incursions into Britain.

350–400: The *Déisi*, an Irish tribe from the region of Waterford, emigrate to Dyfed and Gwynedd. Wales reorganizes its defences against attacks by the *Déisi*.

361–363: Romano-Brythonic troops help to elevate Julian the Apostate as Roman Emperor in Paris. He restores paganism.

367: *Conspiratio Barbarica* (The Barbarian Conspiracy). Roman Britannia is invaded from all directions by a purported alliance of Picts, Irish, and Saxons. A 4th-century Roman historian named Ammianus Marcellinus mentions that General Theodosius, the father of the Roman Emperor, is sent to Britannia to reorganize its defences. As confirmed from excavations in houses of the towns of Verulamium (St Albans) and Cirencester, this leads to a new period of urban prosperity which continues even after the withdrawal of the Roman troops in 410.

383: The Romans may have organized a population movement from south-eastern Scotland (Votadini-Gododdin, cf. **211**) towards north Wales after Magnus Maximus (*Macsen Wledig* in Welsh) leads the Romano-Brythonic army to the continent. This explains the close dynastic and cultural ties between the Welsh and Britons of *Yr Hen Ogledd* (the Old North). Cunedda, the King of Gododdin, is said to have had seven sons who found the seven kingdoms of Wales:

1) *Ceredig* > Ceredigion

2) *Meirion* > Meirionnydd

3) *Edern* > Edeyrnion

4) *Rhufon* > Rhufoniog

5) *Dunod* > Dunoding

6) *Dogfael* > Dogfeiling

7) *Afloyg* > Afflogion[15]

383–388: Magnus Maximus[16] is the *Dux Britanniarum*. As with several governors who preceded him (cf. 244–284), his troops name him as Roman Emperor. At the time, there are already two Emperors of Rome vying for supremacy. Maximus meets the first contender, Gratian, and slays him in battle near Trier, now southern Germany. He rules the northern part of the

Roman Empire from Trier until he attacks Rome in 388. During this expedition, he is killed by Emperor Theodosius (379–395) at Aquileia in northern Italy. Some historians believe his persona may have served as a foundation for stories about King Arthur's campaigns in Gaul and against Rome.

405: Irish marauders under King Niall of the Nine Hostages (*Noígíallach* in Irish, 379–405 or 428)[17] plunder the west coast of Britain, including Wales. More Irish settlers from the *Déisi* tribe arrive in Dyfed and in the Llŷn Peninsula (Llŷn comes from the Irish name *Laigin* which also gave its name to the province of Leinster in Ireland). The kings of Dyfed and Brycheiniog[18] (for example, Eochaid Allmuir, Vortipor, and Tewdos ap Rhain) until the 8th century are direct descendants of the Irish dynasty of Leinster, as is Uí Liatháin (in Anglesey), and are mentioned in the *Historia Brittonum*. Ogham inscriptions written in Irish are found in Pembrokeshire and Carmarthenshire (cf. **549/550**).

Chapter 4

Wales during the Dark Ages

By the mid-5th century, Roman political and cultural domination over Britain had waned. After the Roman army departed, the Britons were forced to defend themselves against marauding Gaelic-speaking Irish and Pictish raiders who attacked the island from the north and west. The greatest threat came from Germanic-speaking Anglo-Saxons who settled the island from mainland Europe.

From the Welsh perspective, the Dark Ages can be marked by several phases:

o   The Christianization of the Britons (4th – 6th centuries)

o   The Anglo-Saxon colonization of the island (5th – 8th centuries)

o   The Christianization of the Anglo-Saxons (7th century)

o   The Viking invasions (8th – 11th centuries)

The gradual decline of Brythonic language and culture in what is today England and south-eastern Scotland had the paradoxical effect of encouraging a distinct Brythonic identity in the west and north, where the Celtic-speaking inhabitants called themselves the *Cymry*, the Welsh.

406–411: Constantine (*Custennin Fendigeid* 'the blessed' in Welsh tradition), whose dynasty is based in Devon (Dumnonia) is commander of the Romano-Brythonic forces. This marks the only truly successful Brythonic attempt to place an emperor on the throne.

o Roman Emperor Honorius recognizes Constantine as ruler of Britain and Gaul. Like Magnus Maximus, ruler of Britain 23 years before him, Constantine leads the army of Britain into Gaul. He makes an alliance with the Gaulish *Bagaudae* (groups of peasants, former slaves, and deserters from the Roman army) and defeats the Germanic invaders who are attempting to occupy Gaul.

o Tensions arise between Constantine and his general, Gerontius (*Gereint* in Middle Welsh). Gerontius's roots are also in *Dumnonia* (Devon), the region of Britain which supplies the greatest number of colonists to Armorica.

o Constantine sends Gerontius to Spain to fight the Germanic *Alans* and *Suebi*. Gerontius is unsuccessful in this attempt and is held responsible by Constantine.

The two then enter into open conflict in 409. Gerontius and his troops recognize Maximus as the new Roman Emperor in Tarragon, Spain.

o The Gothic king, Alaric, captures Rome in 410. During this same year, Emperor Honorius writes his famous letter to the Britons announcing that Roman forces will withdraw and that, henceforth, their defence will be their own responsibility.

o Mounting pressure in Italy leads Emperor Honorius to seek temporary reconciliation with Constantine who controls much of Gaul. Nevertheless, Honorius sends a new army to Arles (south of France) and manages to sow discord between his two enemies, Constantine and Gerontius. After an epic battle, Gerontius is slain along with his wife, Nonnichia. This event has been proposed to be at the origin of the story of the *Mabinogion*'s *Gereint ac Enid* (cf. also Chrétien de Troyes, *Erec and Enid*).

o With Gerontius dead, Honorius turns against Constantine whom he slays in Arles in 411.

418: Pelagius (354–420), a Brythonic monk, goes to Jerusalem in 412, and is declared a heretic during the Council of Carthage in 418. He translates the work of the Greek fathers into Latin and is best known for his role in the so-called 'Pelagian heresy'. Pelagius does not believe in the notion of original sin (man does evil or good by choice, not because it is in his nature). Neither does he believe in the necessity to baptize children at an early age (like modern Baptists).

420–450: Britain is ruled by a Brython by the name of Vortigern. This is not a personal name but rather a Brythonic translation of the *Dux Britanniarum* meaning 'overlord' (*Gwrtheyrn* in Middle Welsh). In keeping with Roman tradition, Vortigern invites Germanic warriors (called *foederati*, mercenaries) to Britain to defend the eastern parts of the island. His authority is strongest in the south of the island. He is opposed by less Romanized Brythonic chiefs in the west and north who call themselves the *Cum-brogi*, 'the compatriots' (*Cymry*).

428: According to the Welsh historian Nennius (author of the *Historia Brittonum* / History of the Britons), Vortigern offers the Isle of Thanet off the coast of Kent to the Anglo-Saxons. In exchange, he requests their assistance in fighting the Picts, Gaels and other Germanic warrior bands. This event is attested by Gildas, Bede, Nennius, and the *Anglo-Saxon Chronicle*.

o St Germanus of Auxerre (*Garmon* in Welsh) is sent by Pope Celestin I to Britain, along with Bishop Lupus of Troyes, to put an end to the Pelagian heresy and to lead a military expedition against the Picts. He accomplishes his missions successfully. Constantius of Lyon mentions in his *Vita Germani* (Life of Saint Germanus) that, before Germanus becomes the Bishop of Auxerre (around 420), he is the lord / commander of the territory extending from Armorica to modern Rouen (*Dux Tractus Armoricani et Nervicani*). That is probably one of the reasons why he is chosen to lead a military expedition against the Picts and the Saxons. According to traditional accounts, the latter flee when they hear Germanus's newly-converted Christian soldiers sing 'Alleluia' near Mold (north Wales).

o One of Germanus's first disciples is Dubricius (*Dyfrig* in Welsh, 425–505; *Saint Devereux* in French). Based in Erging (Archenfield, corresponding to modern Herefordshire), he evangelizes south-eastern Wales. He is said to have died on Bardsey Island.

o Brioc, originally from Ceredigion, is another of Saint Germanus's disciples. Several towns in Brittany still bear his name: Saint Brieuc (Côtes-d'Armor) and Briec (north of Quimper). Llandyfriog in Wales is named after him.

o Germanus's successor is named Illtud, another of his disciples. He consolidates the foundations of Brythonic Christianity on the island and founds the monastery of Llanilltud (Llantwit Major) in the Vale of Glamorgan (cf. 12th century for early map of monastic establishments). It is here that the colonization of Brittany is organized (cf. Lanildut, on the north-west coast of Brittany). Almost all the early leaders of Irish monasticism were trained in Wales.

Somewhere between 445 and his death in 448,

Germanus of Auxerre leads a final mission in Britain with Severus of Trèves (Trier) although recent scholarship questions the occurrence of this second expedition. There are four churches in north Wales dedicated to Saint Germanus. Once the seat of a bishop, Saint Germans[1] in Cornwall also honours this saint (cf. also Sant Jermen, Finistère, Brittany).

446: In his *Ecclesiastical History of England*, the Venerable Bede (*c.*710–730) writes that the Saxons, Angles and Jutes establish kingdoms in Britain, respectively in modern East Anglia, Mercia, and Northumbria.

- o According to Gildas's *De Excidio et Conquestu Britanniae* (*c.*540, Part I), the Britons send a letter to Agitius[2] ('the last of the Romans') to request his help.

- o Ambrosius Aurelianus[3] (*Emrys Wledig*[4] in Welsh) is well known thanks to Gildas who also calls him the 'last of the Romans' and credits him with a great victory over the Anglo-Saxons at Mount Badon. This same victory is later attributed by Nennius to King Arthur (cf. **496**).

449: Based on the Venerable Bede and the *Anglo-Saxon Chronicle*, this is the traditional date given for the arrival of the Anglo-Saxon chieftains, Hengist and Horsa.

- o Nennius relates how 'the tyrant' (Vortigern), founder of the kingdom of Powys, becomes enthralled by the beautiful Rowenna, daughter of Hengist. At some point between 400 and 430, he agrees to organize a banquet for Brythonic and Anglo-Saxon chieftains. All pledge to disarm to avoid potential conflict. However, in exchange for Rowenna's romantic favours, Vortigern allows the Anglo-Saxons to conceal their weapons. In the middle of the banquet, they suddenly turn on their unsuspecting Brythonic guests killing 300 of their chieftains. This story of Saxon deceit, known as the 'treachery of the long knives', was never forgotten by the Welsh and the term was later applied to a 19th-century English government study on Welsh education (cf. the 1847 Treachery of the Blue Books).

460–480: Another wave of Brythonic migration to Armorica (Brittany) takes place. These migrations, however, were probably not due to direct pressure from the Anglo-Saxons, as is often claimed. At this time, the Anglo-Saxons controlled only certain coastal areas in eastern Britain. The Britons who left for Armorica originated from areas in the south-west and west of the island that had remained relatively unaffected by their presence (cf. Chadwick, 1969). Fleuriot (1980) suggests that, if there was military pressure on the Britons during this time, it came from Irish raiders and colonists coming from the west.

469: According to Jordanes, a 6th-century chronicler, Riothamos, the King of Britons, sends 12,000 troops to help Emperor Anthemius in Gaul against the Goths. Fleuriot believes that *Riothamus* (< **Rigo-thamos*), like Vortigern (Overlord), is a Brythonic title given by his troops, the meaning being 'Great or all-powerful king', his personal name being Ambrosius Aurelianus. His warriors are said to have settled in Brittany.

470: Cadwallon Llawhir (the long hand, d. 534), King of Gwynedd (and grandson of Cunedda, cf. **383**), defeats the Irish at Cerrig y Gwyddel, near Trefdraeth, Anglesey. He supposedly expels them from Wales and brings Anglesey into the kingdom of Gwynedd.

470–540: The *Annales Cambriae* and Nennius's *Historia Brittonum* claim King Arthur (if he really existed) lives during this period. Medieval authors later romanticize his deeds in

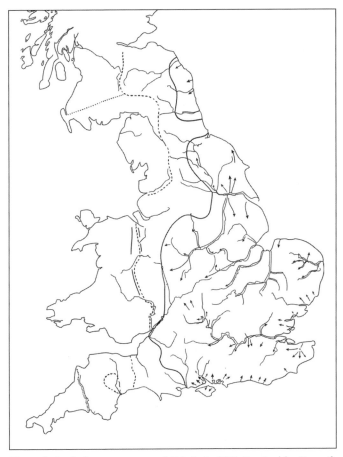

Figure 6: Anglo-Saxon conquest of Britain (c.449) (inspired by Kenneth Jackson, 1953)

the Arthurian Cycle. Examples of Welsh-language literary texts are 'Culhwch and Olwen' and 'The Dream of Rhonabwy', both of which are preserved in 'The White Book of Rhydderch' and

'The Red Book of Hergest'. French author Chrétien de Troyes shares the same (unknown) sources as the Welsh tales of Peredur (French *Perceval*), Owain[5] (French *Yvain*) and Gereint and Enid (cf. **406**).

490 (or 500)–570: Gildas, originally a Strathclyde[6] Brython, is thought to have founded the monastery of Rhuys, near Vannes, Brittany. It is one of the three principal monasteries in Brittany along with St Méen (*Sant Mewen*) and Landevennec. Gildas is the author of the *De Excidio et Conquestu Britanniae* (*c.*530), the most detailed contemporary source for the Anglo-Saxon conquest of Britain. Many towns and parishes of Brittany still bear his name (Saint Gildas de Rhuys, St Gildas des Bois, Loqueltas, etc). Gildas attributes the invasions to the sinfulness of the Brythonic kings. In a ferocious diatribe he attacks Maglocunos (*Maelgwn Gwynedd* or *Maelgwn Fawr* in Welsh), Cunedda's great-grandson (cf. **534–549**). In the 12th century, Caradog of Llancarfan writes his *Vita Gildae*. Another tradition tells that he was the student of Illtud at Llanilltud (Llantwit Major) in Glamorgan, along with St David, St Samson and St Paul-Aurelian.

495: The Saxon king, Cerdic (d. 534), founds the House of Wessex and gains authority over the area of Hampshire. Some scholars propose that his name may be Brythonic suggesting that he may have been an Anglicized Brython.[7]

496: Gildas claims that the Britons, led by Ambrosius Aurelianus (*Emrys Wledig*), a Romano-Brythonic leader, win an overwhelming victory over the Anglo-Saxons at the Battle of Mount Badon (maybe Badbury Rings, near Bath), fought in the year of his birth. Scholars propose that the battle was fought between 490 and 516. Writing at the beginning of the 9th century, the Welsh historian Nennius claims King Arthur was the victor. Thereafter, in Welsh, French and English histories and romances, it is Arthur who is credited with this victory.

508: According to the *Anglo-Saxon Chronicle*, the King of Britons, Natanleod, and 5,000 of his men are killed by Cerdic of Wessex and his son, Cynric.

515–530: According to the *Annales Cambriae*, Arthur is killed at the Battle of Camlan. Some situate this site near the River Camel, Camelford, in Cornwall.

515–590: According to Sir Ifor Williams (1975), Taliesin (534– 599), a Brythonic bard, composed heroic poems dedicated to various Brythonic kings of his age, presumably his patrons: Kynan Garwyn (king of Powys, *c.*550–*c.*600, cf. *Trawsganu Kynan Garwyn mab Brochfael*), Urien Rheged and Owain ab Urien Rheged (cf. *Marwnat Owein*).

520: Samson of Dol (Brittany) is a student at the abbey of Llantwit (Llanilltud) Major. Like David (Dewi), he is a disciple of Illtud. His fellow student is Paulinus Aurelianus (a native of Glamorgan) who also emigrates to Brittany and whose name is preserved in the town of St Pol-de-Léon in north-western Brittany.

530–589: David (*Dewi* in Welsh), a disciple of Illtud, founds a monastery at Glyn Rhosyn where an important Christian community develops. He is a contemporary of Teilo, Padarn and Deiniol. According to tradition, David was of the house of Ceredigion and promoted the most ascetic practices of early monastic tradition (hard work, vegetarianism and temperance; cf. **310**). Saint Davids Cathedral, Pembrokeshire (founded in the early 6th century), is at the heart of a long-lasting quarrel with Rome and England concerning the choice for the establishment of an archbishopric of Britain (cf. **597** and **1128** below). He becomes the patron saint of Wales and his saint's day is celebrated every 1 March.

530–700: Another wave of migration to Brittany. These may very well have been precipitated by conflicts with the pagan Anglo-Saxons, but also constant raids from the West by the Irish.

534–549: Maglocunos (*Maelgwn Fawr* in Welsh) is King of Gwynedd. According to Gildas, he becomes King after killing his uncle, perhaps Owain Ddantgwyn (White Tooth), King of Rhos. In his *De Excidio*, Gildas condemns Maelgwn as the archetypal Brythonic king: a vain, power-hungry, sexually immoral murdering tyrant.

541: According to Nennius's *Historia Brittonum*, the poet Aneirin is born in this year. He is said to have composed a collection of panegyric poems dedicated to 300 Brythonic warriors who were slain by the Angles (and perhaps Brythonic allies) at the Battle of Catraeth (Catterick, in North Yorkshire). The collection, preserved in *Llyfr Aneirin* (c.1250), is better known as the *Gododdin*, one of the masterpieces of early Welsh literature. The title itself, the *Gododdin,* takes its name from the Brythonic tribe which ruled over south-eastern Scotland.[8] The oldest form of this tribal name is *Votadini,* given by Ptolemy in the first century. The capital of *Gododdin* was *Din Eidyn*, modern Edinburgh. Aneirin and Taliesin belong to the Early Poets (*Y Cynfeirdd*), composers of the Old Poetry (*Hengerdd*).

Y Gododdin (VIII)

Gwŷr a aeth Gatraeth, oedd ffraeth eu llu,
Glasfedd eu hancwyn a gwenwyn fu,
Trichant trwy beiriant yn catäu,
A gwedi elwch tawelwch fu.
Cyd elwynt lannau i benydu,
Dadl ddiau angau i eu treiddu.

Warriors went to Catraeth, their host was swift,
Fresh mead was their feast and it was bitter,
Three hundred fighting under command,
And after the cry of jubilation there was silence.
Though they went to churches to do penance,
The certain meeting with death came to them.

(Source: A.O.H Jarman, 1990, p. 7)

547: Ida (d. 559 or 560), an Anglian king, creates the nucleus of the kingdom of Bernicia (Brynaich). The name of Bernicia is thought to be of Celtic origin.

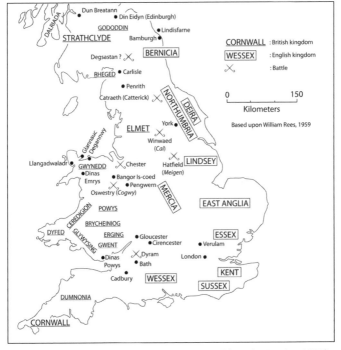

Figure 7: Britons and English, 500–700 (inspired by John Davies, 1993)

549–550: The Yellow Plague (said to come from Egypt) devastates Britain. Maelgwn Gwynedd is said to have died of this plague.

o Vortiporix (*Gwrthefyr* in Welsh, *Gartbuir* in Irish), King of Dyfed, also dies around this time. His name is preserved in an Ogham and a Latin inscription in 1895 in the church of Castell Dwyran (Carmarthenshire) and is now at the Carmarthenshire County Museum in Abergwili. He is thought to have been the descendant of Eochaid Allmuir (*Eochaid [from] Overseas*) mentioned in the Irish genealogy *Expulsion of the Déisi*. About 40 stones with Ogham and Latin inscriptions have been conserved.

550–650: The Saxons occupy and dominate the greater part of southern Britain.

550–850: The inhabitants of western Britain, including Wales, speak western Brythonic Celtic varieties, very early forms of the Welsh language known by linguists as 'Primitive Welsh'.

552; 571: Saxons of Wessex capture Salisbury (Wiltshire, in south-west England) and Aylesbury (Buckinghamshire, in south-east England).

560–630: Saint Tysilio[9] (or Sulio) becomes an important clerical leader. He is the son of the King of Powys, Brochfael Ysgithrog (*c.*540–*c.*560) and the brother of Kynan Garwyn (King of Powys, *c.*550–*c.*600; cf. Taliesin's poem: *Trawsganu Kynan Garwyn mab Brochfael*). It is thought by some to be the oldest poem in the Welsh language.

Trawsganu Kynan Garwyn mab Brochfael
('Book of Taliesin', BT 45)

Kynan kat diffret
am arllofeis ket.
kanyt geu gofyget.
Gwrthelgwn trefbret.
kant gorwyd kyfret
aryant eu tudet.
Cant llen ehoec
o vn o vaen gyffret.
Cant armell ym arffet.
A phympwnt cathet.
Cledyf gwein karrec
dyrngell gwell honeb.
cant kynan kaffat.
kas anwelet
katellig ystret.

Kynan battle-defender
has given me bounty:
for it is not false to praise these things
before the hunting hounds of the household:
one hundred exceedingly fast steeds
with silver trappings,
one hundred purple mantles
each the same in length,
a hundred armlets in my lap
and fifty cats,
a sword with a stone-encrusted sheath
– bright hilted, better than any.
With Kynan one has
a friend most dear
– of the lineage of Cadell…

(Koch and Carey, 2000: 301, lines 1–15)

570: Koch (1997) presents arguments for an early date for the Battle of Catraeth (Catterick) (D. Dumville proposes an even earlier date, *c.*540, using similar historical arguments). Koch suggests that the Battle of Catraeth is another example of the kind of internecine warfare between Britons about which Gildas had complained so bitterly in his *De Excidio*. In this case, the dynasties of the Gododdin, along with their allies from Pictland, Strathclyde and Anglian Bernicians, would have confronted an alliance led by the famous Urien Rheged (*Reget* in Old Welsh) and Gwallawg Elfed (Old Welsh *Elmet*) and their Anglian allies from Deira (south-eastern Yorkshire). If Koch is right, this battle was won by Urien (who is also known in the Taliesin poems as 'the Lord of Catraeth') against the northern Britons.

o   According to this view, the fighting would have been sparked by a quarrel of succession between Gwallawg Elfed, supported by Urien, and Madog Elfed who was supported by the men of Gododdin. At this time, Urien Rheged was considered the most powerful warrior of Britain. The kingdom of Rheged included all the lands extending from Lancashire (Erechwydd) and Cumbria (Llwyvenydd) as far north as Aeron (Ayrshire).

o   Koch believes that the 'Battle of Gwen Ystrat', a praise poem to Urien Rheged found in the *Canu Taliesin*, is in fact another name for the Battle of Catraeth as viewed by the victors.

572–592: Battles between the Britons of the Old North (*Gwŷr y Gogledd*)[10] and the Anglian kingdoms in the north-east of England, Deira (Deifr) and Bernicia (Brynaich). The *Historia Brittonum* mentions that a Brythonic coalition led by Urien Rheged pushed the Bernician King Theodoric onto the island of Lindisfarne where the latter is besieged for three days.

Urien's cousin, Morcant of Gododdin, jealous of his military successes, has him assassinated (cf. *Canu Llywarch Hen* below).

o   Urien (Urbgen) of Rheged and his son, Owain, fight Theodoric (son of Ida) and his kinsmen, forming the historical context for eleven of the twelve Taliesin poems.

Marwnat Owein (in 'Book of Taliesin', BT 67)

Eneit owein ap yryen.
gobwyllit y ren oe reit.
Reget ud ae cud tromlas.
nyt oed vas y gywydeit.
Iscell kerdglyt clotuawr
escyll gawr gwaywawr llifeit.
cany cheffir kystedlyd.
y vd llewenyd llatreit.
Medel galon geueilat.
eissylut y tat ae teit.
Pan ladawd Owein fflamdwyn…

The soul of Owein son of Uryen.
may the lord consider its need.
The chieftain of Reget that the dense green [grass] conceals:
it is not frivolous to praise him in verse;
the cist-grave of the hero who was renowned in song,
vastly praised, whose whetted spears were like the rays of dawn,
for no equal can be found
To the lord of Llwyenydd…
the reaper whose custom was seizing the foe –
like in nature to his father and grandfather.
When Owain slew Flamdwyn…

(Koch and Carey, 2000: 354, lines 1–11)

573: Rival Brythonic kings fight each other in Gwenddoleu ap Ceidio's kingdom at the Battle of Arfderydd (now Arthuret, near Carlisle, in Cumbria). Gwenddoleu confronts a coalition consisting of Peredur and Gwrgi, sons of Eliffer, allied to King Rhydderch Hael of Strathclyde. According to the *Annales Cambriae* Gwenddoleu ap Ceidio is killed during this battle. Owing to the ferocity of the fighting, the bard Lailoken goes mad during the fighting and flees into the forest of Celyddon (Caledonia). This story very probably was attributed to Merlin, also called Llallawc or Llallogan Vyrddin (Lailoken Merlin) in early Welsh tradition.[11] Lailoken is also mentioned in Saint Kentigern's 'Life of Jocelyn' written around 1185. Kentigern was a northern Brythonic saint known as *Cyndeyrn Garthwys* in Welsh.

577: Battle of Dyrham (near Bristol). The Saxons defeat the Brythonic kings Conmael, Condidan, and Farinmail, who are all killed. This allows the Saxons to capture Bath, Cirencester and Gloucester, thus cutting the Welsh off from the south-western Britons.

593: After the death of Urien Rheged, Aethelfrith of Bernicia (d. 616), merges the Anglian-dominated kingdoms of Deira and Bernicia, thus founding Northumbria. Both names have Brythonic origins.

597: Pope Gregory I sends Augustine (d. 605) to England to evangelize the Anglo-Saxons. He lands in Kent where he is welcomed by King Aethelbert. It is Augustine who lays the foundations for the Christianization of the Anglo-Saxon kingdoms. Canterbury is chosen to be the seat of the archbishopric and the Pope gives Augustine authority over all the Christians of Britain, including those of Wales. Given that Christianity had long been established there, the Welsh clerics of Saint Davids feel betrayed with what they consider to be a cruel injustice. This disagreement marks the beginning of a religious feud between Canterbury and the Welsh that spans 13 centuries (cf. **1406** and **1920**).

600: Elmet (*Elfed* in Welsh) stretches from north Wales across southern Lancashire and Yorkshire. Sir Ifor Williams suggests this date for the Battle of Catraeth and the original composition of the *Gododdin*. (For an earlier date, cf. **570**)

601: Augustine, Archbishop of Canterbury, baptizes Aethelbert of Kent.

602: The laws of Aethelbert refer to his Brythonic subjects proving that they were not exterminated or forced to flee as 19th-century English historians asserted (cf. William Stubbs, E. A. Freeman, and John Richard Green). [12]

603: Aethelfrith of Bernicia defeats Aedan, King of the Scottish Gaels (Áedán mac Gabráin, King of Dál Riata) at the Battle of Degsastan.[13]

610: One of the earliest saints' lives, the *Life of St Samson,* is written in Brittany. It states that Samson is from Glamorgan, south Wales. He studies at Llanilltud (Llantwit Major) and is sent to Brittany where he founds the bishopric of Dol (cf. **520**).

616: Aethelfrith, King of Northumbria, kills King Selyf of Powys (son of Cynan Garwyn, cf. Taliesin poems) and King Cadwal of Rhos at the Battle of Chester. Aethelfrith's daughter marries the King of Strathclyde and his son Eanfrith weds a Pictish princess demonstrating that these kingdoms must still have been considered to be powerful adversaries (cf. **635**).

- o According to Bede, Aethelfrith orders the slaughter of a large number of Welsh monks of Bangor Is-Coed.

- o Aethelfrith is killed in a battle against Raedwald, the

King of East Anglia (600–624). Edwin succeeds him as King of Northumbria and reigns until 633.

o   Raedwald is mentioned by Bede and the *Anglo-Saxon Chronicle* as *Bretwalda*, 'Overlord of Britain', a concept which is intolerable to the Britons. It is thought that he may be the individual who was buried in the famous Sutton Hoo ship burial (in modern-day Suffolk).

617: Ceredig ap Gwallog, King of Elmet, is driven from his kingdom by Edwin of Deira. Afterwards, this kingdom is annexed by Northumbria. Ceredig's father, Gwallog ap Llaennog (or Gwallawg fab Lleennawg), is known as one of the 'three battle pillars of the island of Britain' (*tri phost cad*) in the Welsh Triads, along with Dunawd Fawr and Cynfelyn Drwsgl.

620: Saint Malo, a native of Gwent, dies in Brittany. He is a follower of Saint Brendan of Llancarfan and the first Bishop of Saint-Malo in Brittany.

625: Cadwallon ap Cadfan becomes King of Gwynedd.

626 (or **627** according to Bede): Despite claims to the contrary, the Britons do evangelize their Anglo-Saxon enemies. Rhun, son of Urien Rheged, baptizes Edwin, King of Northumbria (mentioned by the *Annales Cambriae* and the *Historia Brittonum*, §63) and 12,000 of his subjects. Some of the most famous monasteries of Wessex may thus have had Brythonic origins. The Anglo-Saxon kingdom of Mercia is also influenced by Welsh Christianity. But the most zealous efforts of the Welsh are for fellow Britons of Cornwall and Brittany and also Galicia (north-western Spain).

629: King Edwin of Northumbria besieges Cadwallon on Puffin Island (*Ynys Glannawg*), one of the islands off the coast of Anglesey.

632–633: Penda, King of Mercia, and Cadwallon form an alliance against Edwin. Penda may also have had Brythonic origins. Cadwallon ap Cadfan of Gwynedd kills King Edwin of Northumbria at Hatfield Chase, Yorkshire, alongside his heirs, Osric of Deira and Eanfrith of Bernicia. Cadwallon leads a bloody campaign across Northumbria. Bede claims that Cadwallon's goal was to exterminate the entire Angle population in what is present-day Yorkshire. Koch proposes that Cadwallon's ultimate objective was to liberate the Brythonic territory of Elmet (*Elfed*) that had just been lost to the Angles.

634: Cadwallon ap Cadfan of Gwynedd is killed by Oswald, the son of Aethelfrith and brother of Eanfrith of Bernicia, at the Battle of Heavenfield (near Hexham, Northumberland). Aidan goes from Iona to Lindisfarne to evangelize the Angles.

635: The kingdom of Rheged is absorbed by the kingdom of Northumbria, most probably through the marriage of Oswy, son of King Aethelfrith, and Rhianfellt, a great-granddaughter of Urien. This would explain how all of north-western Britain passed peacefully into Anglian hands in such a short time.

638: Edinburgh (*Din Eidyn, Eidin Vre*), capital of the Britons of Gododdin, is seized by Oswy of Northumbria. This marks the end of the kingdom of the ancient *Votadini,*[14] a kingdom which played such an important role in early Welsh literature.

640: Death of Beuno, abbot of Clynnog Fawr, in Gwynedd. He serves Kings Cadfan and his successor, Cadwallon. It is said that earlier in his life, after hearing the voices of Anglo-Saxon heathens for the first time near the River Severn, Beuno fled in horror to Gwynedd.

642: Battle of Maserfield (*Maes Cogwy*, near Oswestry). The Welsh, among them Cynddylan of Powys, are allied to Penda of Mercia against Oswald of Northumbria. Oswald is killed by them during the battle.

655: Penda of Mercia is killed by Oswy of Northumberland, the brother of Oswald, at the Battle of Winwaed Field (*Maes Gai*). Oswy goes on to capture and destroy Pengwern, 'Hall of Cynddylan' (near Shrewsbury, formerly part of Powys), where Cynddylan is said to have died.[15] This tragic event is the subject of one of the most moving collections of early Welsh poetry, known as the *Canu Heledd* cycle. Cynddylan's sister, Heledd, evokes her impressions upon beholding the ruins of Cynddylan's hall. It is one of the rare pieces of early European literature which present a woman's perspective. The cycle is part of *Canu Llywarch Hen* (cf. Llywarch Hen poems) which Sir Ifor Williams believed may have been first put into writing around 850 (cf. below).

Stafell Gynddylan ('Hall of Cynddylan', in *Canu Heledd*)

Stauell Gyndylan ys tywyll heno,
Heb dan, heb wely.
Wylaf wers; tawaf wedy.

Stauell Gyndylan ys tywyll heno,
Heb dan, heb gannwyll
Namyn Duw, pwy a'm dyry pwyll?

Stauell Gyndylan ys tywyll heno,
Heb dan, heb oleuat.
Etlit a'm daw amdanat.

Stauell Gyndylan ys tywyll y nenn.,
Gwedy gwen gyweithyd,
Gwae ny wna da a'e dyuyd.

The Hall of Cynddylan is dark tonight,
Without fire, without bed.
I weep awhile, then I am silent.

The Hall of Cynddylan is dark tonight,
Without fire, without candle.
Save god, who will give me sanity?

The Hall of Cynddylan is dark tonight,
Without fire, without songs,
Tears wear away cheeks.

Hall of Cynddylan, each hour I am grieved
Deprived of the joyful company
That I saw on thy hearth.

(Source: G. Jenkins, 2007: 36)

Marwnad Cynddylan ('Elegy of Cynddylan', in *Canu Heledd*)

Dyhedd deon diechir by[g]eledd,
Rhiau, a Rhirid, a Rhiossedd,
A Rhygyfarch lary lyw eirassedd.
Ef cwynif oni fwyf i'm derwin fedd,
O leas Cynddylan yn ei fawredd.

Mawredd gyminedd! A feddyliais
Myned i Fenai, cyn ni'm bai fais.
Carafi a'm enneirch o dir Cemais,
Gwerling Dogfeiling, Cadelling trais.
Ef cwynif oni fwyf i'm derw llednais,
O leas Cynddylan, colled annofais.

War of unyielding menacing noblemen,
Rhiau and Rhirid and Rhiosedd
and Rhigyfarch, the generous leader, the chariot driver,
I shall lament until I lie in my oaken coffin
for the slaying of Cynddylan in his greatness

Grandeur in battle! Did I think
of going to Menai, though there was no ford for me?
I love those of the land of Cemais who give me welcome,
The dynast of Dogfeiling, violator of the descendants of Cadell,
I shall lament until I shall be in my unassuming silence
for the slaying of Cynddylan, profound loss.

(Source: Koch and Carey, 2000: 364)

655–682: Cadwaladr ap Cadwallon becomes King of Gwynedd. Not much is known about him except that there are two plagues during his reign, one in 664 (mentioned by Bede) and another in 682 of which he himself dies (according to the *Annales Cambriae*). In his book *Historia Regum Britanniae* (History of the Kings of Britain, 1136), Geoffrey of Monmouth indicates that he is the last of the Brythonic kings. In his legendary history, Cadwaladr is named (along with Cadwallon and Arthur) as one of the kings descended from Brutus of Troy, who will save the Britons from the Anglo-Saxons.

664: At the Synod of Whitby, Northumbria, the Northumbrians convert to Roman Christianity and accept the Roman calendar. They also agree that it is Saint Peter, and not Saint Aidan, who holds the keys of Heaven. In 688, Strathclyde also accepts the authority of Rome, and the north of Ireland and the Church of Iona follow suit in 697 and 716 respectively.

685: Carlisle (Welsh: *Caerliwelydd*), the old capital of Rheged, is occupied by the Angles. It may have served as a staging area to launch attacks on Brythonic Strathclyde.

690: Ine (reigned 688–726), the Anglo-Saxon King of Wessex, writes a code of laws around this time in which there are eight clauses referring to the rights of his Brythonic subjects. This is further proof that large numbers of Britons retained their identity (and probably their language) in England long after the Anglo-Saxon conquest. They were, over time, culturally and linguistically assimilated by the Old English-speaking newcomers.

705–709: Rhodri Molwynog (d. 754), King of Gwynedd, leads a series of Welsh attacks on Mercia.

716–757: Aethelbald, King of Mercia, builds Wat's Dyke to defend Mercia from the Welsh attacks.

730: Bede writes his *Historia Ecclesiastica Gentis Anglorum* (Ecclesiastical History of the English People) at the monastery of Jarrow, Northumbria (i.e. Sunderland). Bede expresses anti-Welsh sentiments, probably on account of Welsh resistance to the Roman Catholic Church regarding the calendar and other points of worship but also, perhaps, because of the brutality of the Welsh incursions into his native Yorkshire a generation before.

o The King of Morgannwg (Glamorgan), Morgan ab Athrwys (or Morgan Mwynfawr, 'the benefactor'), dies in this year. The county takes its name from him although some historians say it could have been named after Morgan ab Owain (cf. **942**).

740: The *Book of St Chad* (or *Lichfield Gospels*) is an insular gospel book housed in Lichfield Cathedral (in Staffordshire, England). In the margins of the manuscript are found some of the oldest glosses written in Old Welsh. The bishops of Lichfield still swear their oaths on this book. It may have been written in Llandeilo Fawr, Carmarthenshire, and contains the first phrases written in Old Welsh.

750–800: The Brythonic kingdoms of Cornwall, Wales, Cumbria, and Strathclyde are still unconquered by the Anglo-Saxons.

755–809: According to *Brut y Tywysogyon* (Chronicle of the Princes), Elfodd (or Elbodius), Bishop of Bangor, persuades the Welsh Church to adopt the date of Easter proposed by Rome. Nennius claims that he himself was a student of Elfodd and that this bishop was a dedicated student of Bede's work. As we have seen, Bede had always attacked the Welsh for having refused to accept the Roman calendar.

757: Offa, King of Mercia (d. 796) rules Northumbria.

760: Offa is defeated by the Welsh at Hereford.

776 or **784:** According to the *Annales Cambriae*, King Offa builds an earthen wall which stretches along the current Welsh border in order to protect Mercia from Welsh attacks. It is still known as Offa's Dyke.

> **Commentary:** Wales, as we know it now, did not yet exist as such. For this reason, the inhabitants of Wales have a dual identity from an early period calling themselves both Britons[16] (i.e. Ancient Britons), stressing a broader pan-Brythonic identity, and also *Cymry* (>*cumbrogi* meaning the 'comrades'). According to Kenneth Jackson[17] (1969), Cymry is a name that is attested as early as the 6th century and refers to all the Britons of north-western Britain: Wales, north-western England and southern Scotland.
>
> By the end of the Roman period, it is likely that the Britons of these regions, the *Cymry*, felt themselves to be culturally and linguistically different from their more Romanized kinsmen to the east, hence the distinction. The term *Lloegr* may have its origins during this period and may refer not only to the dominant Anglo-Saxons but also the Romanized Britons who inhabited the area. The territorial and national identity of the *Cymry* becomes more marked as the invading Anglo-Saxons systematically occupy and anglicize regions in what is today England.
>
> The term 'Welsh', on the other hand, comes from Old English *wealh* meaning 'foreigner', a word known in all the Germanic languages. It probably dates back to a time when it referred to all the inhabitants of the Roman Empire whether Gauls, Britons or Romans.

Chapter 5

The Viking Age (789–1066)

The Viking Age marks a new phase in the development of Welsh nationhood during which the Christian Welsh and Anglo-Saxons are increasingly drawn closer in their struggle against a common non-Christian enemy. While relations between the old rivals often remain hostile, a status quo arises resulting in the progressive consolidation of Welsh territorial, linguistic and political distinctiveness which concludes with the establishment of an increasingly Welsh, as opposed to Brythonic, identity.

789: The Vikings ravage the coast of England.

796: King Offa of Mercia is killed at Rhuddlan by the Welsh.

850–1150: Traditional dates for the Old Welsh language (700–1150 according to Willis, 2009).

808–855: Cyngen becomes King of Powys. In 854, he is the first Welsh king to go on a pilgrimage to Rome where he dies in 855. He also erects Eliseg's Pillar in honour of his great-grandfather Elisedd ap Gwylog, near Valle Crucis Abbey, in Denbighshire.

825–844: Merfyn Frych is King of Gwynedd. He marries Cyngen ap Cadell's sister, Nest.

829: Egbert of Wessex (802–839) temporarily conquers Mercia (until 830). He is also King of Kent (825–839). According to the *Anglo-Saxon Chronicle*, he is named *Bretwalda*, meaning 'Overlord of Britain', an Anglo-Saxon term corresponding roughly to the Brythonic term *Vor-tigern*, literally 'over-Lord').

c.830: The *Historia Brittonum* (History of the Britons) is written. Attributed to the Welsh historian, Nennius, this famous book contains the first historical reference to King Arthur and is one of the principal sources of Geoffrey of Monmouth's *History of the Kings of Britain* (cf. **1136**).

840–886: Hywel ap Rhys, King of Glywysing, reigns during this period. He is buried in the monastery of Llanilltud (Llantwit) Fawr.

844: Rhodri the Great (*Rhodri Mawr*) becomes King of Gwynedd, Powys (855), and Seisyllwg (856) and reigns over these regions until 877.

c.850: *Canu Llywarch Hen* is composed around this period. It is divided into several parts. A series of poems recalling the death of Urien Rheged is (incorrectly) attributed to Llywarch Hen, the grandson of Coel Hen (i.e. 'Old King Cole' mentioned in the English nursery rhyme). Many of the poems concern the successive deaths of Llywarch Hen's sons in battle in defence of Powys. For more details on the *Canu Heledd* cycle, see **642** and **655** above.

856: Rhodri Mawr, King of Gwynedd and Powys, wins a great battle on Anglesey against the Danish Vikings and kills their king, Horm. Rhodri marries Angharad, the sister of Gwgon, King of Seisyllwg. This event is mentioned by Sedilius Scotus, an Irish scholar at the court of Charles the Bald at Liège (in modern Belgium), who calls him Roricus in two poems celebrating his victory. He is also mentioned in the Ulster Chronicle.

865: Danish Vikings colonize north-eastern England and call it *Danelaw*. Their territory stretches from Northumberland down to East Anglia.[1]

871–99: Alfred the Great reigns as King of Wessex. He is the son of Egbert of Wessex.

872: Rhodri fights against the Danes.

878: Rhodri Mawr and his son, Gwriad, are killed in a battle against the Anglo-Saxons of Mercia. The exact place where they were killed is unknown.

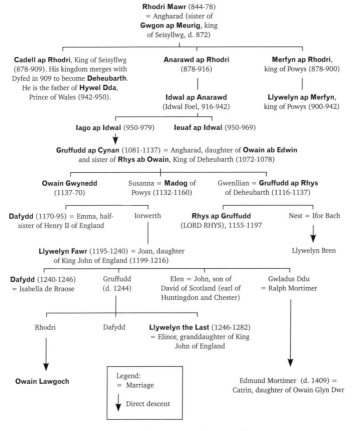

Figure 8: Genealogical tree of the House of Gwynedd

878–916: Anarawd ap Rhodri succeeds Rhodri Mawr as King of Gwynedd.

879: Anarawd defeats the Anglo-Saxons near Conwy (north Wales).

880: Asser, the Welsh scholar and Bishop of St Davids, is invited by King Alfred of Wessex to serve as his advisor. Aside from his intellectual skills, Asser is chosen in part to rally the Welsh kings to support Alfred as their overlord. Around 893, he writes *The Life of King Alfred.* Many of the kings of south Wales submit to Alfred as a result of their fear of Anarawd of Gwynedd and the Mercians.

881: In revenge for the death of their father, Rhodri Mawr, Anarawd and his brothers defeat the Mercians on the banks of the River Conwy. Hyfaidd of Dyfed and Eliseg of Brycheiniog seek an alliance with King Alfred against Anarawd and accept him as their overlord.

885: Anarawd makes an alliance with the Northumbrian Danes under Guthrum (or Gudrum, d. 890) but receives no benefits from it, and it quickly dissolves.

892–96: Wales is again attacked by Danish Vikings. At some time during this period, Anarawd and his brothers submit to King Alfred.

894: King Alfred defeats a Viking army at Chester which retreats into north Wales, pillaging the territory of their former Welsh allies.

899: King Alfred of Wessex dies and is succeeded by his son, Edward. Edward organizes a marriage between his sister, Atheflaed, and the King of Mercia, thus uniting Wessex and Mercia. This means that the men of Wessex and Mercia can organize co-ordinated attacks at any point along the Welsh border.

900: Hywel Dda becomes King of Seisyllwg. Hywel Dda, Owain of Gwent and Idwal Foel (son of Anarawd) of Gwynedd submit to King Edward of Wessex.

902: From their bases in Ireland, the Vikings raid the Welsh coast.

904: Llywarch ap Hyfaidd of Dyfed dies. Hywel Dda marries his sister, Elen, and Dyfed comes into the hands of Hywel Dda.

911: Rollo the Norseman and Charles the Simple, King of France (898–922), sign the treaty of Saint Clair-sur-Epte, thus founding the Duchy of Normandy.

914: The *Anglo-Saxon Chronicle* mentions that an army of Vikings based in Brittany plunders the shores of Morgannwg and Gwent, capturing Bishop Cyfeiliog. King Edward of Wessex pays a ransom of 40 pounds to liberate him. The Vikings leave for Waterford (Ireland) at the end of the year 916.

916: Anarawd ap Rhodri, King of Gwynedd, is killed in Brycheiniog, near Llyn Safaddan (Llangors Lake), in a battle against the Vikings.

916–942: Idwal Foel, the son of Anarawd ap Rhodri, becomes King of Gwynedd.

924–939: Athelstan, the grandson of Alfred, is crowned King of Wessex, and is the first monarch to be called 'King of all of Britain'.

927–935: Hywel Dda, Owain ap Hywel of Gwent and Glywysing (later his son, Morgan ap Owain, 930–974), Idwal Foel of Gwynedd, Constantine II of Scotland (King of the Gaels and Picts) and Owain, King of the Strathclyde Britons, are obliged to attend numerous councils in Wessex where they are forced to recognize Athelstan as their overlord. They are often accompanied by Anglian and Danish kings. These are frequently mentioned in the English royal charters and in the *Anglo-Saxon Chronicle*.

927: According to William of Malmesbury, Athelstan levies a heavy tax on the Welsh (this yearly tax includes 20 pounds of gold, 300 pounds of silver and 25,000 oxen).

*c.*935: *Armes Prydein Fawr* (The Great Prophesy of Britain) is composed. It is one of the great vaticinatory poems, predicting the expulsion of the Anglo-Saxons by the Britons, Gaels and Danish Vikings, probably in response to the dispute over taxes with Athelstan of Wessex.

> Gofynnant [y Cymry] yr Saesson py geissyssant,
> pwy meint eu dylyet or wlat a dalyant?
> cw mae eu herw pan seilyassant?
> cw mae eu kenedloed py vro pan doethant
> yr amser Gwrtheyrn genhyn y sathrant...

> *They [the Cymry] ask the Saxons what it was they had been*
> *   seeking,*
> *how much of the country do they hold by right?*
> *where are their lands, From whence they set forth?*
> *where are their peoples? From what country do they come?*
> *Since the time of Gwrtheyrn [Vortigern] they have oppressed*
> *   us...*

> (I. Williams and Rachel Bromwich, l. 133–7, pp. 11–12)

> Dysgogan derwydon meint a deruyd.
> o Vynaw hyt Lydaw yn eu llaw yt vyd.
> o Dyuet hyt Danet wy bieiuyd.
> o Wawl hyt Weryt hyt eu hebyr.
> Llettawt eu pennaeth tros yr echwyd.
> Attor ar gynhon Saesson ny byd...

> *Wise men foretell all that will happen;*
> *they (the Brythons) will possess all from Manaw [Gododdin] to*
> *   [Armorican] Brittany.*
> *from Dyfed to Thanet, it will be theirs;*

from the Wall to the Forth, along their estuaries,
their dominion will spread over Yr Echwydd.
There will be no return for the tribes of the Saxons…

(I. Williams and Rachel Bromwich, l. 171–6, Ibid. pp. 14–15)

937: Athelstan, King of Wessex, crushes a Celto-Scandinavian alliance composed of the King of Scotland (Constantine II, 900–943), the Brythonic kingdom of Strathclyde (Owen I, d. 937) and Olaf Guthfrithsson (King of Dublin, 934–941) at the Battle of Brunanburh. The site of the battle has recently been identified with Bromborough (formerly Brunanburh) in the Wirral Peninsula near Chester. This event is mentioned in the *Anglo-Saxon Chronicle* and the *Brut*.

939: King Athelstan dies and is succeeded by his 18-year-old brother, Edmund. It is believed that Idwal Foel of Gwynedd may have allied himself with Olaf Guthfrithson against Edmund. At the very least, it seems that he refused to swear allegiance to him.

940: Olaf Guthfrithson, who survived the terrible slaughter at Brunanburh, returns with another army of Danes and ravages Mercia and Wessex.

942: Morgan ap Owain (or Morgan the old, 930–974), King of Glywysing (Glamorgan) unites the kingdoms of Gwent and Glywysing under the name of Morgannwg. According to T. M. Charles-Edwards (2013), however, Morgannwg could have been formed under the rule of his father, Owain ap Hywel.

o   In this year, Idwal Foel and his brother, Elisedd, are killed by the Mercians. Llywelyn ap Merfyn, King of Powys (900–942), also dies in battle. The same year, Hywel Dda, King of Deheubarth, annexes Powys and Gwynedd, thus becoming Prince of nearly all of Wales

(942–950). In doing so, Hywel exiles Idwal's sons, Iago and Ieuaf.

945: An assembly is held at Whitland (Carmarthenshire), where Hywel Dda and six men from every commote of Deheubarth are present. The Laws of Wales, known as *Laws of Hywel Dda* are redacted here. These are a collection of traditional Welsh (ancient Brythonic) laws which, for the first time, are codified in writing. They also present a fascinating portrait of Welsh society during the 10th century. Some 35 Latin/Welsh manuscripts (13th century onwards) are preserved mainly in the National Library of Wales. This code of laws is divided into two sections:

- o 'Laws of the Court': these concern the rights and duties of the king and his court.

- o 'Laws of the Country': Welsh society is divided into four main orders:

    1) King (Brenin)

    2) Landowners (*Breyr* or *Bonheddig*)

    3) Serfs or villeins (*taeog*)

    4) Foreigners (*alltud*)

946: Hywel attends the coronation of Edred of Wessex who is king until 955.

950: Hywel Dda dies. His sons, Owain (950–986), Rhodri (950–953) and Edwin (950–954) rule jointly over Deheubarth (Dyfed and Seisyllwg) and probably Powys. At the same time, Morgan ap Owain rules over Glamorgan.

- o After Hywel's death, Idwal Foel's sons Iago ab Idwal (950–79) and Ieuaf ab Idwal (950–969) return from exile and rule Gwynedd jointly.

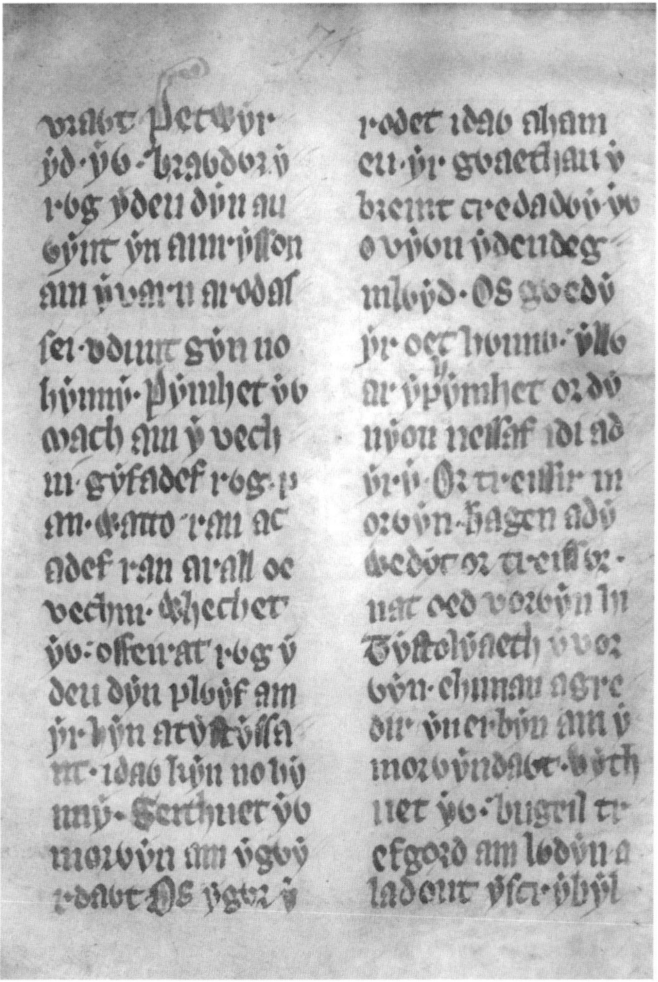

Figure 9: Extract from the Laws of Hywel Dda (National Library of Wales)

951: The sons of Hywel Dda (Owain, Rhodri and Edwin) attempt to invade Gwynedd but are defeated by Iago ab Idwal and Ieuaf ab Idwal at the Battle of Nant Carno (Carno, Powys).

952: Iago ab Idwal and Ieuaf ab Idwal lead an attack on Deheubarth. In response, the sons of Hywel Dda attack Gwynedd again in 954, but they are once again defeated in a battle at Llanrwst, Gwynedd.

955: Morgan ap Owain of Morgannwg, Owain ap Hywel Dda of Deheubarth, and Iago ab Idwal go to Edred's court to submit to his authority. Edred of Wessex dies a couple of months later.

961: The *Annales Cambriae* were written in Latin during the second half of the 10th century by several copyists at St Davids, the abbey of Neath, and the abbey of Whitland. The *Annales* cover the events in Wales and northern Britain between *c*.450 and *c*.955.

969: Iago captures his brother Ieuaf ab Idwal, who dies in captivity around 988.

973: Iago ab Idwal submits to King Edgar of Wessex's authority at Chester, near the River Dee. His nephew Hywel ap Ieuaf, King Kenneth II of Scotland and King Mael Coluim I of Strathclyde do the same.

979: Iago ab Idwal is captured by Hywel ab Ieuaf, who becomes King of Gwynedd until 985. Hywel's brother, Cadwallon ap Ieuaf, succeeds him in 986.

982; 988; 992; 999: The Church of Saint Davids in Menevia (Welsh: Mynyw, Pembrokeshire) is sacked four times by the Vikings and, in 999, its bishop, Morgenau, is killed.

986–999: Maredudd ab Owain, son of Owain ap Hywel

Dda, and grandson of Hywel Dda, succeeds in uniting his grandfather's kingdom. For the first time most of the territory of Wales, as we know it, is united under one leader.

987: The Vikings seize 2,000 men from Anglesey (Ynys Môn) and sell them as slaves.

988: The Vikings plunder Llanbadarn (near Aberystwyth, Ceredigion), St Dogmaels (Pembrokeshire), Llancarfan (Vale of Glamorgan), and Llanilltud Fawr (Llantwit Major, Vale of Glamorgan) destroying priceless objects and manuscripts.

989: Maredudd ab Owain of Deheubarth is obliged to pay a penny poll tax (a bribe) to the Vikings in order to keep them away.

993: The Vikings pillage Anglesey once again.

1013–1016: Canute of Denmark and Norway leads a series of successful military campaigns against Æthelred of England. After Æthelred's death in 1014, Canute wages war against Æthelred's son, Edmund, who dies in 1016. Emma, Queen of England and daughter of the Duke of Normandy, is now alone to confront the Vikings.

1016: Canute marries Emma of England, and Canute of Denmark and Norway is crowned King of all England (1018–35).

1039: Gruffudd ap Llywelyn becomes King of Powys and Gwynedd. He is the son of Llywelyn ap Seisyll, King of Gwynedd and Deheubarth (1018–23) and Angharad,[2] the daughter of Maredudd ab Owain. He is the first Welsh ruler since Cadwallon to intervene militarily in the affairs of the English. The same year, he defeats the forces of Leofric, Earl of Mercia, at Rhyd-y-groes near Welshpool.

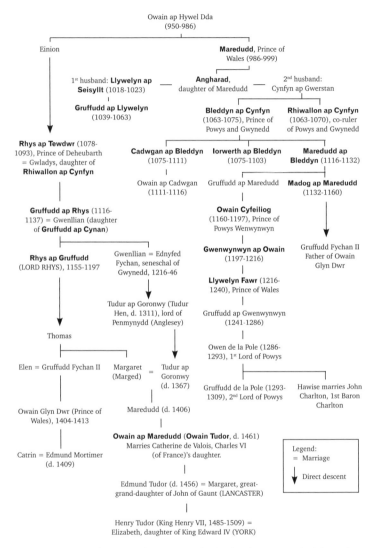

Figure 10: Genealogy tree of the House of Deheubarth, Powys and of the Tudors

1042–1066: Edward the Confessor, the son of Ælthelred II 'the Unready', is the last king of the house of Wessex.

1055: Gruffudd ap Llywelyn makes an alliance with Aelfgar of Mercia, Leofric's son, who returns from exile. Together they attack and defeat a joint Norman-French and Anglo-Saxon coalition in Herefordshire and Gloucestershire. He captures the kingdom of Deheubarth in the same year.

1057–1063: Gruffudd ap Llywelyn is the king of all of present-day Wales, an achievement which was never reduplicated by any Welsh ruler after this. He is recognized by King Edward the Confessor of England as the only King of Wales. Gruffudd bases his court at Rhuddlan in north Wales.

1062: The very ambitious Anglo-Saxon earl, Harold son of Godwin (Godwinson) attacks Gruffudd's court by surprise and destroys his fleet.

1063: Harold leads an expedition of Anglo-Saxon warriors into Wales. Gruffudd is killed near Snowdonia.

1063–1075: Bleddyn ap Cynfyn becomes King of Powys and Gwynedd. He rules with his brother Rhiwallon until the latter's death in 1070. They ally themselves with the kingdom of Mercia in an unsuccessful attempt to keep the Normans at bay.

Chapter 6

Wales and the Anglo-Normans (1066–1485)

The Norman Conquest marks a new phase in the Welsh struggle for cultural and political independence. Paradoxically, the destruction of Anglo-Saxon political hegemony over England by the Normans eventually leads to an even greater long-term threat to Welsh independence and identity.

The first assaults are led by William the Conqueror himself and later by the French Angevin Plantagenets. Welsh affairs become inextricably involved in Anglo-Norman political intrigues. It is important to recall that until the 14th century Norman-French remains the dominant language of the 'English' court.

1066: Edward the Confessor names William, Duke of Normandy as his successor. Harold Godwinson breaks an oath of fealty to William that he made during an earlier visit to Normandy and usurps the throne upon Edward the Confessor's death. Harold Hardrada (Fairhair) of Norway also covets the throne of England and lands with a Viking army in Yorkshire (East Riding), but is defeated by Harold Godwinson at the Battle of Stamford Bridge (25 September).

- o Three days later (28 September), the Norman army lands in Pevensey (East Sussex) and Harold's battle-weary warriors cover 360 miles in 17 days to fight the Normans. At Hastings (in East Sussex, 14 October) the Anglo-Saxon army is crushed and King Harold Godwinson is slain. This marks the end of the dominance of Anglo-Saxon culture and language in

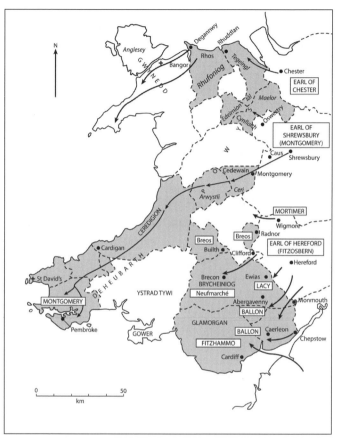

Figure 11: Map of the Norman-controlled areas of Wales, 1067–1099 (inspired by John Davies, 1993)

England. Norman French replaces Old English as the language of the aristocracy. The Anglo-Saxon defeat is to have radical consequences for Wales.

1067–1099: During this period the Normans push westwards and establish their authority along the Welsh border region, known as the Welsh Marches. On the order of William the Conqueror, the Norman Marcher Lords (William Fitzosbern, Earl of Hereford;[1] Roger of Montgomery, Earl of Shrewsbury;[2] Hugh of Avranches, Earl of Chester[3]) build forts on the Welsh border and launch assaults on Wales (for contemporary accounts, cf. Orderic Vitalis, Anglo-Norman clerk, 1075–1141).

1070: Rhiwallon ap Cynfyn is slain during the Battle of Mechain (Powys). His enemies, the two sons of Gruffudd ap Llywelyn of Gwynedd, are also killed. Rhiwallon's brother, Bleddyn ap Cynfyn, rules alone over Powys and Gwynedd until 1075.

1070–1300: The Normans found about 80 towns in Wales.

1072: Maredudd ab Owain ab Edwin, King of Deheubarth from 1063 to 1072, is killed during the Battle of Rhymney by Caradog ap Gruffydd of Gwynllwg and Upper Gwent, a pretender to the throne of Deheubarth from 1072 to 1081. He remains King of Gwent from 1075 to 1081.

1074: Caradog ap Gruffydd seizes Glamorgan from Cadwgan ap Meurig.

1075: Bleddyn ap Cynfyn, King of Powys and Gwynedd, is killed by Rhys ab Owain (a direct descendant of Hywel Dda and member of the Dinefwr dynasty) in Ystrad Tywi. Rhys rules over Deheubarth from 1072 to 1078. Bleddyn's son, Cadwgan ap Bleddyn (1075–1111), is crowned Prince of Powys.

o   The same year, Gruffudd ap Cynan, grandson of Iago ab Idwal ap Meurig, King of Gwynedd, 1033 to 1039, attempts to reclaim the throne of Gwynedd but is exiled to Ireland by his rival Trahaearn ap Caradog (who is also Bleddyn ap Cynfyn's cousin). Trahaearn ap Caradog remains King of Gwynedd until 1081.

o   There are many family ties between Gruffydd ap Cynan, born in Dublin, and the royal family of Ireland. Gruffydd's mother, Ragnaillt (or Ragnhild), is the daughter of the Hiberno-Norse King Olaf Sigtryggsson.

1078: Caradog ap Gruffydd slays Rhys ab Owain, King of Deheubarth, and rules over Deheubarth until 1081.

1081: Gruffudd ap Cynan and Rhys ap Tewdwr of Deheubarth, while in exile in Ireland, make an alliance and both return to Wales the same year. During the Battle of Mynydd Carn (north of St Davids), they kill Trahaearn ap Caradog of Gwynedd and Caradog ap Gruffydd. Gruffudd ap Cynan becomes King of Gwynedd (1081–1137) and William the Conqueror recognizes Rhys ap Tewdwr as the new ruler of Deheubarth. Shortly afterwards, the Norman Lord Hugh of Chester captures Gruffydd ap Cynan and imprisons him for nearly ten years.

1087: William II becomes King of England following his father's death.

1088–1095: The Norman Bernard de Neufmarché (Newburgh, in English), attacks Deheubarth and conquers the kingdom of Brycheiniog (Brecknockshire).

1090: Rhygyfarch (Ricemarch) of Llanbadarn writes *The Life of St David*.

1092–1108: Hervé Le Breton becomes Bishop of Bangor. He is detested by the Welsh. Bangor remains under the authority of the Diocese of Canterbury until 1920.

1093: Rhys ap Tewdwr, King of Deheubarth (1078 to 1093) is killed at the Battle of Brecon by the Normans led by Bernard de Neufmarché. Gruffudd ap Rhys replaces him as King of Deheubarth. Around 1093 the Norman Lord of Gloucester, Robert Fitzhamon, occupies Glamorgan until his death in 1107.

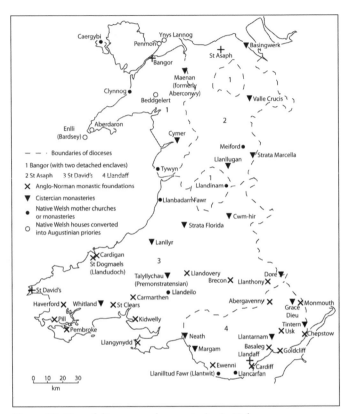

Figure 12: Map of dioceses and monasteries in Wales
(inspired by G. Jenkins, 2007)

1094: Gruffudd ap Cynan of Gwynedd escapes from prison (cf. **1081**) and allies himself with Cadwgan ap Bleddyn of Powys. Together they lead a revolt against the Normans and drive them out of Wales.

1095–1097: William II sends Norman forces to Wales in an unsuccessful bid to put down the Welsh.

1098: Gruffudd ap Cynan of Gwynedd and Cadwgan ap Bleddyn of Powys attempt to renew a revolt against the Normans but are forced to flee to Ireland. The Norman earls of Chester and Shrewsbury are routed on the banks of the Menai straits by a Scandinavian army led by Magnus Barefoot, King of Norway (1093–1103), allied to the Welsh.

1100–1135: King Henry I of England (Beauclerc) succeeds his father William II and becomes more involved in Welsh affairs.

1105: According to *Brut y Tywysogyon* (The Chronicle of the Princes), King Henry I allows a colony of Flemings to settle in the south of Dyfed (modern Pembrokeshire), which becomes the foundation of 'Little England beyond Wales'.

1120: The three dioceses of Wales (Llandaff, St Davids and Bangor) are incorporated into the archdiocese of Canterbury.

1125: *Llyfr Llandaf* (The Book of Llandaff) contains documents (mainly from the 8th and 9th centuries) concerning the lives of saints such as Dyfrig (Dubricius) and Teilo as well as 149 land grant charters. It is particularly rich in Welsh personal names and place-names and contains passages written in Old Welsh.

1128–1148: A Norman by the name of Bernard (b. 1115) is appointed Bishop of Saint Davids. During the last 20 years of his life he struggles to have Rome recognize Saint Davids as an archbishopric on the grounds that the Welsh have their own language, law and customs. They are thus a *natio*, nation.

1132–1160: Madog ap Maredudd is the ruler of Powys. In 1156, he asks Henry II's support to thwart the ambitions of his rival, Owain ap Gruffydd ap Cynan (Owain Gwynedd), Prince of Gwynedd. This marks the beginning of successful Anglo-Norman interference in Welsh dynastic rivalries.

1135: Henry I dies. A dynastic conflict ensues between his daughter, Matilda, and Stephen of Blois, which ends in a victory for Matilda.

1136: In October of this year, Gruffudd ap Rhys, King of Deheubarth (1116–1137), Owain Gwynedd, and his brother Cadwaladr ap Gruffudd (killed in 1172) defeat the Normans at Crug Mawr (near Cardigan). Profiting from the conflict in England between Stephen de Blois and Matilda, Owain Gwynedd annexes Ceredigion. He is also the first Welsh ruler to use the title 'Princeps Wallensium' (Prince of the Welsh).

o   Gwenllian is the sister of Owain Gwynedd and wife of Gruffudd ap Rhys. She is sometimes described as the 'Welsh Joan of Arc' because she leads an army against the Normans at Kidwelly where she is captured and then executed by order of Maurice de Londres.

o   Geoffrey of Monmouth, Bishop of St Asaph (Denbighshire), writes his famous *Historia Regum Britanniae* (History of the Kings of Britain). Geoffrey, who is probably of Breton descent, presents the Britons in a very favourable light. His book, which relates the history of Britain as a succession of single Brythonic (i.e. British, cf. footnote 2, Chapter 5) kings, serves as the official history of the kings of England until the reigns of the Tudors and Stuarts. It is also the basis for the Arthurian Cycle which becomes one of the greatest literary successes of the Middle Ages. For centuries the successive kings and queens of England seek to tie their genealogies to those of the kings of Britain as presented in this book. Geoffrey's patron, Robert, the illegitimate son of Henry I, the King of England, is the first Earl of Gloucester and Lord of Glamorgan.

1148: Geoffrey of Monmouth writes his *Vita Merlini* (Life of Merlin).

1150: There are 17 Benedictine houses in Wales (named after Saint Benedict of Nursia, in 529), mainly in south Wales.

The House of Plantagenet

1154: In December of this year, Henry II Plantagenet (or Henry Fitz Empress), Duke of Normandy and Aquitaine, Count of Anjou, becomes King of England. Like his precedessors, he speaks only French and is a descendant of the Counts of Anjou. He is the son of Matilda and Geoffrey V Plantagenet, Count of Anjou.

o   Henry II receives oaths of allegiance from Rhys ap Gruffudd of Deheubarth (1155–97) and Owain Fawr of Gwynedd (1137–70).

1155–1200: Cynddelw Brydydd Mawr (*fl.* 1155–95) and Gwalchmai ap Meilyr (*fl.* 1130–1180) are the two greatest poets of their time. The Welsh poets of this age are known in Welsh as *Beirdd y Tywysogion* (Poets of the Princes) or *Y Gogynfeirdd* (Less Early Poets).

Gwalchmai ap Meilyr, *I Owain Gwynedd*

Arddwyreaf hael o hil Rodri,
Arddwyad gorwlad, gwerlin deithi,
Teithïawg Prydain, twyth afrdwyth Owain,
Tëyrnain ni grain, ni grawn rëi.

Tair lleng y daethant liant lestri,
Tair praff prif lynges i'w bres brofi:
Un o Iwerddon, arall arfogion
O'r Llychlynigion, llwrw hirion lli,

A'r drydedd dros fôr o Norddmandi,
A'r drafferth anferth anfad iddi.

I exalt the generous descendant of Rhodri,
ward of the Marches, his quality kingly,
right master of Britain, doom-buoyant Owain,
his princes nor grovel, nor hoard their wealth.

Three legions came, ships of the deep sea,
Three prime stout fleets, avid to spoil him:
One was of Ireland, another was war-manned
With Norsemen of Lochlyn, lank steeds of the flood;

A third over seas sailed here from Normandy,
And, for their pains, vast trouble it cost them –

(in J. E. Caerwyn Williams, 1978. Translated into English by Anthony Conran, 1967, p. 24)

1157: With Madog ap Maredudd's assistance, Henry II enters Wales with an Anglo-Norman army. Owain Gwynedd surrenders and pays homage to the King of England. He gives up his territories between the Rivers Clwyd and Dee.

1160: After the death of Madog ap Maredudd, Powys is divided into two parts:

o Powys Wenwynwyn (southern Powys, until 1283), the capital of which is Welshpool.

o Powys Fadog (northern Powys, until 1277), the capitals of which are Dinas Brân (near Llangollen), and Glyndyfrdwy.

1160–1195: Owain Cyfeiliog, Prince of Powys Wenwynwyn, is the nephew of Madog ap Maredudd and is known for his poem *Hirlas Owain* (the Blue Horn of Owain). However, this poem also could have been written by Cynddelw Brydydd Mawr (born in Powys).

Dywallaw di'r corn ar Gynfelyn
Anrhydeddus feddw o fedd gorewyn;
Ac o mynni hoedl hyd un flwyddyn,
Na ddidol ei barch, can nid perthyn.
A dyddwg i Ruffudd, waywrudd elyn,
Gwin a gwydr golau yn ei gylchyn;

Fill thou the horn for Cynfelyn
Honoured in drunkeness with foaming mead;
And wouldst thou live yet but a single year,
Scant not this honour, for that beseems not.
And bear to Gruffudd, red-lance 'gainst the foe,
Wine in a goblet of shining glass.

(Source: Thomas Parry, 1955, p. 63)

1162–1170: Thomas Becket, an Anglo-Saxon and close friend of Henry II, is named Archbishop of Canterbury. Tensions arise between Thomas Becket and King Henry II and this episode weakens Henry's authority over Wales. In 1163, while Thomas Becket is in exile in France, Owain Gwynedd nominates Arthur of Bardsey as Bishop of Bangor and because Becket refuses to recognize him, Owain sends him to Ireland to be consecrated. Becket, who takes his new office seriously, incurs the wrath of the King and is murdered by some of the king's followers.

1164: The Abbey of Strata Florida (Welsh: Ystrad-fflur, Ceredigion) is founded. It is thought that *Brut y Tywysogyon* (The Chronicle of the Princes) was compiled in this abbey. It includes events between 682 and 1332. The descendants of Lord Rhys are buried here.

1165: Owain Gwynedd leads an alliance which includes Madog, the Prince of Powys, and Rhys ap Gruffudd of Deheubarth, also known as Lord Rhys. Together, they defeat Henry II's army in the Berwyn Mountains (in north-east Wales) and he is forced to retreat. In 1166, the alliance captures the castles of Rhuddlan and Prestatyn.

1168: Owain Gwynedd sends a letter to King Louis VII of France (1137–1180), seeking to form an alliance against Henry II. Though this alliance never materializes, this is the first time that a Welsh prince seeks an alliance with a European leader.

1169–1171: Dermot MacMurrough (d. 1171), the 'High King' of Ireland, is forced to flee his kingdom after a *coup d'état* in 1166–1167 by Rory O'Connor. He goes to King Henry II's court to seek support. Afterwards, Dermot asks Rhys ap Gruffudd to free Robert Fitzstephen, a Norman knight who is being held prisoner in Cardigan. He forms an army composed of Welshmen and Normans, including Richard De Clare, second Earl of Pembroke (d. 1176, better known as 'Strongbow'). They land on the Irish coast and capture Wexford, Waterford and Dublin. This is considered to be the beginning of the Norman invasion of Ireland. In 1170, Strongbow marries Aoife, Dermot's daughter. They have three children including Isabel de Clare, fourth countess of Pembroke (1185–1220). Noticing that the Norman barons in Ireland are becoming too powerful, Henry II lands with a Norman army in 1171 and kills Dermot McMurrough. Strongbow's arrival in Ireland is related in a 13th-century poem called 'The Song of Dermot and the Earl'.

The following is a translation of the Irish:

> But before King Dermot
> 375] Crossed over the salt sea,
> He spake to a king in Wales
> Who was very brave and courteous.
> This man was called Rhys,
> And was acknowledged King of Wales.
> 380] At this time King Rhys
> Had a knight of great renown.
> The king kept him in prison,

Robert the son of Stephen was his name.
In his prison he was keeping him,
385] He wished him to submit.
I know not how the king took him.
In a castle in his country.
Concerning him I will not here relate
How he was taken nor in what way;
390] But the rich King Dermot
Then besought King Rhys
As much as he could on behalf of the knight
That he might be able to depart freely.
Not to tell you an untruth
395] I know not if he was liberated then:
At the request of the rich king,
If he was liberated at that time;
But afterwards the knight
To Ireland came to aid the king.
400] Then King Dermot returns.
To St. Davids as soon as he could.
To Ireland then he crossed
With as many men as he had.
But Dermot, the noble king,
405] Did not bring with his warriors
Any Englishmen on this occasion,
According to the account of my informant,
Except one Richard, as I have heard say,
A knight of Pembrokeshire,
410] Richard the son of Godibert,
A knight he was of good parts...

(Source: website of the University of Cork, Ireland)

1170: After the death of Owain Gwynedd, his son, Hywel ab Owain Gwynedd, becomes, for a brief period, the new ruler of Gwynedd. He is well known for his poem, *Gorhoffedd Hywel ab Owain* (The Exultation of Hywel ab Owain). Hywel is killed in battle by his half-brothers.

Ton wen orewyn a orwlych bedd,
Gwyddfa Rhufawn Befr, ben tëyrnedd.
Caraf, drachas Lloegr, lleudir gogledd heddiw,
Ac yn amgant Lliw lliaws calledd.
Caraf a'm rhoddes rybuched medd,
Myn y dyhaedd mŷr, maith gyfrysedd.
Caraf ei theulu a'i thew annedd ynddi,
Ac wrth fodd ei rhi rhwyfaw dyhedd.

A foaming white wave washes over a grave
the tomb of Rhufawn Pebyr, regal chieftain
I love today what the English hate, the land of the North,
and the varied growth that borders the [river] Lliw
I love those who gave me my fill of mead,
where the seas reach in long contention
I love its household and its strong buildings
and at its lord's wish to go to war

(Translated by Gwyn Williams, 1974, lines 1–8)

o   According to legend, Madog ab Owain Gwynedd discovers America during this period (see **1577** and **1792**).

o   The Cistercian abbey of Strata Marcella is founded near Welshpool in Powys.

1170–1195: The new ruler of Gwynedd is Dafydd ab Owain (d. 1203), another son of Owain Gwynedd. For a short time, he rules jointly with his brothers, Maelgwn and Rhodri. After their father's death, they turn on each other and Dafydd exiles Maelgwn and imprisons Rhodri.

1171: Rhys ap Gruffydd (or Lord Rhys, 'Yr Arglwydd Rhys' in Welsh), the Prince of Deheubarth (cf. **1154**), builds a castle at Dinefwr, in Llandeilo, Carmarthenshire. After being confiscated by Edward I from Lord Rhys's descendants in 1277, the castle is given back by Henry VII to Rhys ap Thomas in

Figure 13: Photograph of the castle of Dinefwr (*c.*1171)

1485. However, in 1531, Henry VIII takes it and orders Rhys's arrest and execution for treason. By then the castle had been replaced by the mansion of Newton, near the castle. Rhys ap Thomas's descendants anglicize the name Rhys to Rice, and are made peers of Great Britain in 1780 under the name of Baron Dynevor.

1173–1174: Richard the Lionheart and John Sans Terre (Lackland or Softsword), and Henry II's wife, Eleanor of Aquitaine, lead a revolt against Henry II. The Welsh support the king.

1174: Dafydd ab Owain marries Emma of Anjou, the French-speaking daughter of King Henry II, thus becoming his son-in-law. He swears an oath of allegiance to him in 1177.

1175: Rhodri ab Owain Gwynedd escapes from prison and seizes all of western Gwynedd from his brother Dafydd.

1176: Lord Rhys (cf. **1154** and above) holds the first eisteddfod in Cardigan.

1189: Richard I Lionheart is crowned King of England. He speaks only French. He is best known for his participation in the third crusade (1189–92), but also for the romantic image we have of him in Sir Walter Scott's *Ivanhoe*. He spent relatively little time in England during his reign. His body lies in the Abbey of Fontevraud (Touraine, France) alongside his parents, Henry II and Eleanor of Aquitaine.

1191: Gerald of Wales (or Giraldus Cambrensis, 1146–1223), a clergyman and chronicler, writes his famous *Itinerarium Cambriae* (Journey through Wales). Born in Pembrokeshire, his father is Norman and his mother is Welsh. He speaks Latin, Norman French, English and Welsh and perhaps some Breton (which he describes as rougher sounding and older than Welsh).

1194: Gerald of Wales completes his *Journey through Wales* with his *Descriptio Cambriae* (Description of Wales). The same year, Dafydd ab Owain Gwynedd is defeated by his nephew, Llywelyn ap Iorwerth, at the Battle of Aberconwy (the estuary of the Conwy).

1195–1240: Llywelyn ap Iorwerth, later known as Llywelyn Fawr (The Great) is successively Prince of Gwynedd, Prince of Powys Wenwynwyn and Prince of Wales.

1197: Dafydd ab Owain Gwynedd, Llywelyn's uncle, is imprisoned by Llywelyn, and after his liberation by the Archbishop of Canterbury, he is exiled to England where he dies in 1203.

1198: Gwenwynwyn ab Owain, King of Powys Wenwynwyn (1195–1216), is defeated near Painscastle by the Anglo-Norman Marcher Lords and the Justiciar of England (the King of England's right-hand man). Gwenwynwyn's defeat allows Llywelyn Fawr to expand his power throughout all of Wales.

1199: Henry II's third son, Geoffrey II, is named Duke of Brittany following his marriage to Constance of Brittany (daughter of Conan II). They name their first son Arthur whom King Richard the Lionheart names as his successor. The idea is to placate the Bretons, Cornish and Welsh whose poets continue to predict that a Celtic leader by that name will fulfil Merlin's prophecy by becoming King of England. Richard's brother, the very ambitious John Lackland, takes this as an affront and seizes the throne of England after Richard's death during the siege of Châlus, Anjou. Like the Anglo-Norman kings who precede him, he speaks only French.

1201: While in exile in England, Dafydd ab Owain Gwynedd, Llywelyn I's uncle, swears an oath of allegiance to King John.

o   The Cistercian abbey of Valle Crucis is founded during this year by Madog ap Gruffydd Maelor, Prince of Powys Fadog, at Llantysilio, in Denbighshire. It is currently one of the UNESCO World Heritage sites. The Princes of Powys are buried here.

1202: To ensure the stability of the throne, King John captures his nephew Arthur (whom Richard the Lionheart had named as his successor), and has him blinded. Arthur is assassinated the following year.[4]

1205: Llywelyn I marries King John's daughter, Joan, who becomes Princess of Wales and Lady of Snowdon.

1213–1216: King John attempts to retake Normandy from Philip Augustus but he is defeated by the French at the Battle of Bouvines. This French victory consolidates Philip's control of territories formerly belonging to the Plantagenets: Brittany, Anjou, Maine, Poitou, and the Duchy of Aquitaine. This leads to divisions among the Norman Lords in England who are now cut off from their original homeland. To make matters worse, the crown jewels of England are lost in the Wash, in East Anglia, during King John's disastrous retreat from France. This happened in 1216, just before his death.

1215: Llywelyn I allies himself with Philip Augustus of France and, thus strengthened, makes a pact with the Normans barons of England. Llywelyn then proceeds to capture Shrewsbury. This event, among others, forces King John to sign Magna Carta, the objective being to limit the king's power and grant more authority to the barons. King John is also forced to liberate Llywelyn's son, Gruffydd (who is said to be the son of Llywelyn Fawr's mistress, Tangwystl). Gruffydd had been held hostage in England since 1211. Llywelyn's control over Gwynedd is thus consolidated after this confrontation.

1215–1217: Judging that he had signed Magna Carta under duress, King John obtains the Pope's permission to break his oath. This event leads to the First Barons' War. In December 1215, Llywelyn leads a confederation of Welsh princes who capture the Norman-held castles of Carmarthen, Kidwelly, Llanstephan, Cardigan and Cilgerran. The Norman barons of England, in turn, offer the throne of England to Prince Louis of France, Philip Augustus's son. Prince Louis arrives with an army of French troops who occupy the Isle of Thanet. They proceed to capture London and Winchester and extend their control over most of the south of England. Prince Louis is proclaimed King of England in a ceremony at St Paul's cathedral in London. His crowning is not official, however, since his father, Philip, is still King of France.

1216: Llywelyn Fawr is crowned Prince of Wales and reigns until 1240. King John dies shortly after his retreat from France in October. As a result, the Norman barons of England abandon their support of Louis and recognize John's son, Henry III, as the rightful King of England. Prince Louis and his French troops return to France. Henry III and Llywelyn I are brothers-in-law thanks to Llywelyn's marriage to Henry's sister, Joan (cf. **1205**).

1218: The King of England signs the Treaty of Worcester in which he recognizes Llywelyn I's authority over Wales.

1220: Henry III supports Llywelyn I in his efforts to ensure that his son, Dafydd, should be the sole heir to Gwynedd.

1222: This agreement is approved by Pope Honorius III (1216–1227).

1226: Dafydd ap Llywelyn receives oaths of allegiance from the *uchelwyr* (literally, high men, the noblemen) of Wales.

1227–1228: King Henry III gives Hubert de Burgh (1180–1243)[5] the title of Lord of Montgomery in Powys. This is a means for the King to encroach upon Llywelyn's lands. Anticipating this ploy, Llywelyn I captures Hubert during the fighting and forces King Henry III's relief force to retreat back into England.

1229: Dafydd ap Llywelyn marries Isabella, the first of the four daughters of William de Braose, the Lord of Brycheiniog (Breconshire), Abergavenny (Monmouthshire) and Builth Wells (Powys). William de Braose is hated by the Welsh who call him 'Gwilym Ddu' (Black William). William is hanged in Gwynedd by Llywelyn I after he surprises him in bed with his wife, Joan, the daughter of King John. His death in 1230 is mentioned in the chronicle of Ystrad-fflur.

1231–1234: Llywelyn I leads his forces in a military campaign in south Wales against Hubert de Burgh. He burns Brecon, marches through Glamorgan and destroys Neath. Henry III is seriously concerned and appeals to Ireland for help, offering Anglo-Irish knights the right to own any lands they might win in Wales.

- o In 1231, Richard Marshal becomes Earl of Pembroke after his brother William's death.

- o In 1232, Hubert de Burgh is removed from the earldom of Kent and is later put in gaol. Peter de Rivaux, a native of Poitou, France, succeeds him.

- o A conflict arises in 1233 between Richard Marshal (supported by Llywelyn) and Peter de Rivaux (supported by King Henry III).

- o In 1234, Richard Marshal and Llywelyn I seize Shrewsbury. After Richard is killed in Ireland the same year, Henry III and Llywelyn I agree to sign in Shropshire a two-year truce called 'the Peace of Middle' (on 21 June) which results in a *status quo*. Llywelyn continues to rule over Powys Wenwynwyn, but he subjects the Lords of Powys Fadog and Deheubarth to his authority through bonds of allegiance and obtains possession of Gwrtheyrnion, Builth, and Maelienydd.

1237: Llywelyn suffers a stroke following the death of his wife Joan. He decides to order an assembly at Strata Florida to ask the *uchelwyr* to swear allegiance to his son Dafydd.

1240: Llywelyn I and Henry III meet in Gloucester. The King recognizes that Dafydd will possess the territories owned *de jure* (legally) by his father. Llywelyn I dies at the Cistercian abbey of Aberconwy. Dafydd becomes King of Gwynedd.

1241: In August of this year, Henry III invades Wales and obliges Dafydd ap Llywelyn to give up all his possessions outside Gwynedd. Moreover, Dafydd must also hand over his elder brother, Gruffudd ap Llywelyn, as a hostage to the king. Gruffydd ap Llywelyn is the father of the future Llywelyn II, the 'Last Prince of Wales'.

1244 (1 March): Gruffudd ap Llywelyn falls to his death while attempting to escape from the Tower of London.

1246: Gruffudd's son Llywelyn ap Gruffudd is recognized as Prince of Wales, thus becoming Llywelyn II. He inherits Gwynedd and is the last prince to rule over most of what is today modern Wales.

1247: Henry III signs an armistice at Woodstock Palace with Llywelyn II and his brother, Owain ap Gruffudd. This treaty obliges the Prince of Wales to give the King of England the territories of Gwynedd between the River Conwy and River Clwyd. Llywelyn must also share some of his territories with Owain ap Gruffudd.

***c.*1250:** *Llyfr Du Caerfyrddin* (The Black Book of Carmarthen) is redacted. It includes the 'dialogue between Merlin and Taliesin' (*Ymddiddan Myrddin a Thaliesin*) and poems related to the *Hen Ogledd* (The Old North, northern England and Scotland). It is the oldest of the four great books of Wales. In this year, Matthew Paris, a Benedictine monk from Saint Albans, Hertfordshire, draws the first map of Wales, suggesting that, by this time, Wales is viewed, abroad at least, as having a definite Welsh (as opposed to Brythonic) cultural, political and linguistic identity.

1255: Dafydd and Owain ap Gruffudd plot against their brother in an attempt to remove him from power. Llywelyn II defeats them at the Battle of Bryn Derwin, imprisons them, and conquers back Owain's territories (cf. Treaty of Woodstock, above).

Figure 14: Map of Britain by Matthew Paris (British Library)

1257: Llywelyn II defeats an Anglo-Norman army led by Stephen Bauzan at the Battle of Cadfan. The latter is killed in the engagement.

1264–1267: The King of England faces a second baronial revolt in England which is led by Simon de Montfort, sixth Earl of Leicester (d. 1265). The latter receives Welsh support.

1264: King Henry III and his son, Edward (the future King Edward I), are taken prisoner by Simon de Montfort at the Battle of Lewes.

1265: Llywelyn II and Simon de Montfort sign the Treaty of Pipton in which they form an alliance against Henry III.

o   *The Book of Aneirin* is redacted about this time. It contains the masterpiece of early Welsh poetry entitled *Y Gododdin*. It is a large collection of panegyric poems for the Brythonic warriors who died at the Battle of Catraeth (cf. the years **541**, **570** and **600** above for the possible dates of this battle).

1267: The Treaty of Montgomery results in a compromise in which Henry III recognizes Llywelyn II as Prince of Wales. Llywelyn in turn acknowledges that he is a vassal of Henry III, King of England.

1267–1271: For his fidelity to Henry III during Simon de Montfort's revolt, Gilbert de Clare[6] (1263–1295) is given the castles of Abergavenny (modern-day Monmouthshire) and Brecknock (modern-day Powys). In revenge, Llywelyn II seeks to conquer northern Glamorgan. In September 1268 he seizes Senghennydd, provoking a conflict with Gilbert de Clare.

1272: Edward I (Longshanks) becomes King of England upon the death of his father, Henry III. Although his first language is French, Edward is the first King of England to be fluent in English.

1274: Dafydd ap Gruffydd (Llywelyn II's brother), a relative of his, Gruffudd ap Gwenwynwyn (of Powys Wenwynwyn) and Gruffudd's son, Owain (also known as Owen de la Pole), make an unsuccessful attempt to kill Llywelyn II.

1275: Conscious of the arrangement of a future marriage between Llywelyn II and Eleanor de Montfort, Simon's daughter, Edward I takes her prisoner in a strategic move to isolate Llywelyn II.

1277: The King conquers Powys Fadog (Denbighshire). This leads to the signing of the Treaty of Aberconwy between the King and Llywelyn II on 9 November. The consequences are:

o   Llywelyn II retains his title of Prince of Wales but the *uchelwyr* (except four of Powys Fadog and one from Deheubarth) cease their allegiance to him.

o   The western part of Gwynedd still belongs to Llywelyn II. The eastern part of Gwynedd is divided between Edward I and Dafydd ap Gruffudd, Llywelyn's brother.

o   Eleanor de Monfort is freed.

1278: Llywelyn II marries Eleanor de Montfort.

1282: Probably as the result of a conspiracy between Edmund Mortimer[7] and Edward I, Llywelyn II, the last Prince of Wales, is tracked down and murdered by Edward's men near Cilmeri in Breconshire. A beautiful lament concerning his death is composed by Gruffudd ab yr Ynad Coch.

> O Iaith Llywelyn cof dyn ni'm daw.
> Oerfelawg calon dan fron o fraw,
> Rhewydd fal crinwydd y sy'n crinaw.
> Poni welwch-chwi hynt y gwynt a'r glaw?
> Poni welwch-chwi'r deri'n ymdaraw?
> Poni welwch-chwi'r môr yn merwinaw'r tir?

Poni welwch-chwi'r gwir yn ymgweiriaw?
Poni welwch-chwi'r haul yn hwylaw'r awyr?
Poni welwch-chwi'r sŷr wedi'r syrthiaw?

With Llywelyn's death, gone is my mind.
Heart frozen in the breast with terror,
Desire decays like dried-up branches.
See you not the rush of wind and rain?
See you not the oaks lash each other?
See you not the ocean scourging the shore?
See you not the truth is portending?
See you not the sun hurtling the sky?
See you not that the stars have fallen?

(Translated by Joseph Clancy in: Ceri W. Lewis, 1992:154–5)

o   Dafydd III, Llywelyn's brother and successor, continues the war against Edward I. He too is betrayed by one of his men and is arrested at Cadair Idris in 1283. At the end of September, he is executed for high treason.

1282–1350: The *Hendregadredd* Manuscript is redacted. It contains an anthology of the poetry of the 'Poets of the Princes'. It was probably written in the Cistercian abbey of Strata Florida in Ceredigion.

1282–1400: One hundred and six Welshmen are known to have studied at Oxford and Cambridge universities (and also at European universities in Paris, Lyon, Perugia and Bologna).

Chapter 7

The Political Assimilation of Wales by the Anglo-Normans (1284–1400)

After the slaying of the last native Prince of Wales, Llywelyn II (*Y Llyw Olaf*) in 1282, the Anglo-Normans under Edward I succeed in pitting Welsh leaders against one another and, as a result, encroach on large regions of Wales (cf. 1284) and, in particular, along the border with England known as the Welsh Marches. Intermarriage between Anglo-Norman and Welsh noble families becomes increasingly common, the result being the further erosion of the cultural identity of the Welsh nobility.

1284: The Statute of Rhuddlan declares that Wales is to be incorporated into England. The consequences of the statute are as follows:

o   The Laws of Hywel Dda, which had served as the basis for all legal transactions in Wales since 945 (and before), are replaced by English common law.

o   Edward I creates new lordships: Denbigh (for Henry de Lacy, Earl of Lincoln), Rhuthun (for Reginald de Grey), Bromfield and Yale (for John de Warenne, Earl of Surrey), and Chirk (for Roger Mortimer). As a result, a chain of lordships is created between England and the recently conquered territories of west Wales.

o   The principality is divided into five counties: Anglesey, Caernarfon, Meirionnydd, Cardigan and Carmarthen.

o A justice is appointed at Chester for the three northern counties (Anglesey, Caernarfon and Meirionnydd), and the county of Flint.

1286: Gruffudd ap Gwenwynwyn dies. His son, Owain de la Pole (d. 1293) becomes Lord of Powys. Edward I organises a marriage between Owain's daughter, Hawise de la Pole (known as the 'The Lady of Powys') and John Charlton, one of Edward I's faithful vassals. This marriage is part of the King of England's successful strategy to disinherit Owain de la Pole's son, Gruffudd (the rightful Welsh heir) and bring Powys under the direct sway of the English throne.

1287–1288: Rhys ap Maredudd of Deheubarth revolts against King Edward I.

1292: Rhys ap Maredudd of Deheubarth is finally captured and put to death for treason at York.

1294–1295: Madog ap Llywelyn (based in Welshpool, d. 1312), Maelgwn ap Rhys Fychan (based in Ceredigion), and Morgan ap Maredudd (based in Glamorgan, d. 1316), all Welsh princes, lead a revolt in Wales against Edward I. At the head of 35,000 men, the King defeats the rebels at the Battle of Maes Moydog (5 March 1295) in Caereinion (Powys Wenwynwyn). Maelgwn ap Rhys Fychan is killed during the summer of the same year in Carmarthen by English soldiers.

The Political Assimilation of Wales into England (1297–1400)

1297: 5,300 Welsh soldiers fight alongside Edward I in Flanders.

1298: With the help of 10,000 Welsh archers, the Anglo-Normans win the Battle of Falkirk against the Scottish rebels led by William Wallace.

1300–1600: Poets of the Nobility (*Beirdd yr Uchelwyr*) are also called '*Cywyddwyr*' because of their use of their favourite metre, the *Cywydd* (rhymed couplets). Among the best known of these are: Iolo Goch (*c.*1320–*c.*1398), Dafydd ap Gwilym (*c.*1330–*c.*1360), Gutun Owain (*fl.*1450–98), Guto'r Glyn (*c.*1435–*c.*1493), Dafydd Nanmor (*fl.*1450–1480), Lewys Glyn Cothi (*c.*1420–1489), Dafydd ab Edmwnd (*fl.*1450–97), Tudur Aled (*c.*1465–*c.*1526).

1307: Edward I dies in July of this year. Edward II is crowned King of England. There follows a period of continuous conflict between the new king and his barons.

1308: Edward II marries Isabella, the daughter of King Philip 'the Fair' of France.

1309: Gruffudd de la Pole dies. Powys passes directly into the hands of John Charlton, husband of Hawise de la Pole (cf. **1286**). The Charlton family rules over Powys until 1421.

1314: Edward II is defeated by the Scots at the Battle of Bannockburn. Gilbert de Clare (1291–1314), Lord of Glamorgan, is slain here.

1314–1321: Glamorgan passes into the hands of Payne de Tuberville of Coety.

1315–1318: A series of poor harvests across Europe causes great desolation in Wales.

o   The Scottish king, Robert Bruce, sends his brother Edward Bruce to invade the lordship of Ireland (under Anglo-Norman control). The latter becomes High King of Ireland, under the Gaelic name of *Edubard a Briuis* (1315–1318). His goal is to use Ireland as a second front in his war against England. He attempts to win over the Welsh and sends a letter to Gruffudd Llwyd,[1]

Lord of North Wales (from Tregarnedd, Anglesey, d. 1335). The response of the latter is positive. Gruffudd Llwyd appears to have been motivated by his hatred of Roger Mortimer rather by than any disloyalty to King Edward II. Despite this, Gruffudd is imprisoned from 1316 to 1318 for having conspired against the king.

1316–1317: Llywelyn Bren, the great-grandson of Ifor Bach,[2] leads an unsuccessful revolt against Edward II. He is hanged at Cardiff castle on the orders of Hugh Despenser the younger, leaving six sons: Gruffydd, John, Meurig, Roger, William and Llywelyn.

o Dafydd ap Gwilym (*fl.* 1330–1360), was born in Ceredigion. He is considered by many to be the greatest Welsh poet of all time. He is a Welsh *Uchelwr* and a descendant of Ednyfed Fychan, the seneschal of Gwynedd. Most of his poems are *cywyddau* (rhymed couplets). One example is *Merched Llanbadarn* ('The Girls of Llanbadarn').

Extract from *Merched Llanbadarn* (The Girls of Llanbadarn)

Plygu rhag llid yr ydwyf,
Pla ar holl ferched y plwyf!
Am na chefais, drais drawsoed,
Ohonun yr un erioed.
Na morwyn, fwyn ofynaig,
Na merch fach na gwrach na gwraig.
Pa rusiant, pa ddireidi.
Pa fethiant na fynnant fi?
Pa ddrwg i riain feinael
Yng nghoed tywylldew fy nghael?
Nid oedd gywilydd iddi
Yng ngwâl dail fy ngweled i.

I am bent with wrath,
a plague upon all the women of this parish!
for I've never had (cruel, oppressive longing)
a single one of them,
neither a virgin (a pleasant desire)
nor a little girl nor hag nor wife.
What hindrance, what wickedness,
what failing prevents them from wanting me?
What harm could it do to a fine-browed maiden
to have me in a dark, dense wood?
It would not be shameful for her
to see me in a bed of leaves.

(Lines 1–12, website: www.dafyddapgwilym.net, poem 137; translated by Huw Meirion Edwards)

1321: Gilbert de Clare's brother-in-law, Hugh Despenser the younger (the Earl of Gloucester), becomes Lord of Glamorgan.

o The 'Despenser War' begins this year and ends in 1322. Under the rule of Edward II, there is strong rivalry between the supporters of Hugh Despenser, known as the 'Despensers' (supported by the King) and the Mortimers, represented by Roger Mortimer.

o **March:** The Marcher Lords led by Thomas, second Earl of Lancaster (also Lord of Denbigh) along with Roger Mortimer of Wigmore, his uncle Roger Mortimer of Chirk, and Humphrey de Bohun, Earl of Hereford, start a rebellion against the Despensers and the King.

o **Summer:** The Mortimers and the Earl of Hereford attack the lands owned by the Despensers in Glamorgan, capturing Newport, Cardiff and Caerphilly. Under duress, the King is forced to exile the Despensers in August until their return to England in October.

January 1322: The Mortimers surrender to Edward II at Shrewsbury (Shropshire) and are imprisoned in the Tower of London. Gruffudd Llwyd, now free (cf. **1315–18**), with the support of Edward II, leads an attack against the Anglo-Norman castles of Welshpool, Chirk (in Wrexham, belonging to Roger Mortimer of Chirk), and those of the Earl of Hereford.

- o Roger Mortimer of Wigmore escapes the same year from the Tower of London and in 1324 flees to the court of Charles IV of France.

- o The last diehard supporters of the Mortimers are finally defeated at the Battle of Boroughbridge (near York) where the Earl of Hereford is killed and the Earl of Lancaster is captured and executed.

- o A Parliament is held at York where there are 48 representatives from Wales.

- o Einion Offeiriad writes the first Welsh bardic grammar (*Gramadeg y Penceirddiaid*).

1325: Edward II sends his wife, Queen Isabella, on a diplomatic mission to negotiate a peace treaty with her brother, King Charles IV of France (1322–8). The objective of the voyage is to regain the lost Anglo-Norman territories in France such as Aquitaine. In order to achieve this goal, Isabella's son Prince Edward, the future King of England, pays homage to the King of France instead of his father. While at the court, Isabella meets Roger Mortimer of Wigmore who has been in exile since his escape from the Tower of London in 1322. They become lovers. Charles IV gives Isabella, Roger Mortimer and Prince Edward a sum of money to raise an army and they organize a landing on the English coast the following year.

1326: In September, they execute the plan and overthrow Edward II and the Despensers. With the help of Llewelyn

Bren's sons, Queen Isabella and her lover, Roger Mortimer of Wigmore, arrange to have the Despensers executed.

o   Edward II is captured in south Wales and officially abdicates on 24 January 1327 at Kenilworth castle (Warwickshire). He is imprisoned at Berkeley castle on the banks of the Severn. In September of this same year, the King dies and is buried at St Peter's monastery, Gloucester, and his tomb becomes a place of pilgrimage for his supporters, the Welsh in particular.

o   Carmarthen is recognized as Wales's chief commercial port. Each year, several ships arrive with wines from Bordeaux.

o   The Queen of England, Isabella of France, is intensely disliked at the Anglo-Norman court because of her pro-French activities.

1327–1330: Her son, Edward III, becomes king under the regency of Roger Mortimer. This sets the stage for the Hundred Years' War. At the end of this period (1330), Edward III orders the arrest of his mother, Queen Isabella, and Roger Mortimer. Shortly afterwards, Edward has the latter hanged at Common Gallows in London and Isabella is exiled to Rising castle (Norfolk) where she dies in 1358.

The Hundred Years' War

1337: Although the actual fighting begins in 1340, the Hundred Years' War begins as the result of an Anglo-Norman versus French dynastic struggle between the Plantagenet kings of England and the Valois kings of France. Large numbers of Welsh soldiers fight for the King of England, the role of Welsh archers being of prime importance in many of the Plantagenet victories over the French (Crécy, Poitiers and Agincourt).

Nevertheless, not all Welshmen fight on the Anglo-Norman side. Owain Lawgoch is a notable exception and serves Charles V of France. He is the last direct heir of the Princes of Gwynedd (cf. **1360**).

1342: During the War of Succession in Brittany, 600 Welshmen fight for the Breton contender, John IV of Montfort (supported by the Anglo-Normans), against Charles de Blois (supported by the French).

1343–1376: Edward, known as the 'Black Prince',[3] the eldest son of Edward III, is Prince of Wales. He leads many campaigns in France and Flanders during the first half of the Hundred Years' War. He is also the father of Richard de Bordeaux (the future Richard II) who succeeds Edward III in June 1377, a year after the Black Prince's death.

1346: At the Battle of Crécy, 3,550 Welshmen and 3,450 men from the Welsh Marches serve alongside the Anglo-Normans, mainly as archers.

1347: Iolo Goch composes a panegyric in honour of Edward III, entitled *I'r Brenin Edward y Trydydd* (To King Edward III).

Iolo Goch, *I'r Brenin Edward y Trydydd* (To King Edward III)

Edwart ab Edwart, gwart gwŷr,
Ab Edwart, anian Bedwyr;
Edwart ŵyr Edwart ydwyd,
Edwart Trydydd, llewpart llwyd;
Gwisgaist, a ririaist yr aer,
Crest gwedy cwncwest cancaer;
Ar awr dda, arwraidd iôr,
Aur gwnsallt, eryr Gwynsor...

Edward son of Edward, men's guardian
son of Edward, Bedivere's nature;
you are Edward grandson of Edward,
Edward the Third, brown leopard;

you wore, and you reared war,
a crest after the conquest of a hundred castles;
it was at an auspicious hour – heroic lord,
golden surcoat, Windsor's eagle…

(lines 1–8, translated by Dafydd Johnston, 1993, p. 2)

1347–1349: The Black Plague reaches Carmarthen and Abergavenny in March 1349. The population of Wales decreases from 300,000 to less than 100,000 people. According to the medieval French historian, Jean Froissart, the plague kills a third of the inhabitants of Europe.

o There is a drop in the number of tenants (or sharecroppers), either because they flee their lands (for instance, it falls from 104 to seven in Ceredigion) or because they die of the plague (36 out of 40 tenants die in Caldicot castle, Monmouthshire). This provokes a fall in the rent of the landlords (example: by a quarter in the lordship of Pembroke in 1349–50).

1350: *Llyfr Gwyn Rhydderch* (The White Book of Rhydderch) is redacted. It contains the masterpiece of medieval Welsh prose, the *Mabinogion,* a collection of eleven prose tales relating the adventures of numerous Welsh/Brythonic heroes. It is currently kept at the National Library of Wales; it formerly belonged to Robert Vaughan (cf. **1667**).

*c.***1354:** Owain Glyndŵr is born in Glyndyfrdwy (in present-day Denbighshire). He marries Margaret Hanmer, daughter of David Hanmer (a barrister) from Maelor, Flintshire. They have five sons (Gruffudd, Madog, Maredudd, Thomas, John) and five daughters (Alice, Jane, Janet, Margaret, and Catrin). Note that the names among the nobility are increasingly Norman-French.

1355: Carmarthen obtains the monopoly for wool exports (replaced later by Shrewsbury and Rhuddlan). The same year, about 90 Welshmen (60 from north Wales and 30 from Flintshire) participate in a campaign in Gascony led by the Black Prince, including Hywel ap Gruffudd[4] 'of the axe', the Constable of Criccieth castle, and Rhys ap Gruffudd[5] of Llansadwrn.

1356: The Welsh serve in large numbers at the Battle of Poitiers (1356) where the King of France, John II 'le Bon' (the Good), is captured by the Black Prince.

Figure 15: Welsh archers at the Battle of Poitiers (an illuminated manuscript by Jean Froissart, Bibliothèque Nationale de France)

Figure 16: Photograph of the abbey of Nouaillé, the Black Prince's headquarters

1357: Thomas Ringstead (d. 1366), an Englishman, is appointed Bishop of Bangor by Pope Innocent VI, and is the first non-Welsh bishop there since Hervé Le Breton (1092–1108).

1360–1403: Owain Lawgoch (born Owain ap Thomas ap Rhodri, 1330–78) leads a company of Welshmen (or *Compagnie de Galle*) who serve the King of France, Charles V. Known in France as Yvain de Galles (i.e. Owain of Wales), he is the grandson of Llywelyn ap Gruffudd's brother Rhodri, thus being the only heir of Gwynedd. Owain fights against the Anglo-Normans in 1370–1 in Maine and Anjou and in 1373 in Guyenne, alongside the Breton, Bertrand du Guesclin. He is assassinated in 1378 by the Scot, Jon Lamb, at Mortagne-sur-Gironde (south-western France). To honour his memory a monument was inaugurated here in 2003 by the French government, represented by the French Minister of Defence, and the National Assembly for Wales, represented by Dafydd Wigley.

1361; 1369; 1379; and **1391:** Return of the plague.

Anglo-Normans develop an English identity and adopt the English language

1362: Edward III is the first King of England to address Parliament in English. In this year he also enacts the Laws of Pleading, requiring the laws of England to be written in the English language, and not in Norman French. This is not fully adhered to, and French is used by many as the legal language until the beginning of the 17th century.

> **Commentary:** The king's address to Parliament in English and the Laws of Pleading are symbolic acts marking the point when the Anglo-Norman ruling classes begin to reject their French origins in favour of a new sense of 'Englishness', which is neither Anglo-Saxon nor Norman. This can be explained by the fact that generations of Anglo-Normans had been born and raised in England by 1362 and many were bilingual. The geographical and linguistic isolation from their kinsmen on the continent, compounded by the bitter fighting against the French (who no longer viewed the Anglo-Normans as 'Frenchmen'), contributed to the cultural estrangement of the latter.
>
> For this reason, the Anglo-Normans and their subjects in England will be referred to, from this point on, as 'Englishmen'. Nevertheless, it is significant to note that only the ruling classes ever spoke French, a figure which never exceeded five to ten per cent (cf. Blake, 1996). Despite 300 years of Anglo-Norman domination over England, the mass of the population had continued to speak multiple dialects of English since Anglo-Saxon times.

1375–1425: *Llyfr Coch Hergest* (The Red Book of Hergest) is redacted. Along with *Llyfr Gwyn Rhydderch* (cf. **1350** above), it contains prose tales making up the *Mabinogion* (for example, 'The Dream of Rhonabwy', 'Culhwch and Olwen'), some 'Poets of the Princes', the Welsh Triads, and a Welsh translation of Geoffrey of Monmouth's *History of the Kings of Britain*. It is currently held at the Bodleian Library, Oxford.

1377: Richard II, son of the Edward, the Black Prince (the oldest son of Edward III), succeeds his grandfather. His uncle, John of Gaunt (the fourth son of Edward III), becomes his regent. Gaunt is also Geoffrey Chaucer's brother-in-law.[6]

1378–1417: Crisis of the Papacy between Avignon and Rome (great schism).

1380: Around this time there are 13 Cistercian monasteries and about 70 monks in Wales.

1382–1395: The Englishman John Wycliffe translates the Bible into Middle English, the first to do so since Richard Rolle of Hampole, northern England, in the early 14th century (*c.*1320s–30s). This is to have a profound influence on Christianity in Britain as a whole. Wycliffe dies in 1384. The Catholic Church strongly condemns such translations into vernacular languages which are not viewed as being worthy of expressing God's word.

1385: The poet Gruffudd Llwyd (*fl.*1380–1410)[7] from Montgomeryshire, composes a poem honouring Owain Glyndŵr.

1386: Two Welsh students at Oxford, John Gunderhumber and John Coneway, are excommunicated from the Catholic Church because they are followers of Wycliffe. This marks the beginning of the persecution of the Lollards (followers of Wycliffe).

1389: King Richard II starts ruling without his regents. He wins the support of the landowners of Wales, men such as the sons of Tudur ap Goronwy of Anglesey, ancestors of the Tudors.

***c.*1390:** The poet Iolo Goch composes a poem entitled *Llys Owain Glyndŵr* (Owain Glyndŵr's court), describing his court at Sycharth, near Llangedwyn, in Powys.

> Iolo Goch, *Llys Owain Glyndŵr* (Owain Glyndŵr's court)
>
> Fo all fy naf, uchaf ach,
> Eurben claer, erbyn cleiriach;
> Clod bod, cyd boed alusen,
> Ddiwarth hwyl, yn dda wrth hen.
> I'w lys ar ddyfrys ydd af,
> O'r deucant odidocaf,
> Llys barwn, lle syberwyd,
> Lle daw beirdd aml, lle da byd;
> Gwawr Bowys fawr, beues Faig,
> Gofuned gwiw ofynaif.
>
> *My liege can, highest lineage,*
> *bright golden head, receive an old codger;*
> *it is praiseworthy, though it be but alms,*
> *course without shame, to be kind to the old.*
> *I will go to his court in haste,*
> *the most splendid of the two hundred;*
> *a baron's court, place of refinement,*
> *where many poets come, place of the good life;*
> *queen of great Powys, Maig's land,*
> *promise of good hope.*
>
> (Lines 13–22, translated by Dafydd Johnston, 1993, p. 38)

1391: A priest of the bishopric of Lincoln and disciple of Wycliffe, William Swinderby[8] is excommunicated by the Catholic Church because of his attempts to spread Wycliffe's ideas in Wales.

1399: John of Gaunt dies. Richard II exiles Henry of Bolingbroke (son of John of Gaunt and Blanche of Lancaster) and assumes control of the house of Lancaster. In July of this year, while Richard is campaigning in Ireland, Henry of Bolingbroke lands on the coast of Yorkshire, allied with Thomas Arundel (former Archbishop of Canterbury, 1397) and opponents of the king. Meanwhile, learning of this threat, Richard lands in Wales to seek support. In September, Richard II surrenders at Flint castle to Henry of Bolingbroke and is dethroned.

o   Henry of Bolingbroke is crowned King of England, thus becoming Henry IV. On 15 October 1399, his son, the future Henry V (b. 1386), is invested as Prince of Wales.

1400 (January): Richard II is murdered at Pontefract castle (in the city of Wakefield, West Yorkshire).

Chapter 8

The Revolt of Owain Glyndŵr (1400–1413)

The English crown neutralizes and dilutes the power of the Welsh lords thus further weakening Welsh resistance to the throne. During this time of increasing tension with England, the Welsh nobleman, Owain Glyndŵr, organizes his supporters to resist the King of England's encroachments on Welsh independence. This period of revolts is divided into three phases:

o   1400–1405: victorious years for the Welsh rebels led by Owain Glyndŵr (b. *c.*1354)

o   1405–1408: the English wear down the insurgents

o   1408–13: the rebellion is crushed

In spite of this popular uprising, large numbers of Welshmen continue to fight alongside the English in the Hundred Years' War (1337–1453).

1400 (16 September): Owain Glyndŵr begins his revolt in Glyndyfrdwy (i.e. Glyn-dŵr-Dwy, Valley of the River Dee), his birthplace.

o   22 September: The Welsh rebels attack the eight towns of north-eastern Wales.

o   October: English soldiers arrive in Wales. Henry of Monmouth, the Prince of Wales, establishes his headquarters at Chester.

1401 (Good Friday): Conwy castle is attacked by Rhys and Gwilym ap Tudur ap Goronwy, Owain's cousins.

o June: The Welsh defeat the English at the Battle of Mynydd Hyddgen (in the mountains of Pumlumon, Ceredigion).

o Owain receives a warm welcome from the inhabitants of the Tywi Valley (in Carmarthenshire).

o 2 October: Henry IV visits Wales. He bases his headquarters at Strata Florida (near Aberystwyth).

1401–1402: The English Parliament passes two series of laws, known as 'the Penal Laws'. In 1401, they forbid Welshmen from owning lands in the Welsh Marches in order to force them to submit to English authority. In September of the following year, new laws forbid Welshmen from bearing arms, living in fortified towns, holding office, and meeting in assemblies. Englishmen cannot marry Welsh women. These laws are repealed during the reign of James I in 1624.

1402 (April–November): Owain captures Reginald Grey (of the Grey family of Powys), and liberates him after receiving a ransom of 10,000 marks (approx. £6,700).

o 22 June: Owain captures Edmund (1376–1409), the brother of Roger Mortimer (d. 1398), during the Battle of Bryn Glas (Pilleth, Powys).

o August: Owain's leadership and authority is recognized by most of the Welsh.

1403 (July): Henry Percy[1] Earl of Northumberland (nicknamed 'Hotspur'), is stationed at Chester and leads a rebellion against the King. He starts discussions with the Welsh rebels concerning a possible alliance between the Welsh and the northern English. He is defeated and killed on 21 July at the

Battle of Shrewsbury before he can receive help from Wales and Northumberland.

o October–November: Owain, with the assistance of Breton sailors, attacks the English at Caernarfon and Kidwelly (near Swansea).

1404: The castles of Aberystwyth and Harlech fall into Owain's hands. The area between these two castles becomes a centre of his authority. He is crowned Prince of Wales in Machynlleth in the presence of envoys from France, Scotland, and Castile. It is also there that he founds a parliament. Gruffudd Young, a cleric (1370–1435), is named chancellor and he bases his chancery and his centre of administration in Aberystwyth until 1408.

o May: Owain appeals to Charles VI (King of France, 1380–1422) for help and asks for weapons and soldiers. He sends his two representatives: Gruffudd Young and John Hanmer, his brother-in-law. They are both welcomed by the French king to negotiate an alliance.

o By 1404, Gruffudd Young enlists John Trefor, Bishop of St Asaph, and John Byford, the Bishop of Bangor, as allies in order to win the support of the Catholic Church.

1405 (February): Henry Percy (Earl of Northumberland, father of Hotspur), Edmund Mortimer and Owain make an alliance which consists in dividing the territories of the kingdom into three regions:

1) Edmund Mortimer: southern England;

2) Henry Percy (not to be confused with his son, Hotspur), Earl of Northumberland: central and northern England;

3) Owain will reign over Wales and five counties on the border with England.

Figure 17: Illustration of Owain Glyndŵr (*c.*1404)

1405–1408: The English wear down the insurgents

1405 (spring): The Battle of Pwllmelyn near Usk ends in the defeat of the insurgents and the death of John ap Hywel, the abbot of Llantarnam.

o June: Henry Percy, Earl of Northumberland fails in his attempt to organize a revolt. He flees to Scotland where there is considerable interest in Owain's cause. In the meantime, Gruffudd Young and John Byford are sent to the Scottish court in 1405. Following the capture of the heir to the King of the Scots by the English in 1406 (the future James I of Scotland), hopes of Scottish assistance evaporate.

o July: 2,600 Bretons and Frenchmen sail from Brest to assist the Welsh rebels and bring equipment.

o August–November: French soldiers disembark at Milford Haven (Pembrokeshire). They march towards England with the hope of rallying the English followers of Richard II against Henry IV. At the end of the month, they and the forces of Owain arrive in Worcester. Nevertheless, English support for their cause does not materialize and they retreat back into Wales.

1406: The peripheral regions of Owain's principality slip from his grasp.

o March: Owain Glyndŵr sends a letter (in Latin) to the King of France, Charles VI. It is better known as 'the Pennal Letter'[2] (because it was written at Pennal, in Gwynedd). In exchange for more French aid, he promises that the Welsh Church will swear allegiance to Pope Benedict XIII of Avignon, who is supported by Charles VI, rather than the Pope of Rome (supported by the King of England and Canterbury). In so doing, he hopes to re-establish Saint Davids as the rightful centre of Christianity for all Britain.

'And because, most excellent prince, the metropolitan church of St David was, as it appears, violently compelled by the barbarous fury of those reigning in this country, to obey the church of Canterbury, and *de facto* still remains in this subjection. Many other disabilities are known to have been suffered by the Church of Wales through these barbarians [i.e. the English], which for the greater part are set forth fully in the letters patent accompanying.

[…] 'Again, that the Church of St David shall be restored to his original dignity, which from the time of Saint David, archbishop and confessor, was a metropolitan church, and after his death twenty-four archbishops succeeded him in the same place, as their names are contained in the chronicles in the ancient books of the Church of Menevia, and we cause these to be stated as the chief evidence, namely, Eliud, Ceneu, Morfael, Mynyw, Haerwnen, Elwaed, Gwrnwen…'

This is remarkable proof that, at this late date, the Welsh had still not forgiven Pope Gregory for having appointed Augustine as the first Archbishop of Canterbury, rather than supporting the long-established Church of Wales. (cf. AD **597**).

o Owain also calls for the creation of two Welsh universities.

[…] 'Again, that we shall have two universities or places of general study, namely, one in North Wales and the other in South Wales, in cities, towns, or places to be hereafter decided and determined by our ambassadors and nuncios for that purpose.'[3]

o October: Considering the lack of success of their previous incursions, the French decide to cease furnishing further aid to the Welsh. Meanwhile, the inhabitants of Anglesey and those living on the coast of southern Wales yield to Henry IV.

1408–1413: The end of the rebellion

o **1408** (September): Aberystwyth castle surrenders to the King. Owain and his court move to Harlech castle but surrender in 1409 when the Prince's family is captured. Edmund Mortimer, who is in the castle during the siege, dies of starvation.

o Owain Glyndŵr, along with Gruffudd Young, John Trefor, Philip Hanmer, and the sons of Tudur ap Goronwy, escape into the mountains of north Wales and, until about 1413, unleash sporadic attacks upon local centres of power.

o After 1413, nothing more is heard of Owain Glyndŵr, although it is speculated that he may have died in September 1415, possibly in Monnington, Herefordshire, where his daughter, Alys Scudamore, lived.

'For the Welshmen of all subsequent ages, Glyndŵr has been a national hero, the first, indeed, in the country's history to command the willing support alike of north and south, east and west, Gwynedd and Powys, Deheubarth and Morgannwg. He may with propriety be called the father of modern Welsh nationalism.' (John Edward Lloyd, *Owen Glendower: Owen GlynDŵr*, 1931)

Chapter 9

The Second Half of the Hundred Years' War and the Wars of the Roses (1413–1485)

The second half of the Hundred Years' War begins well for England, but gradually the tables are turned when Joan of Arc rallies French forces and inflicts several defeats upon the English armies under Lord Talbot. Lord Talbot is slain in the final battle against the French at Castillon in 1453.

Two years after the end of the Hundred Years' War, the Wars of the Roses break out (1455–1485). They are sparked by a dynastic quarrel between the descendants of Edward III's sons, John of Gaunt, Duke of Lancaster (red rose) and Edmund of Langley, Duke of York (white rose).

The poets Dafydd Nanmor and Lewys Glyn Cothi (c.1420–90) are supporters of the Lancastrians.

The warrior-poet Guto'r Glyn (from Glyn Ceiriog, near Wrexham) is pro-Yorkist and writes poems honouring Edward IV and William Herbert.

This civil war further divides the Welsh nobility and the ensuing political confusion and turmoil weaken Welsh national development.

1413: Henry V, of the House of Lancaster, is crowned King of England. He was born in Monmouth and considers himself to be a Welshman, a point which was not lost on Shakespeare who has the King boast of this fact in his history play, *Henry V.*

1414–1418: The Council of Constance marks the end of the schism between Avignon (France) and Rome and only the Pope in Rome is recognized.

1415: The French suffer another crushing defeat at the Battle of Agincourt. 251 archers are recruited from Carmarthenshire and 102 from Ceredigion to serve in Henry V's army. The personality of Fluellen, one of the main characters in Shakespeare's play, *Henry V*, might have been inspired by Dafydd Gam, a Welsh soldier who sacrificed his own life to protect Henry V during the battle.

1421: Powys passes from the Charlton family into the hands of the Grey family.

1422: Henry V dies. Until 1437, Henry VI is placed under the authority of his mother, Catherine de Valois (daughter of King Charles VI of France). She appoints Henry's uncles as his regents: John of Lancaster, Duke of Bedford (1422–35); Humphrey, Duke of Gloucester[1] (1435–37) and Bishop Henry Beaufort (who becomes cardinal in 1426).

1429: Henry VI is crowned King of England and France.

1430–1445: The soldier-poet, Guto'r Glyn, fights in France during the second part of the Hundred Years' War. 120 of his poems are known to have been composed by him either in France or in Wales.

o   He dedicates one poem to Matthew Gough of Maelor, in north-eastern Wales (captain of Bayeux, 1439 to 1442; d. 1450) and two to Sir Richard Gethin of Builth (captain of Mantes, near Paris, between 1432 and 1437). Both defeat the French at Verneuil (1424) in Normandy, but are forced to surrender to Joan of Arc's forces following the siege of Beaugency near Orléans (1429).

Moliant i Fathau Goch o Faelor
(In praise of Matthew Gough of Maelor)

Pan sonier i'n amser ni
Am undyn yn Normandi,
Mathau Goch, mab maeth y gwin,
Biau'r gair yn bwrw gwerin.
Eryr yw ar wŷr ieuainc,
Arthur ffriw, wrth aerau Ffrainc,
Enaid y capteiniaid da
A blaenor y bobl yna;
Broch a'i bâr coch yn bwrw cant,
Brwydr elyn, brawd i Rolant.
Gwayw a chorff Mathau Goch hael
A gyfyd Lloegr a'i gafael.
Â'r bêl o ryfel yr aeth
Â'i baladr o'i fabolaeth.

When there's talk in our time,
of a certain man in Normandy,
the fame for striking soldiers belongs to,
Matthew Gough, a son nurtured on wine.
He is an eagle leading young men,
facing the armies of France, with Arthur's countenance,
he is the darling of excellent captains
and the leader of the people there;
a badger with his blood-stained spear striking a hundred men,
an enemy in battle, brother to Roland.
The spear and body of generous Matthew Gough
will lift England and her inherited land.
Since his youth he has returned from war
with victory with the help of his spear.

(Source: www.gutorglyn.net, poem 3, lines 1–14)

1431: Owen Tudor (born Owain ap Maredudd) marries Catherine de Valois (Henry V's widow). He is the grandfather of Henry VII (Henry Tudor). They have two sons: Edmund[2] and Jasper, Henry VI's half-brothers (cf. genealogical chart).

1441: Guto'r Glyn participates in an expedition to Normandy under the leadership of Richard, Duke of York. Three of his patrons are said to have been among his companions: William ap Thomas of Raglan (father of the pro-Yorkist William Herbert, cf. **1461**, **1466–68**), Henry Griffith[3] of Bacton (Herefordshire), and Thomas ap Watkin of Llandewi Rhydderch, in Gwent.

1450: The English aristocratic families divide the Welsh principality amongst themselves and much intermarriage takes place.

- o The partisans of the Duke of York (the Yorkists) are based in Ludlow (territories extending from Denbigh to Caerleon).

- o The House of Lancaster: Henry VI is also Lord of Monmouth, Kidwelly, and Brecon.

- o The Marcher Lords: Humphrey Stafford, 1st Duke of Buckingham (Newport, Mowbray); John de Mowbray, 3rd Duke of Norfolk (Chepstow, Gower); the Neville family, Earl of Warwick (lordships of Glamorgan and Abergavenny).

1450–1490: The poet, Dafydd Nanmor, from Nanmor, Gwynedd, writes mainly love poems, such as *Gwallt Llio* (Llio's Hair) and praise poems. Here is an extract of 'an encouragement to Rhys ap Rhydderch of Tywyn' (*Anogaeth i Rys ap Rhydderch o'r Tywyn*):

> Rhys wyd, flodeuyn rhos haf,
> Ŵyr Rhys, nid o'r rhyw isaf:
> O fonedd y'th sylfaenwyd
> Aberth holl Ddeheubarth wyd
> Tref tad a chartref wyt ynn,
> Troed deau tir y Tywyn.

You are Rhys, flower of the summer rose,
Grandson of Rhys, not of ignoble stock:
You have been reared from nobility,
You are the offering of all Deheubarth.
You are a patrimony and a home for us,
The right foot of the land of Tywyn.

(Translated by Marged Haycock, in: H. Tristam, 1991:167)

1450/51: Dafydd ab Edmwnd wins the bardic chair at the eisteddfod organized by Gruffudd ap Nicolas in Carmarthen. He is a great poet of the 15th century, known for his poem *Y Cusan* (The Kiss). He is close to the Hanmer family (from Flintshire), and an uncle of Tudur Aled (cf. **1526**). Tudur Aled and Gutun Owain are both his pupils.

Dafydd ab Edmwnd, *Marwnad Siôn Eos*

Drwg i neb a drigo'n ôl
Dau am un cas damweiniol.
Y drwg lleiaf o'r drygwaith
Yn orau oll yn yr iaith.

O wŷr, pam na bai orau
O lleddid un na lladd dau?
Dwyn, un gelynwaed, a waeth,
Dial un dwy elyniaeth.

It's hard for those left behind,
the trouble of a chance enmity;
the smallest of all crimes,
but the best man in all our tongue.

O men, why isn't it better,
if one is killed, not to kill two?
he took one enemy's blood,
avenged our dual enmity.

(Translated by Gwyn Williams, 1974: 74)

In **1453** the English army suffers a severe defeat at Castillon near Bordeaux, ending the Hundred Years' War. Thousands of English and Welsh veterans return from France with little prospect of a future and turn to brigandage and pillaging. A war succession breaks out opposing the House of Lancaster and the House of York. These soldiers are quickly enrolled on both sides.

The Wars of the Roses

1455: The first battle is fought at St Albans (in Hertfordshire, England) and ends in a victory for the Yorkists.

1456: Gruffudd ap Nicolas (1400–1456) dies. He was the sheriff of Carmarthenshire (1436–56) and deputy Justice of the South (1437–56). He established his authority over south Wales and ruled from his castle in Carmarthen. One of his grandsons is Rhys ap Thomas (cf. **1485**).

> Here is an extract from Lewis Glyn Cothi's *Marwnad Siôn y Glyn* (Elegy of Siôn, the son of Lewis Glyn Cothi):
>
> Yngo y saif angau Siôn
> Yn ddeufrath yn y ddwyfron.
> Fy mab, fy muarth baban,
> Fy mron, fy nghalon, fy nghân,
> Fy mryd cyn fy marw ydoedd,
> Fy mardd doeth, fy moeth im oedd.
>
> *Siôn's death stands near me*
> *like two barbs in my breast.*
> *My son, child of my hearth,*
> *my breast, my heart, my song,*
> *my one delight before my death,*
> *my knowing poet, my luxury.*
>
> (Translated by Gwyn Williams, 1974: 78)

1460 (December): Richard, the Duke of York, is killed by the Lancastrians at the Battle of Wakefield.

1461: Richard of York's son, Edward IV, is crowned King of England. He marries Elizabeth Woodville, whose family has allies in Wales, notably Thomas Stanley[4] and his brother, William Stanley.

o The second Battle of St Albans ends in a Lancastrian victory. Later in the year, the Yorkists defeat the Lancastrians at Mortimer's Cross (in Herefordshire, England). The Lancastrian Owen Tudor (Henry VII's grandfather, cf. **1431**), is slain here.

o King Edward IV rewards the pro-Yorkist William Herbert (1423–69), by making him Lord of Raglan. He is the son of William ap Thomas (d. 1445) who built the castle of Raglan (1435). He is also the grandson of Dafydd Gam on his mother's side (cf. **1415**).

1466: William Herbert's son, also named William (1451–91), marries the Queen's sister, Mary Woodville.

1467: William Herbert (father) is appointed Chief Justice of Wales and becomes Earl of Pembroke (1468–69).

1468: Harlech castle falls into the hands of the Yorkists.

Guto'r Glyn composes his *Moliant i William Herbert o Raglan, iarll cyntaf Penfro, ar ôl cipio castell Harlech* (In Praise of William Herbert of Raglan, first Earl of Pembroke, after the Capture of Harlech castle):

> Na ad, f'arglwydd, swydd i Sais,
> Na'i bardwn i un bwrdais.
> Barna'n iawn, brenin ein iaith,
> Bwrw 'n y tân eu braint unwaith.
> Cymer wŷr Cymru'r awron,
> Cwnstabl o Farstabl i Fôn.

Dwg Forgannwg a Gwynedd,
Gwna'n un o Gonwy i Nedd.
O digia Lloegr a'i dugiaid,
Cymru a dry yn dy raid.

Do not, my lord, allow any office to an Englishman,
nor give any burgess his pardon.
Judge rightly, king of our nation,
cast their privilege into the fire once and for all.
Take now the men of Wales,
constable from Barnstaple to Anglesey.
Take Glamorgan and Gwynedd,
make all one from the Conwy to the Neath.
If England and her dukes are angered,
Wales will come to your need.

(www.gutorglyn.net, poem 21, lines 61–70)

1469: The Lancastrians are victorious at the Battle of Edgecote Moor, near Banbury (Oxfordshire, England). This leads to the restoration of Henry VI. The Lancastrians kill William Herbert along with 168 Welsh followers.

1470: Edward (the future Edward V, 1483) is invested as Prince of Wales shortly after his birth.

1471: Battle of Tewkesbury (in Gloucestershire, England) ends in a decisive victory for the Yorkists.

1472: The Council of Wales and the Marches is created and continues until its dissolution in 1689. Headed by the Prince of Wales, it serves to rule the lands held under the principality of Wales which had been directly administered by the English crown since the Edwardian conquest of 1284.

1483: The Yorkist, Richard III, seizes the crown from his 13-year-old nephew, Edward V. It is thought that he has the latter assassinated.

1485: The Lancastrian, Henry Tudor, lives in exile at the court of Francis II, Duke of Brittany. In the same year, he lands at Milford Haven, Pembrokeshire, with a 4,000-man army composed mainly of Welshmen, Frenchmen, and Bretons. They rally Welsh support (Rhys ap Thomas) and Henry leads his army to Leicestershire, where he defeats and kills Richard III at the decisive Battle of Bosworth Field, thus ending the Wars of the Roses.

o   Before the Battle of Bosworth Field, the bard Robin Ddu had written:

> Y mae hiraeth am Harri,
> Y mae gobaith i'n hiaith ni,
> Y ddraig goch ddyry cychwyn
>
> *For Henry there is longing.*
> *There is hope for our tongue.*
> *The red dragon made the first move*

Archaeologists discovered Richard III's body in 2012 near Greyfriars Church in Leicester where he was killed. Dafydd Johnston points out that the slash marks on his skull may correspond to the description given in Guto'r Glyn's poem *Moliant i Syr Rhys ap Tomas o Abermarlais* in which the poet describes how the 'Boar has been shaved', the boar being Richard III's nickname. From the appearance of his skull, it would seem that he literally was.

> Cwncwerodd y Cing Harri
> Y maes drwy nerth ein meistr ni:
> Lladd Eingl, llaw ddiangen,
> Lladd y baedd, eilliodd ei ben,
> A Syr Rys mal sŷr aesawr
> 'r gwayw'n eu mysg ar gnyw mawr.
>
> *King Henry won the day*
> *through the strength of our master:*

killing Englishmen, capable hand,
killing the boar, he shaved his head,
and Sir Rhys like the stars of a shield
with the spear in their midst on a great steed.

(www.gutorglyn.net, poem 14, lines 35–40)

William Shakespeare's representation of the battle in his play, *Richard III* (Act V, Scene 3) is interesting in that the playwright emphasizes the close bonds between Henry Tudor and his Breton allies perhaps emphasized because of the old prophecy which held that the future liberator of Britain would come from Brittany.

Speech by Richard III to his troops

What shall I say more than I have inferr'd?
Remember whom you are to cope withal;
A sort of vagabonds, rascals, and runaways,
A scum of Bretons, and base lackey peasants,
Whom their o'er-cloyed country vomits forth
To desperate ventures and assured destruction.
You sleeping safe, they bring to you unrest;
You having lands, and blest with beauteous wives,
They would restrain the one, distain the other.
And who doth lead them but a paltry fellow [Henry Tudor],
Long kept in Bretagne at our mother's cost?

(Wells & Taylor, 1999)

Chapter 10

Wales and the Tudors (1485–1603)

In multiple Welsh sources – Nennius's *Historia Brittonum* (Merlin's prophecy), the *Armes Prydein Vawr*, the Triads of Wales – generations of Welsh historians and poets had predicted the return of a Welsh hero who would drive the English out of Britain and reclaim the sovereignty (*unbeiniaeth*) of Britain which was symbolized by the 'crown of London'. Largely based on Breton and Welsh sources, Geoffrey of Monmouth's *Historia Regum Britanniae*, one of the most influential books of the Middle Ages, also predicted the return of a descendant of a Cynan or Cadwaladr who would re-establish the sovereignty of Britain.

In Henry Tudor the Welsh poets saw an answer to the age-old prophecy. As Geraint Jenkins has expressed it: 'his paternal grandfather, Owain Tudor of Penmynydd, Anglesey, could claim descent from Cadwaladr the Blessed, held to be the last native king of Britain' (2007: 127). The symbolic importance to the Welsh is largely linked to the re-establishment of a lost order which resulted from the Anglo-Saxon conquest and colonisation of England.

The final Lancastrian victory and crowning of Henry Tudor gives the Welsh new hope and enhanced prestige. Large numbers of the the Welsh nobility flock to the royal court in London. The unintended result of this is that many high-born Welsh nobles are anglicized during this period. Many abandon the Welsh language and adopt English names. A direct consequence of this process is that the age-old tradition of maintaining household poets falls out of fashion and the bardic class of poets slowly falls into decline. In 1536 and 1543 Henry VIII passes the Acts of Union between England and Wales, which has profound linguistic, cultural and political effects on Wales.

This period also sees the beginning of the Protestant Reformation a process of religious conversion which by degrees deeply alters Welsh identity on a massive scale. Having said this, the Welsh cling to their Catholic faith until well into the 18th century.

The entire period can be seen as one of transition, from ancient and medieval Wales to the early modern period.

1485: Henry Tudor becomes King of England under the name of Henry VII. His Welsh ties lead many Welsh noblemen to seek their fortunes in London, not in Wales. Many abandon the Welsh language and adopt Anglo-Norman names.[1]

1489–1502: Fully conscious of the Welsh/Brythonic sovereignty myth, Henry VII names his first son Arthur, Prince of Wales, but he dies at the age of 13.

1504: Arthur's brother Henry (the future Henry VIII) is invested as Prince of Wales.

1509: Henry VIII is crowned King of England.

1521: Edmund Stafford, Duke of Buckingham, is executed for treason. His territories in Brecon and Newport are added to those of the crown.

1523; 1567: Two eisteddfodau, sponsored by the Mostyn family and authorized by the British Crown, take place in Caerwys, Flintshire, to secure the professional status of Welsh bards.

1526; 1534–1536: William Tyndale translates the Bible into

English at a time when the Catholic Church deems this to be heresy.

- o Death in Carmarthen of Tudur Aled, a poet from Llansannan, Denbighshire (b. 1465). His main patrons are the Salisburys of Dyffryn Clwyd.

1532–1540: Thomas Cromwell[2] first Earl of Essex (1485–1540) becomes chief administrator of the kingdom. He serves Henry VIII as Chancellor of the Exchequer (1533) and Lord Privy Seal (1536).

- o Cromwell plays an important part in the Act of Union of 1536 under the reign of Henry VIII, and also in the Reformation.

- o In 1539 he attempts to arrange a marriage between Anne of Cleves and Henry VIII. His failure ends in his disgrace and execution.

1532–1536: After the Pope refuses to allow King Henry VIII to divorce Catherine of Aragon, he instigates the schism with the Catholic Church, thus becoming the supreme head of the Church of England. At the instigation of Thomas Cromwell, a series of statutes abolish the authority of the pope in the territories of the Crown of England. Anti-Catholic sentiments begin to spread in Wales (cf. the dissolution of the monasteries below).

1534–1543: Rowland Lee, the Bishop of Lichfield, is appointed President of the Council of Wales and the Marches. The powers of the Marcher Lords are also radically reduced.

1536: First Act of Union passed. The term, Acts of Union, was coined in 1901 by the Welsh historian Owen M. Edwards. In fact, it is only one of a series of articles designed to absorb Wales into England. Here are some of its consequences:

o The Marcher Lordships are abolished and new shires are created: Denbighshire, Montgomeryshire, Radnorshire, Brecknockshire, Monmouthshire, Glamorganshire and Pembrokeshire. Carmarthenshire, Anglesey, Caernarfonshire, Merionethshire, Flintshire and Cardiganshire had been in existence since the Statute of Wales in 1284. Now there were 13 shires in Wales (see map).

o The office of the Justice of the Peace is created (nine for each county). According to John Davies, it is 'a key institution in the local government of England, until the establishment of the county councils in 1889' (1993: 231).

o The Welsh can send members to the English Parliament at Westminster (27 members in 1543).

o English becomes the official language of law and administration, although the Welsh language is still used in the courts by monoglot Welsh speakers and their testimony is translated into English:

'[...] *from henceforth no person or persons that use the Welsh Speech or Language, shall have or enjoy any manner office or fees within this realm of England, Wales, or other the King's dominion, upon pain of forfeiting the same offices or fees, unless he or they use and exercise the English speech or language*' (section 20, §3). Ironically, Norman-French is still used in courts of law in England until the early 17th century. See the year **1362**, 'The Laws of Pleading'.

1536–1539: All but three of the 32 monasteries in Wales are dissolved including Valle Crucis abbey (1537). The three abbeys that remain are at Neath (in the Clydach Valley), Strata Florida and Whitland (Llanboidy).

1540: Thomas Cromwell (cf. **1532**) is executed for treason.

1543: The remaining monasteries, friaries and reliquaries are all destroyed.

- o The Second Act of Union is adopted by the English Parliament and brings two modifications to the first one:

  The Court of Great Sessions is established at Ludlow, Shropshire, until its abolition in 1830. It judges criminal offences. It meets twice a year in each county. There are four main courts that represent three counties each: in Chester (for the counties of Flintshire, Denbighshire, and Montgomeryshire), north Wales (for the counties of Anglesey, Caernarfonshire, and Merionethshire), Brecon (for the counties of Breconshire, Glamorganshire and Radnorshire), and Carmarthen (for the counties of Carmarthenshire, Cardiganshire and Pembrokeshire). Monmouthshire is excluded from the Court of Great Sessions, and added to the Oxford Circuit of the English Assizes.

  The Council of Wales and the Marches (cf. **1472** and **1689**) has full recognition after the second act of 1543. It is composed of the lord president and his deputy, 20 members nominated by the King who represent the royal household, the bishops of Wales, and the justices of the Court of Great Sessions.

1546: John Prys (or John ap Rhys) of Brecon publishes what is considered to be the first printed book in the Welsh language.

1546–1660: Davies (1993: 239) indicates that 108 printed books are published in Welsh during this period (only four in Scottish Gaelic, 11 in Irish).

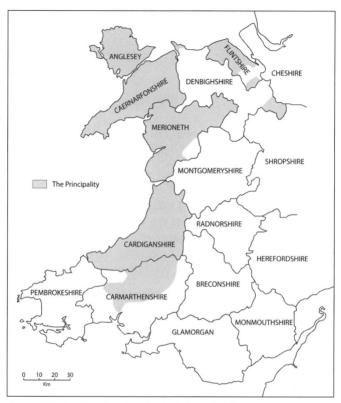

Figure 18: Map of Wales after the 1536 Acts of Union
(inspired by G. Jenkins, 2007)

1547: Edward VI is crowned King of England.

o William Salesbury,[3] a Welsh scholar well versed in
traditional Welsh bardic poetry, writes his *A Dictionary
in Englyshe and Welshe*. This is the first Welsh-English
dictionary. It is very precious in that he spells the
English words using Welsh orthography providing

linguists with a clear idea of the way Welsh-English was pronounced in his day.

1549: The first version of the *English Prayer Book* is published.

1550: William Salesbury publishes a pamphlet on the ancient laws of Hywel Dda.[4]

1551: William Salesbury writes *Kynniver Llith a Bann*, a translation into Welsh of the epistles and gospels taken from the *English Prayer Book* of 1549.

1553: Mary I, the daughter of Henry VIII and Catherine of Aragon, becomes Queen of England. A devout Catholic, she marries Philip of Spain, son of the emperor Charles V. In this same year, the statutes *De Haeretico Comburendo* are revived during the first meeting of her Parliament. It abrogates Edward VI's protestant laws and papal power is restored.

o   Almost 500 of her subjects flee to Europe, among them a dozen Welshmen, notably Richard Davies.[5] Mary has about 300 Protestant heretics burnt at the stake. The majority of the Welsh, many of whom are Catholic sympathizers, support her.

The Elizabethan Era (1558–1603)

1558: Elizabeth I is crowned Queen of England. Some of her advisors, such as William Cecil, 1st Baron Burghley, are of Welsh descent. His name is an anglicization of *Sisyll*. His family originates from Allt-yr-ynys, at Walterstone, in Herefordshire. During the reign of Elizabeth, British clearly means 'Brythonic' or 'Welsh' and she, as a descendant of the Tudors, sees herself as a 'British' queen. This ties in well with Geoffrey of Monmouth's *History of the Kings of Britain* (cf. **1136**). See also Spenser's 'Faerie Queene'.

1559: Elizabeth launches her 'Religious Settlement', a movement to unify the Anglican Church. The new *English Prayer Book* is published.

1561: Morys Clynnog, the Catholic Bishop of Bangor since 1558, goes into exile in Rome.

1562–1624: The Welsh wool industry is dominated by the Shrewsbury Drapers' Company.

1563: Thirty-nine articles are written to define the doctrine of the Anglican Church. Catholics such as Gruffydd Robert and Owen Lewis (a teacher of law at Oxford) exile themselves to Europe. The Act of 1563 is passed by Parliament, thanks to the efforts of Richard Davies (Bishop of St Davids, 1561–1581). It allows him, William Salesbury, and Thomas Huet (dean of St Davids), to translate the New Testament into Welsh in 1567. Also in 1567 William Salesbury translates the *English Book of Common Prayer* (Lliver Gweddi Gyffredin) into Welsh. This is a revised version of *Kynniver Llith a Bann* (cf. **1551**).

1567–1590: Gruffydd Robert's *Gramadeg Cymraeg* (Welsh Grammar) is printed in Milan.

1568: Morys Clynnog and Gruffydd Robert (the confessor of the Archbishop of Milan) write a 63-page booklet entitled *Athrawaeth Gristnogawl* (Christian Doctrine). It is published in Rome. Louis Lucien Bonaparte, Napoleon I's nephew, owned a facsimile of *Gramadeg Cymraeg* and an original copy of *Athravaeth Gristnogol* which are now held by the Newberry Library in Chicago. He was a famous linguist who worked on Celtic languages and on the Basque language.

1570: Queen Elizabeth I is excommunicated by Pope Pius V. This coincides with the beginning of the persecutions against the Catholics. Nevertheless, relatively few (about 15) members of the Catholic clergy of Wales are stripped of their possessions, among them Morys Clynnog and Gruffydd Robert.

Another group of English Catholics flees to Europe where they are later joined by Hugh Owen and Thomas Morgan, both well-known for their involvement in plots against Elizabeth I.

Puritanism begins as a religious trend within the Anglican Church. The Puritans are inspired by Calvinism and its theocratic republic in Geneva (1536–64). They are influential among members of the court, merchants and aristocrats. In Wales, Puritanism first develops in towns such as Cardiff, Swansea, Wrexham and Haverfordwest.

1571: Jesus College, Oxford, is founded by Hugh Price, a native of Brecon. The first royal charter is signed on 27 June. According to the Jesus College website, 24 Principals of the college came from Wales or were of Welsh descent. Generations of Welshmen have been educated here. John Rhŷs was Principal and first holder of the Chair of Celtic (see **1877**). Oxford University, especially Oriel and All Souls Colleges (founded in 1324 and 1438 respectively), has always had a strong Welsh component since the 13th century.

1573: The first detailed map of Wales, entitled *Cambriae Typus* (Model Image of Wales) is drawn by Humphrey Lhuyd and published in Antwerp by Abraham Ortelius as an appendix to his atlas entitled *Theatri Orbis Terrarum* (Theatre of the World, 1570).

1577: The Welshman John Dee coins the term 'British Empire' on the grounds that King Arthur had conquered a huge empire in the North Atlantic. The idea is based on the legend surrounding Madog ab Owain Gwynedd's voyages (cf. 1170) to North America and his claim of these sovereign territories for the Welsh. In Dee's mind, 'British' still implies a strong connection with Celtic Britain.

1578: The English college in Rome is established. Morys Clynnog is at its head until he resigns in 1579.

The Struggle between Anglicanism and Catholicism in Wales

1581–1587: A bardic controversy arises between Edmwnd Prys, a graduate of Cambridge, and William Cynwal (d. 1587 or 1588, poet and disciple of the poet Gruffudd Hiraethog). It results from a confrontation between two generations of bards: the old school led by Cynwal versus the new school led by Prys. The latter is inspired by new European poetry. Moreover, Prys speaks or reads eight languages, including Latin and Hebrew!

1584: Richard Gwyn, a Cambridge University-educated teacher from Montgomeryshire, is executed at Wrexham for his Catholic beliefs and on the grounds that he is plotting the overthrow of the Anglican establishment.

David Powel, vicar of Ruabon, writes his *Historie of Cambria now called Wales*. The book is published by William Wynne in 1697, and republished between 1702 and 1832. Although he expresses dislike for the English, he nevertheless favours the union with England, arguing that it provides Wales with good administration and modernity.

Copper starts to be smelted in Neath, south Wales, under the control of the Society of Mines Royal. Gold, zinc, and silver are also extracted.

1584–1587: Edward Dunn Lee is MP for Carmarthen. During the Parliamentary session of 1586–7 he presents his *Aequity of* *an Humble Supplication* to Parliament, a treatise in which he pleads for preachers to 'expound the gospel to the Welsh'.

1585: Another Catholic, the recusant Robert Gwyn, writes *Y Drych Gristianogawl* (The Christian Mirror).

1586: Catholics Thomas Salisbury of Llewenni (Denbighshire) and Edward Jones of Plas Cadwgan (Denbighshire) are executed for their alleged role in the Babington Plot (named after its Catholic leader, Anthony Babington) to overthrow the Queen and replace her with Mary Stuart, Queen of Scots. Mary's beheading the following year is justified by the plot.

William Camden writes *Britannia*, a topographical masterpiece. It is translated from Latin into English in 1610 by Philemon Holland. In this book, he details the tribal division of Roman Wales. Along with Polydor Vergil (c.1470–1555), an Italian historian, he also calls into question certain points in Geoffrey of Monmouth's *History of the Kings of Britain*, a book which had served as the official history of the sovereigns of Britain for centuries.

1588: By the order of Queen Elizabeth, the Welsh translation of the Bible is published. The translators involved in the project are all well-versed in traditional Welsh poetry. Their work is considered to be a masterpiece to this day and provided a recognized literary standard for all those who followed. William Morgan adds his own translation of the Old Testament to the New Testament.

1593: John Penry, a graduate of Cambridge and native of Breconshire, is accused by the Anglicans of being too close to the Puritans. He is accused of being the author of the *Marprelate Tracts* (1588–89) and is obliged to flee to Scotland. When he returns in 1592, he is arrested in London and

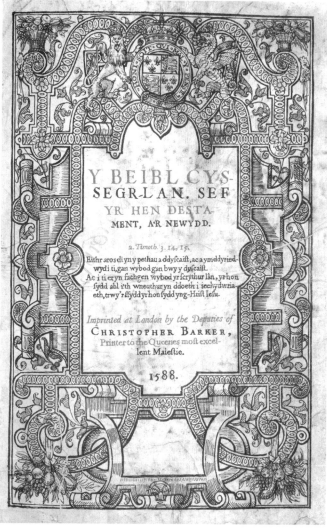

Figure 19: Cover of the 1588 Welsh Bible (National Library of Wales)

executed in 1593. During this year, the plague returns as well as devastating attacks of typhus and smallpox.

During this year, William Davies, a Catholic priest, is hanged for treason in Beaumaris, Anglesey.

1594–1602: During the Nine Years' War, 6,611 Welshmen are recruited to fight alongside the Elizabethan forces in Ireland against the Irish chieftains (led by Hugh O'Neill). Most of the battles take place in Ulster where the English seek to replace the native Irish with British (English, Welsh, Scottish) settlers.

1595: Morris Kyffin writes *Deffynniad Ffydd Eglwys Loegr*, a translation into Welsh of Bishop John Jewel's book, *Apology or Defence of the English Church* (1562).

Philip Sidney's *Apology for Poetry* is published posthumously (he had died in 1586). One of the greatest poets of the Elizabethan era, he is the son of Sir Henry Sidney, President of the Council of Wales and the Marches (1560–86) and brother of Mary Sidney, wife of Henry Herbert, Earl of Pembroke (and Sir Henry Sidney's successor, 1586–1601). In one of his poems, he praises the Welsh bards:

> In Wales, the true remnant of the ancient Britons,
> There are good authorities to show the long time
> They had poets, which they called bards; so through
> All the conquests of Romans, Saxons, Danes, and
> Normans, some of whom did seek to ruin all memory
> Of learning among them, yet do their poets to this
> Day, last; so as it is not more notable in soon
> Beginning than in long continuing

> (Source: http://www.britannia.com/wales/whist11.html)

1601 (February–March): Robert Devereux, 2nd Earl of Essex rebels against Queen Elizabeth. This leads to his execution and that of his close ally, Gelli Meurig (or Meyrick, c.1556–1601).

1602: George Owen (1552–1613), an antiquarian, author and naturalist from Henllys (near Newport, Pembrokeshire) publishes his *Description of Wales* (originally entitled *The Number of the Hundreds, Castells, Parish Churches and ffayres… in all the Shiers of Wales*).

Chapter 11

Wales and the Stuarts (1603–1714)

The reign of the Stuarts is marked by the clash between Anglicans and Puritans, Cavaliers and Roundheads. In Wales many Welshmen still cling tenaciously to their Catholic faith. By the time of the Glorious Revolution of 1688, Welshmen are slowly converting to various Protestant denominations. One of the consequences of this religious transformation is the creation of a popular religious environment in which the language of worship and the social activities surrounding it is Welsh. This results in the foundation of a remarkably vibrant, popular, literary tradition, the consequence of which is the foundation of a rigorous linguistic standard for the Welsh language, a fact which has guaranteed its survival until the present day.

Following the English Civil War there are only 1,000 Catholics and more than 4,000 Nonconformists (mainly Baptists, Presbyterians, and Independents) in Wales. Around 1560–1660, four per cent of the Welsh population are landowners. Until the Reform Act of 1832, only landowners can elect Members of Parliament to Westminster.

1603: James VI of Scotland becomes King of England under the name of James I, the son of Mary Stuart, thus founding the Stuart dynasty. The Stuarts claim Breton descent (through Alan FitzFlaad, a Breton knight who came to Britain after the Norman Conquest). The Stuarts, like their Tudor predecessors, use Celtic genealogical links and the authority of Geoffrey of Monmouth's *History of the Kings of Britain* to justify their kingship over Britain. Nevertheless, in the wake of the Reformation and the Glorious Revolution, Geoffrey's work (cf. **1136**) is finally discredited as a serious historical source. James I also claims descendance from Henry VII through the marriage of Henry's daughter Margaret Tudor and James IV of Scotland (1503–1513).

1605: The Gunpowder Plot (led by Guy Fawkes) is a failed attempt to murder King James I. Hugh Owen, a Welshman, is involved in the conspiracy but his fate is unknown. He had also participated in an attempt to assassinate Queen Elizabeth (cf. **1570**).

1610: John Roberts, a Welsh Benedictine monk, is drawn and quartered for his religious beliefs. In 1970 he is canonized by Pope Paul VI as one of the Forty Martyrs of England and Wales. Among these is the Welshman Richard Gwyn (cf. **1584**).

1611: John Speed, an Englishman from Farndon, Cheshire, publishes his *Theatre of the Empire of Great Britaine*, which contains maps of Wales, notably of Cardiff, Carmarthen, and Bangor.

1616–1632: Sir William Vaughan (1575–1641), a landowner from Golden Grove, Carmarthenshire, settles in Newfoundland and calls his plantation Cambriol. Several towns such as Cardiff are founded nearby on the island.

1620: Bishop Richard Parry and his brother-in-law, Dr John Davies (rector of Mallwyd, in Gwynedd from 1604 to his death in 1644), publish a revised version of William Morgan's Bible (cf. **1588**), known as 'Parry's Bible', along with a revised version of the *Book of Common Prayer*. It is published 28 times between 1620 and 1800.

1621: Dr John Davies writes his *Antiquae linguae Britannicae*, a Welsh grammar in Latin, showing that Welsh scholars are keen to maintain clear linguistic standards for their language (cf. **1322**, **1567**). In this respect, the Welsh are in the forefront of such work, along with the French.

1621–1626: Edward Wynne, a Welshman, is appointed by George Calvert (future founder of the colony of Maryland) to govern the colony of Ferryman (south-eastern Newfoundland and Labrador).

1621–1630: Sir Eubule Thelwall (a Welshman whose family comes from Plas Coch, Denbighshire) is the Principal of Jesus College, Oxford, and obtains in 1622 a new charter. It becomes the most important college for Welsh students (cf. **1571**).

1625: Charles I is crowned King of England and Wales. He is an Anglican and, like his cousins, Louis XIII and Louis XIV of France, he believes in the 'Divine Right of Kings' (i.e. God himself appoints kings as absolute monarchs and as the sole authorities over their kingdoms).

1628: The House of Commons obliges the King to sign the 'Petition of Right' in order to avoid the absolutist measures of the crown.

1630: Sir Thomas Myddelton and Rowland Heylin, London-Welsh merchants, publish *Y Beibl Bach* (The Little Bible), a smaller and cheaper version of 'Parry's Bible', to allow the Welsh people to have access to it more easily.

1631: Oliver Thomas writes *Carwr y Cymry* (The Welshmen's Friend). It is inspired by *Y Beibl Bach*. It starts with two letters dedicated to the Welsh clergy and the Welsh laity, followed by a dialogue in which a sympathizer (Thomas himself) instructs Welshmen about the Bible.

1632: Dr John Davies writes *Dictionarium Duplex*, a Welsh-Latin dictionary (see also William Salesbury's dictionary, **1547**).

1634–1641: The Welsh gentry are opposed to the Ship Money tax, which is levied to defend English and Welsh coastal towns. Perceived as thoroughly unjust and arbitrary, it is one of the primary causes of the English Civil War.

1639: Walter Cradock,[1] William Wroth and William Thomas (a Baptist) found the first Independent Church in Wales at Llanfaches (near Chepstow, Monmouthshire). Along with Morgan Llwyd and Vavasor Powell, these men argue energetically in favour of the right of an individual to interpret the Bible according to his or her own conscience.

1641: The Irish revolt against the British settlers, many of whom are Welshmen.

1642: By this date, 119 future Welsh Catholic priests are being trained in Europe, 64 of them in Douai, northern France. The rest attend various schools such as Reims (France), Valladolid and Salamanca (Spain) and Rome.

o   Howell Powell (from Brecon) is thought to be the first Welshman to emigrate to Virginia in this year.

Wales and the English Civil War (1642–1649)[2]

The English Civil War is the result of a contest between Parliament, which seeks to limit the powers of the king, and King Charles I's desire to retain absolute power over his kingdom and subjects. As head of the Anglican Church, the King has the support of its clergy. The dissenters (Baptists, Independents, and Quakers) are dedicated to transferring many of the king's powers to Parliament. Once again, the Welsh are divided in two camps:

o The Parliamentarians (Roundheads) led by: Rowland Laugharne; Thomas Myddelton of Chirk (Denbighshire); John Poyer and Colonel Rice Powell (the latter two change camps to become Royalists in 1648).

o The Royalists (Cavaliers) led by: Charles Gerard; Richard Vaughan (Earl of Carbery), who owns estates in Pembrokeshire and Cardiganshire; John Bodvel of Anglesey.

1642: The Summer of this year marks the beginning of the Civil War. King Charles I receives most of his support from Anglicans and Catholics, but also the peasantry and landowners. He bases his headquarters in Shrewsbury. The Puritans stand with the Parliamentarians.

o The Battle of Edgehill (Warwickshire) is fought to prevent the Parliamentarians from seizing London. The latter are led by Robert Devereux, the Earl of Essex.[3] The Royalists, commanded by the king's nephew, Prince Rupert of the Rhine, succeed in blocking the Parliamentarians but their infantry suffers heavy losses. About 1,000 Welsh Royalists (of the 5,000 men engaged) are slain on the battlefield.

1642–1649: The pro-royalist poet Huw Morys (1622–1709), known as 'Eos Ceiriog', writes *The Nightingale of Ceiriog*.

Huw Morys, *I'w Gariad*

Fy nghariad i,
Teg wyt i,
Gwawr ragori, lili lawen,
Bêr winwydden;
Fwynaidd feinwen,
Y gangen lawen lun;
Blodau'r wlad
Mewn mawhad...

My sweetheart,
Fair are you,
Dawn surpassing, joyous lily,
Sweet vine,
Gentle slender white,
The branch of happy form;
The country flowers
In honour...

(lines 1–8, in: Nesta Lloyd, 1997: 108–9)

1643: In March, Richard Vaughan, Earl of Carbery (a Royalist) is defeated by Rowland Laugharne in Pembrokeshire. The latter takes control of Haverfordwest, Tenby and Carew castle, but also Carmarthen and Cardiff.

o   Royalist Edward Somerset (Earl of Glamorgan, Lord Herbert) and his Welsh followers are defeated in Highnam during the siege of Gloucester.

1643–1644: Thomas Myddelton of Chirk (Parliamentarian) decides to capture the main Royalist centres in north Wales (Conwy, Bangor and Caernarfon) in the winter in order to cut off the king's military supplies. A Royalist army of 2,500 men arriving from Ireland forces him to withdraw his troops.

1644: With the support of Rowland Laugharne and a small force of 100 men, Parliamentary leader John Poyer captures Pembroke and its castle from the Royalists.

o   From March to December, the Parliamentarians, under the leadership of Rowland Laugharne, capture all centres of importance in south Wales (Cardigan, Tenby).

o   During the summer, the Parliamentarians, under Thomas Myddelton's command, capture Welshpool and Newtown.

o   In September the Royalist troops are defeated at the Battle of Montgomery and 2,000 of their men are killed, wounded or captured by the Parliamentarians.

o   In October, Thomas Myddelton's Parliamentarians capture Powis castle, Montgomeryshire.

1644–1645: Richard Vaughan is replaced as commander of south-west Wales (Pembrokeshire) by Lieutenant-General Charles Gerard. The latter reimposes Royalist control over Haverfordwest, Cardigan, Carew castle and Picton castle.

1645: Lord Thomas Fairfax is appointed commander-in-chief of the Parliamentarian troops.

o   In April Laugharne has some success against the Royalists, but Charles Gerard gains the upper hand by early summer.

o   In June the Battle of Naseby (Northamptonshire) marks a turning point in the Civil War. Charles Gerard and 12,000 Royalist troops are defeated by 15,000 Parliamentarians. Afterwards, the King is forced to flee successively to Raglan, then to Cardiff, to try to recruit more soldiers. He then flees to Chirk and Chester.

o   In July, disgruntled Royalists from Glamorgan form a 'peaceable army' against their commander, Charles Gerard. They meet Charles I who agrees to remove him and Gerard is replaced by Jacob Astley as the new commander-in-chief.

1646 (May): Charles I surrenders to the Scots Covenanters (Scottish pro-Parliamentarians).

o   After a three-month siege, Raglan castle (Monmouthshire) yields in August to the Parliamentary forces, commanded by Col. Thomas

Morgan. Following this, all the counties of north and south Wales surrender to the Parliamentarians. This marks the end of the first Civil War.

1647: In January, the Scots Covenanters deliver Charles I to the Parliamentary authorities.

o   In March Harlech castle surrenders to the Parliamentary forces and they accumulate victories against the Royalists.

o   After their initial victory the Parliamentarians face internal tensions. The first subject of dissension concerns the Monarchy: the hardliners want to execute the King and the moderates want to simply limit his powers (this occurs after the Glorious Revolution of 1688). This marks the beginning of the second Civil War.

o   George Fox (1624–91) founds the Religious Society of Friends (or Quakers), a denomination which is popular in north Wales.

Figure 20: Photograph of Raglan castle (*c.* 1646)

1648: Revolts break out inside the Parliamentary ranks, notably in south Wales. Disenchanted by the hardliners, some Parliamentarians join the Royalists, such as John Poyer, governor of Pembroke, who declares himself in favour of the King in April. He is joined by former Parliamentarian Colonel Rice Powell, the governor of Tenby castle. They both march to Cardiff, where they are joined in May by Major-General Rowland Laugharne, who also changes camps.

o   Rowland Laugharne and 8,000 Royalists are defeated in May by the Parliamentary army, led by Colonel Thomas Horton, at the Battle of St Fagans, near Cardiff, in south Wales. In the meantime, the Parliamentary fleet in the Downs changes sides and declares its allegiance to the King.

o   Pembroke castle is captured in July after a siege by the Parliamentarians. John Poyer, Rice Powell and Rowland Laugharne, who are in the castle, are taken as prisoners and sent to London.

o   In December, Colonel Thomas Pride removes the 'levellers', the moderate faction of the Parliamentarians, and also all those who do not support the 'Grandees' (these are senior officers of Oliver Cromwell's New Model Army) from the Long Parliament. This is known as 'Pride's Purge', which most historians view as a *coup d'état*.

The Commonwealth (1649–1660)

1649: Charles I is executed on 30 January at the Palace of Whitehall. Of the 59 signatories responsible for the king's execution, only two are Welsh: John Jones,[4] MP for Meirionnydd (since November 1647) and Thomas Wogan,[5]

MP for Cardigan Boroughs (since August 1646). Charles's wife, Henrietta Maria, Louis XIII's sister (d. 1669), returns to her native France. Oliver Cromwell becomes head of the Commonwealth which replaces the monarchy.

o John Miles (1621–83), a native of Herefordshire, founds the first Baptist church at Ilston, Gower, near Swansea (cf. **1663**).

o John Poyer (cf. **1644**, **1648**) is executed by a firing squad at Covent Garden, London.

1650: The English-language poet Henry Vaughan (1621–95) publishes *Silex Scintillans* and *Olar Iscanus* the following year. Born in Newton St Bridget, Breconshire, his work influenced the poetry of William Wordsworth, Alfred Tennyson, and even Siegfried Sassoon. He is part of the Vaughan family of Tretower Court (near Crickhowell, Powys).

1650–1653: Parliament passes *Deddf er Taenu'r Efengyl yng Nghymru* (The Act for the Better Propagation of the Gospel in Wales) in 1650. A Commission for the Propagation of the Gospel is led by Major-General Thomas Harrison (also leader of the Fifth Monarchists[6]) and 70 commissioners. Eleven of these commissioners are governors of towns in Wales. They are Englishmen for the most part. As a consequence 60 schools are established, such as Abergele (Conwy), to teach children reading and writing. These commissioners also replace 278 clerics by preachers (examples: Morgan Llwyd, Vavasor Powell[7], and Walter Cradock). These three men contribute to the growth of the Baptist[8] and Independent congregations. The Commission ceases to be operative in 1653, but part of the work is continued under the supervision of the Commission for the Approbation of Public Preachers, established in 1654.

1650–1689: More than 3,000 Quakers are jailed around

Wales, mainly because they refuse to swear allegiance to any earthly authority (example: the Lloyd family of Dolobran, Montgomeryshire; many leave for Pennsylvania a few decades later).

1653: Morgan Llwyd is the author of an influential book entitled *Llyfr y Tri Aderyn* (The Book of the Three Birds), an allegorical discussion between three birds: an eagle (secular authority), a dove (the Puritans), and a raven (the Anglican establishment).

1654: 2,492 Royalists from the west of England and south-east Wales begin to emigrate to Virginia via Bristol. Others go to Barbados. Most are indentured servants and unskilled workers.

1655: In March, the 'Penruddock rising' occurs in Wiltshire against Cromwell's government. Following this, until 1657, Parliament places Hereford, Worcestershire, Shropshire, and Wales under the authority of Major-General James Berry (d. 1691). John Nicholas serves as his deputy in Monmouthshire and also Rowland Dawkins in Carmarthenshire, Cardiganshire, Glamorganshire, and Pembrokeshire.

1657: George Fox (1624–91), the founder of the Society of Friends (The Quakers) converts many Welshmen and women from mid-Wales and south Pembrokeshire during a missionary tour in Wales. Born in Cefn Mawr (near Ruabon, Denbighshire), John ap John (*c.*1625–97) is a follower of the preacher Morgan Llwyd. He becomes Fox's first Welsh apostle. During the Civil War, he serves as a chaplain in the Parliamentary army and in 1681 meets William Penn in London. He persuades Penn to found a settlement in America (future Pennsylvania).

o Under the Commonwealth, some influential parliamentarians build estates in Wales, among them

Philip Jones of Llangyfelach[9] (1618–74) in Fonmon (Vale of Glamorgan) and Colonel John Jones in Mostyn (Flintshire).

1658: Oliver Cromwell dies.

o Stephen Hughes publishes the first part of Vicar Rees Prichard's collection of popular religious verses, *Canwyll y Cymry* (The Welshmen's Candle). Fifty-two editions are published between 1658 and 1820.

1659 (5–19 August): Following Richard Cromwell's resignation, an insurrection called the Booth Uprising (named after Sir George Booth) takes place in Cheshire, the purpose being to restore the Stuart Monarchy. Sir Thomas Myddelton participates in the revolt in Cheshire and north Wales.

Wales during the Restoration (1660–85)

1660: Charles II is proclaimed King of England, Scotland and Ireland at Wrexham, and is welcomed by most of the inhabitants of Wales. He is crowned on 29 May.

o Edward Lhuyd (cf. **1707**), the founder of Celtic studies, is born in Lopington, Shropshire. His father comes from Oswestry (Shropshire) and his mother from Talybont (Ceredigion).

1661–1665: The Clarendon Code is passed by the pro-Anglican English Parliament to prevent King Charles II (influenced by his French Catholic mother) from imposing Catholicism as the official religion. It bears the name of Edward Hyde, first Earl of Clarendon. It also contains four discriminating laws against Nonconformist Protestants:

o Corporation Act, 1661: Nonconformists are forbidden

from holding public or military offices, unless they swear allegiance to the Anglican Church.

o   Act of Uniformity, 1662: All clergy who do not use the *Book of Common Prayer* during church services are expelled from the Church of England. As a result, over 2,000 clergymen (including more than 100 Puritans) are forced to resign from their parishes.

o   Conventicle Act, 1664: Nonconformists cannot meet in assemblies of more than five persons.

o   Five Mile Act, 1665: Former Anglican clergymen are forbidden from teaching in schools and cannot live in a place more than five miles from their former parish.

1661–1673: Leoline Jenkins from Cowbridge (Glamorgan) is the Principal of Jesus College, Oxford.

1663–1667: Reverend John Miles leaves Wales with 15 members of his Baptist congregation for America where he founds the town of Swansea, Massachusetts.

1666: The last professional Welsh bard, Gruffydd Phylip of Ardudwy (Merionnydd), dies. He is part of the Phylip family (brother of Phylip Phylip, son of Siôn Phylip and nephew of Rhisiart Phylip). All are Welsh bards who compose elegies in honour of the Vaughan family of Corsygedol (Merionethshire) and the Ellis family of Bron y Foel (Caernarfonshire).

1667: Welsh antiquarian Robert Vaughan (1592–1667) of Hengwrt (Old Court) near Dolgellau, Gwynedd, assembles a collection of medieval Welsh manuscripts, including 'The Book of Taliesin', 'The Black Book of Carmarthen', and 'The White Book of Rhydderch' which forms the basis of the Hengwrt-Peniarth Collection, now preserved in the National Library of Wales.

1667; 1671; 1677: Charles Edwards (1628–91), a Welsh Puritan cleric and writer, publishes *Y Ffydd Ddi-ffuant* (The Sincere Faith).[10]

1668–1674: Sir Henry Morgan (Harri Morgan in Welsh), from Abergavenny (Monmouthshire), serves as a privateer for King Charles II. He arrives in Barbados in the 1650s as an indentured servant. He plunders the Spanish cities of Portobelo (1668) and Panama (1671). He is knighted by the King in 1674 and appointed Lieutenant Governor of Jamaica the same year.[11]

1673: The Test Act is passed against the Catholics and Nonconformists. Any person who occupies a civil or military office has to swear allegiance to the Anglican Church.

1674: With the support of Puritans and Nonconformists Thomas Gouge (d. 1681), a former clergyman, and Stephen Hughes, leader of the Independents, found the Welsh Trust.[12] Between 1674 and 1681 about 3,000 pupils attend Welsh Trust schools. The work of John Locke (the son of Puritan parents) is the source of many of their intellectual ideas.

1678–1681: The Bill of Exclusion seeks to bar Charles II's brother, James, Duke of York, from the succession because he is a Catholic. One of the consequences of this religious conflict is the rise of the two-party system. The Tories (modern Conservative Party), support the King. The Whigs generally oppose him.

1679: The law of Habeas Corpus is passed to guarantee individual liberties by limiting arbitrary arrests by the King.

1681: Stephen Hughes publishes all of the verses of Vicar Rhys Prichard's *Canwyll y Cymry* (The Welshmen's Candle).

1681: The Quaker William Penn obtains a vast tract of territory south of New York from the British government. Initially it is called New Wales. It is later renamed Pennsylvania (Penn's Woods).

1682: William Penn and Welsh Quakers from Merioneth, Montgomeryshire and Pembrokeshire emigrate to 'New Wales' (Pennsylvania).

o Some towns established in Pennsylvania bear Welsh names, such as Bryn Mawr[13] or Gwynedd. The following inscription can still be read in Philadelphia's City Hall: 'Perpetuating the Welsh heritage, and commemorating the vision and virtue of the following Welsh patriots in the founding of the City, Commonwealth, and Nation: William Penn, 1644–1718, proclaimed freedom of religion and planned New Wales, later named Pennsylvania. Thomas Jefferson, 1743–1826, third President of the United States, composed the Declaration of Independence. Robert Morris, 1734–1806, foremost financier of the American Revolution and signer of the Declaration of Independence. Gouverneur Morris, 1752–1816, wrote the final draft of the Constitution of the United States. John Marshall, 1755–1835, Chief Justice of the United States and father of American Constitutional Law.'

o Many Welsh families from north Wales settle in Chester and Delaware counties, Pennsylvania, such as Thomas Wynne (William Penn's doctor) and Thomas Lloyd (from Dolobran, Montgomeryshire).

o In this year William Richards, an English Anglican priest, writes *Wallography*, a pamphlet condemning the Welsh language stating that it is inferior to English and the language of the past.

1684: The Welsh Tract, a 40,000-acre territory to the west of Philadelphia where the Welsh language can be used, is founded by John Roberts, the leader of the settlers, as a result of an accord with William Penn.

1685: Charles II converts to Catholicism on his deathbed. James II is crowned King of England. He is openly Catholic and is supported by Louis XIV of France, his first cousin. Faced with intense opposition from the Protestants, the King is increasingly isolated.

1686: Rowland Ellis (1650–1731), a Quaker from Dolgellau (in Gwynedd), and other Quakers sail for Pennsylvania.

The Glorious Revolution (1689–1702)

1688: William of Orange, a Dutch Protestant, is invited to become King of England and lands on the coast of Devon. James II flees to France where he is welcomed at the court of King Louis XIV. William of Orange becomes William III and rules with his wife, Mary II. This event is known as the Glorious Revolution.

o Stephen Hughes translates John Bunyan's[14] *Pilgrim's Progress* (*Taith y Pererin*) into Welsh.

o Around this time Sir Humphrey Mackworth, an industrialist born in Shropshire, develops lead mines in Cardiganshire and establishes the lead and copper industry in Neath, and later in Swansea.

1689: The English Bill of Rights is written. It salutes the removal of James II and establishes a series of fundamental liberties and safeguards against abuses of power by the king.

o The Toleration Act is passed and concerns the freedom of religion which applies to the Baptists and Congregationalists, but not the Quakers, Catholics and non-Trinitarians, who refuse to swear allegiance to the Church of England (owing to the King's primacy over it).

o   The Royal Welch Fusiliers (23rd Regiment of Infantry),[15] one of the most famous regiments in the British army, is created by Edward Herbert, 4th Baron of Cherbury, to confront James II. It changes its name in 1702 when it becomes the Welsh Regiment of Fusiliers (cf. **1776–1783, 2003**).

o   The Council of Wales and the Marches is abolished (cf. **1472**).

1694: The Triennial Act (or Meeting of Parliament Act) is passed by Parliament. Parliament is to meet annually and hold general elections once every three years.

1696: Some influential Welshmen, such as Sir Rowland Gwynne[16] (of Llanelwedd, Radnorshire, 1660–1726), serve William and Mary's administration.

1697: John Cadwalader (from Bala, Merioneth) arrives with his family in Pennsylvania. One of his descendants, also named John Cadwalader, becomes a General during the American Revolution / War of Independence (cf. **1775–83**).

1699: This year marks the foundation of the SPCK (Society for Promoting Christian Knowledge), by an Anglican minister, Thomas Bray, in London.

Chapter 12

Wales during the Age of Enlightenment

The 18th century is marked by the rise of Great Britain as the world's foremost economic, naval and military power a period which coincides with the Age of Enlightenment (1680–1780). In this section, the role played by Welshmen in the development and spread of British colonial power is outlined.

This century also sees the birth of the industrial revolution which affects south-eastern Wales in particular. At the domestic level, we observe increasing religious fervour and rising literacy throughout the nation (cf. Griffith Jones's circulating schools) as well as the rise of Welsh cultural, historical and linguistic consciousness, the consequence of which is the Celtic Renaissance of the following century.

1700–1740: The SPCK establishes 96 schools (1699–1715: 68 schools; 1716–27: 28 schools) throughout Wales, almost half of them are in Pembrokeshire and Carmarthenshire. Both regions are under the influence of the Philipps family of Picton castle (Pembrokeshire). John Philipps[1] is MP for Pembroke Borough (1695–1702) and for Haverfordwest (1702–22), and a member of the SPCK from 1699–1737.

1701: Elihu Yale (1649–1721), whose ancestors are from Plas-yn-Iâl (near Llandegla, Denbighshire) gives his name to Yale University at New Haven, Connecticut.

1703: Ellis Wynne's (1671–1734) masterpiece of Welsh

literature, *Gweledigaetheu y Bardd Cwsc* (The Vision of the Sleeping Bard), is published.

o John Wesley (born this same year) and his brother, Charles, are the founders of the Methodist Church. According to them, the soul can be saved by simply believing that Jesus Christ is one's saviour. Redemption is not based on works.

1706: William Jones (1675–1749), father of a linguist of the same name (cf. **1786**), is a mathematician from Anglesey who is the first to use the symbol 'Pi' in his book *New Introduction to Mathematics*. He also invents the concept of 'longitude', an essential idea for the cartographers who were engaged in mapping vast unexplored regions around the globe.

1707: The English and Scottish Parliaments are unified thus forming 'Great Britain'. In this year, Edward Lhuyd (1660–1709), one of the greatest Welsh intellectuals of all time, and generally acclaimed as the father of 'Celtic studies', publishes his famous *Archaeologia Britannica: an Account of the Languages, Histories and Customs of Great Britain, from Travels through Wales, Cornwall, Bas-Bretagne [sic], Ireland and Scotland*. Moses Williams (1685–1742), born near Llandysul, Ceredigion, is the pioneer of Welsh bibliographical studies. He is one of Lhuyd's disciples and works as a librarian in the Ashmolean Museum (Oxford). He assists Edward Lhuyd during the redaction of his *Archaeologia Britannica* by translating Jesuit father Julien Maunoir's *Breton Grammar* into English. Collectively their work provides new impetus for the study of the Welsh language, literature and culture thus providing a sound scientific foundation for the Celtic Renaissance that follows.

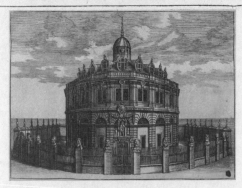

Archæologia Britannica,

GIVING SOME ACCOUNT

Additional to what has been hitherto Publifh'd,

OF THE

LANGUAGES, HISTORIES and CUSTOMS

Of the Original Inhabitants

OF

GREAT BRITAIN:

From Collections and Obfervations in Travels through
Wales, Cornwal, Bas-Bretagne, Ireland and *Scotland.*

By EDWARD LHUYD M.A. of *Jefus College,*
Keeper of the ASHMOLEAN MUSEUM in OXFORD.

VOL. I.
GLOSSOGRAPHY.

OXFORD,
Printed at the THEATER for the Author, MDCCVII.
And Sold by Mr. *Bateman* in *Pater-Nofter-Row, London*: and *Jeremiah Pepyat*
Bookfeller at *Dublin.*

Figure 21: Cover of Edward Lhuyd's *Archaeologica Britannica* (c.1707)

1709–1713: Abraham Darby's coke-smelting process to produce pig iron is first tested in Coalbrookdale, Shropshire. It has a profound effect on the future of industry in south Wales.

1713: A General Election to appoint Members of Parliament is held during this year. Only four of the 27 constituencies of Wales are won by the Whigs. The rest are under Tory control. In Wales the Whig party is led by the Mansels of Margam (near Port Talbot), the Owens of Orielton (Pembrokeshire), the Vaughans of Trawsgoed (Ceredigion), and the Myddeltons of Chirk (Denbighshire). The Tories are represented by the Scudamore family (Duke of Beaufort, Worcester), the Earl of Powis, the Wynns of Wynnstay (Ruabon, near Wrexham), and the Philipps family of Picton castle (near Haverfordwest, Pembrokeshire).

1714: This year marks the beginning of the Hanoverian dynasty. In accordance with the Act of Settlement (1701), George I, the Elector of Hanover, becomes King of Great Britain (son of Sophie, granddaughter of James I). This law also excludes Catholics from the crown. Speaking only German, he is the first King of England since the Plantagenets not to speak English.

1715: The Society of Ancient Britons is founded by Welshmen living in London. Because they are accused of supporting the Jacobites in Scotland, its objective is to demonstrate the loyalty of the London Welsh to the Hanoverian dynasty.

o   There are about 70 Nonconformist chapels in Wales, mainly in south Wales, in the counties of Carmarthenshire, Glamorgan and Monmouthshire where there are 13 chapels per county, whereas there are only eight in the north-eastern Welsh counties, and two in Gwynedd.

o   From this time until the second half of the 19th century, most of the bishops of Wales are non-Welsh Anglicans.

1715–1727: William Wotton (1666–1727), another disciple of Edward Lhuyd (cf. **1709**), translates the laws of Hywel Dda from Welsh and Latin into English. His work is published posthumously in London in 1730 by his son-in-law, William Clarke.

1716: Theophilus Evans (1693–1767), the Anglican curate of Llangammarch (Powys), publishes *Drych y Prif Oesoedd* (The Mirror of the First Age, re-edited in 1740). In this very influential book Evans highlights the ancient and illustrious past of the Welsh (and Breton) language. Following the theory of the Breton abbot, Paul-Yves Pezron,[2] he claims that the Welsh people are direct descendants of Gomer, Noah's grandson, and, for this reason, that Brythonic (the ancestor of Breton and Welsh) is the language of Heaven. This is the basis for the old belief that Welsh is not only the most ancient language of Europe but is the only appropriate language for religious expression. English is the language of worldly preoccupations, with all the negative implications this suggests.

1717: Thomas Newcomen invents the first steam machine, which is used by Lord Mansel in his foundry in Swansea.

1718: Isaac Carter (d. 1741), a native of Carmarthenshire, founds the first printing press in Wales.

1721: Charles Lloyd (of the Lloyd family of Dolobran) starts using the technique which consists in smelting iron ore with coke in Bersham.

o   Ellis Pugh (1656–1718), a Quaker born at Dolgellau, writes *Annerch i'r Cymru* (A Salutation to the Welsh), the first Welsh language book known to be published in Philadelphia. He leaves Wales in 1716, with Rowland

Ellis (of Bryn Mawr) and translates his friend's book into English as *A Salutation to the Britains*, in 1727.

1721–1742: Robert Walpole becomes the first Prime Minister (Whig). Some Welsh MPs are hostile to him, such as Sir Watkin Williams Wynn, 3rd baronet, MP for Denbighshire (Tory, 1716–41; 1742–9). He dies in a hunting accident in 1749, leaving a son, Sir Watkin Williams Wynn, 3rd baronet (cf. **1772**).

1723: Antiquarian Henry Rowlands (1655–1723) publishes *Mona Antiqua Restaurata: An Archaeological Discourse on the Antiquities, Natural and Historical, of the Isle of Anglesey, the Antient Seat of the British Druids*.

1725–1728: Sion Rhydderch publishes the first *English-Welsh Dictionary* and also a *Welsh Grammar Book*.

1730: *Cyd-gordiad Egwyddorawl o'r Scrythurau* (Concordance of the Holy Scriptures) by Baptist minister Abel Morgan (1673–1722), is published posthumously and is the second book printed in British North America. It is dedicated to David Lloyd, chief justice of Pennsylvania (1717–31). Morgan is a native of Alltgoch in Ceredigion. He emigrates in 1711 and becomes pastor of the famous Baptist Church at Pennepek in Philadelphia.

1735: Lewis Morris (1701–65, known as *Llywelyn Ddu o Fôn*) publishes in Holyhead, Anglesey, *Tlysau yr Hen Oesoedd* (The Treasures of the Ancient Ages), the first attempt to establish a Welsh periodical.

1737: Daniel Rowland (of Nantcwnlle, Ceredigion; 1713–90) and Howell Harris[3] (1714–73) meet following Rowland's conversion by Griffith Jones in Llanddowror (Carmarthenshire) the previous year. This marks the beginning of the Methodist Revival. The movement is successful in south Wales (in

Carmarthen, Brecon and Glamorgan), where four-fifths of the 428 *seiadau,* or Methodist societies are located, but less so in north Wales until the 1770s.

o William Williams (Pantycelyn, named after his farm near Llandovery, Carmarthenshire; 1717–91) joins the Methodist movement after he is converted by Howell Harris. Between 1740 and 1743 he serves as the curate of Theophilus Evans (cf. **1716**). He is one of the most famous hymn-writers in Wales. He writes about 90 books and pamphlets, such as *Alleluia* (in six parts, 1744–7), *Hosanna i Fab Dafydd* (Hosannah to the Son of David, 1751). According to Saunders Lewis, he is the first romantic poet in Wales.

William Williams (Pantycelyn), *Cariad at Dduw*

'Rwy'n edrych dros y bryniau pell
Amdanat bob yr awr;
Tyrd, fy Anwylyd, mae'n hwyrhau,
A'm haul bron mynd i lawr.

I look across the distant hills
each hour for thy coming,
come, my loved one, for it's late
and my sun's near to setting.

Diddanwch yn Nghhrist

Melysach nag yw'r diliau mêl
Yw munud o'th fwynhau,
Ac nid oes gennyf bleser sydd
Ond hynny yn parhau.

A phan y syrthio sêr y nen
Fel ffigys îr i'r llawr,
Bydd fy niddanwch heb ddim trai
Oll yn fy Arglwydd mawr.

Sweeter than the honey drops
a minute's joy in thee,
and I've no other pleasure that
lasts everlastingly.

And when the stars of heaven fall
like ripe figs to the sward,
there'll be no ebb to the delight
that's all in my great Lord.

(Source: Gwynfor Evans, 1976: 338)

o Griffith Jones (d. 1761) is a farmer's son from the Teifi Valley, a district counting some of the best educated people in Wales. He is married to John Philipps's sister, one of the founders of the SPCK. Philipps dies in 1737 and Griffith Jones continues his mission of creating new circulating schools, which play an important role in the Methodist Revival. He is also the rector of Llanddowror, in Carmarthenshire. Catherine II of Russia hears about the Welsh schools and in 1764 sends a commissioner to write a report about them. Between 1737 and 1761, 3,325 circular schools are established and attended by 250,000 pupils (which represent more than half of the population). Thanks to their work, by the end of the 18th century, three-quarters of Welsh-speakers are literate in the Welsh language. When Griffith Jones dies in 1761, Bridget Bevan succeeds him until her death in 1779.

1740–1742: Howell Harris writes two masterpieces in Welsh: *Llyfr o Hymneu o Waith Amryw Awdwyr* (collection of hymns) and *Sail, Dibenion, a Rheolau'r Societies*.

1746: The Wales and Berwick Act stipulates that the laws voted in England also apply to Wales.

***c.*1750:** The Methodist movement splits into two different branches until 1763: those in favour of Howell Harris and those in favour of Daniel Rowland. One of the reasons for the split is that Howell Harris purportedly has a love affair with a married woman, Mrs Sidney Griffith of Cefnamwlch (Caernarfonshire), and is also reproached for being too authoritarian. He founds a community in Trefeca, near Brecon, whereas Daniel Rowland establishes himself in Nantcwnlle, Llangeitho (Ceredigion).

o   A copper works is built this year in Holywell, Flintshire (north-east Wales) and is used to sell copper to the British navy and army.

1751: Richard Morris and his brother Lewis (d. 1779) found the *Anrhydeddus Gymdeithas y Cymmrodorion* (Honourable Society of Cymmrodorion) in London. The founders claimed to be the descendants of the original Brythonic inhabitants of Britain. Highly influenced by the Romantic views of the time, they produce articles about the language, culture and history of their Celtic ancestors.

1753: Hymn-writer Dafydd Jones of Caeo (1711–77) translates and publishes the first volume of Isaac Watts's psalms and hymns into Welsh, under the name *Salmau Dafydd*.

1753–1839: Parliament authorizes over 200 schemes to build roads in Wales. The work is financed by tolls on turnpikes (one of the main reasons for the 'Rebecca Riots', cf. **1839–1840**).

1755: Lewis Evans (1700–56), a Welsh surveyor from Caernarfonshire, travels across the British colonies of North America, and produces a *General Map of the Middle British Colonies in America*. The map is used by General Edward Braddock during the French and Indian War.

o   William Edwards (1719–89) builds the bridge over the river Taff at Pontypridd.

1757: Goronwy Owen (d. 1769), born in Anglesey, arrives in Virginia where he buys a plantation and teaches at William & Mary College in Williamsburg. In 1763 his poetry is published in the anthology *Diddanwch Teuluaidd*. It is re-edited in 1817.

o The English poet Thomas Gray composes his poem, 'The Bard', which made English readers aware of the richness of the Welsh literary tradition. It deals with King Edward I's supposed massacre of the Welsh bards. Gray is inspired by Thomas Carte's *The History of England* (1747–55). His poem has a huge influence on the Hungarian poet, Janos Arany. In 1857 the latter publishes his *Walesi Bardok* (The Bards of Wales) in which he compares the treatment of the Hungarian people by Franz-Joseph of Austria to that of the Welsh by Edward I of England.

Cold is Cadwallo's tongue,
That hush'd the stormy main;
Brave Urien sleeps upon his craggy bed:
Mountains, ye mourn in vain
Modred, whose magic song
Made huge Plinlimmon bow his cloud-topt head.
On dreary Arvon's shore they lie,
Smear'd with gore, and ghastly pale:
Far, far aloof th' affrighted ravens sail;
The famish'd eagle screams, and passes by.
Dear lost companions of my tuneful art,
Dear as the light that visits these sad eyes,
Dear as the ruddy drops that warms my heart,
Ye died amidst your dying country's cries –
No more I weep. They do not sleep.
On yonder cliffs, a griesly band,
I see them sit, they linger yet,
Avengers of their native land:
With me in dreadful harmony they join,
And weave with bloody hands the tissue of thy line.

('The Bard', I. 3)

1759: Thomas Lewis and Isaac Wilkinson open the ironworks at Dowlais, in south Wales. By the 1840s 5,000 people work at the Dowlais ironworks.

1760s–1780s: Thomas Edwards (or Twm o'r Nant, 1739–1810) is one of the most famous playwrights and poets of Wales. He was born in Llannefydd, Denbighshire. Three hundred and fifty poems and mainly *anterliwtiau* (interludes), including: *Tri Chydymaith Dyn* (The Three Companions of Man, 1762), *Cyfoeth a Thlodi* (Wealth and Poverty, 1768), *Pleser a Gofid* (Pleasure and Sorrow, 1787), and *Tri Chryfion Byd* (The Three Strong Men of the World, 1789).

1761: John Wilkinson, the son of Isaac Wilkinson, becomes the owner of the ironworks in Bersham (a village near Wrexham, in Clwyd) which becomes one of Europe's leading ironworks by 1780.

  o Morgan Edwards, a Baptist pastor born in Pontypool in 1722, emigrates to the American colonies. Three years later, he co-founds Brown University[4] in Rhode Island, the first Baptist college in America.

1763: The Scot James Macpherson composes the *Songs of Ossian*, thus laying the groundwork for the Celtic cultural and literary revival. His example is followed the following year by Evan Evans (Ieuan Brydydd Hir,[5] 1731–88) who writes *Some Specimens of the Poetry of the Antient Welsh Bards*. He discovers and publishes extracts from the *Book of Taliesin* and Aneirin's *Y Gododdin* (cf. **541**). Influenced by James Macpherson, Edward Williams (best known as Iolo Morganwg, 1747–1826) leads a Welsh cultural revival, and also writes poems and hymns for the Unitarian church.

  o Isaac Wilkinson and John Guest found the Plymouth ironworks in Merthyr Tydfil, which becomes the iron-smelting centre of Britain.

1765: The Englishman Anthony Bacon (1717–86, of Whitehaven, Cumberland) opens ironworks in Cyfarthfa (north-west of Merthyr Tydfil).

o Sampson Lloyd III and John Taylor found Lloyd's Bank in Birmingham. It is then established in London in 1865.

1768: Copper ore is discovered in Mynydd Parys, near Amlwch, Anglesey. In 1801, Amlwch has 5,000 inhabitants and is the fifth town in the country.

1770s: Thomas Williams (1737–1802), an attorney, builds copper works in Anglesey and in Lancashire. In the 1780s, other copper works are established in south Wales in the region between Pembrey (Carmarthenshire) and Tai-bach (Glamorgan), known as Copperopolis. Since the 1730s, Swansea is the main centre in this area that produces 90 per cent of Britain's copper by 1820 (cf. **1688**).

1770–1815: Eighty books are published about tours of Wales showing growing interest in Wales on the part of Englishmen. Among these are Wordsworth, Coleridge, Shelley, Southey, Scott, Peacock, Landor and De Quincey.

1770: The *Gwyneddigion* is founded in London by Owen Jones (Owain Myfyr, 1741–1814). Similar in inspiration to the Cymmrodorion, these cultural enthusiasts seek to revive the glorious Welsh past.

o Peter Williams (1723–96, from Carmarthenshire), a Methodist cleric since 1747, translates a new version of the Bible into Welsh. He is expelled from the Methodist Church in 1791 because he is accused of 'sabellianism', a heretical doctrine which denies that God, Jesus Christ and the Holy Spirit are a single entity.

o Influenced by Le Lorrain, John Constable and William Turner,[6] Richard Wilson (1714–82) is a landscape painter. He paints *Snowdon, Cader Idris, Llyn-y-Cau, Llyn Peris* and *Dolbadarn Castle*. His main disciples are Thomas Jones of Pencerrig (near Builth Wells), Radnorshire (1742–1803), Moses Griffith (1747–1819), Penri Williams (1802–85) from Merthyr Tydfil who works for the Crawshay family, and Hugh Hughes (who paints portraits of Methodist figures such as Thomas Charles of Bala and Thomas Jones of Denbigh between 1812 and 1814).

1772: Sir Watkin Williams Wynn (b. 1749), 4th Baronet, son of Watkin Williams Wynn (cf. **1721–42**), is elected MP for Shropshire until 1774, and MP for Denbighshire from 1774 to 1789. He is also a great patron of the arts.[7]

1774: Bersham ironworks discover a machine that allows them to bore cylinders for James Watt and Matthew Boulton's steam engines in Birmingham (until 1795). They also bore cannons for the British Royal Navy. In 1777, John Wilkinson's brother, William Wilkinson, establishes ironworks for the construction of cannons for the French army (near Nantes, at Indret and le Creusot, Burgundy).

1775: *Twelve Views in Aquatinta*, a painting by Paul Sandby is inspired by a tour of south Wales he went on with Joseph Banks in 1773.[8]

o Dafydd Jones of Caeo writes the second volume of his translation of psalms: *Hymnau a Chaniadau Ysprydol* (Hymns and Spiritual Songs).

1775–1818: Interest in Welsh local history increases. A number of books are written on the histories of the counties of Anglesey, Caernarfon, Meirionnydd, Monmouth, Brecon, Cardigan and Radnor.

1776: Born in Llangeinor, Glamorgan, Richard Price (1723–91) writes *Observations on the Nature of Civil Liberty*. He corresponds regularly with Thomas Jefferson and many other 'founding fathers' of the United States. For this reason he has an important influence on the American Revolution and is invited by the US Congress in 1778 to regulate the financial affairs and the budgets of the 13 newly-created states. His 'Discourse on the Love of our Country' (1789), in support of the French Revolution, inspires Edmund Burke to write his *Reflections on the Revolution in France* (1790).

o The American Declaration of Independence is signed on 4 July 1776. According to the Welsh Society of Philadelphia, 16 of the 56 signatories are of Welsh descent, including Thomas Jefferson (1743–1826) of Virginia, Francis Lewis of New York (1713–1803, born at Llandaff, near Cardiff), William Floyd of New York (1734–1821, whose grandfather was from Breconshire), Button Gwinnett of Georgia (1732–77, from Gloucestershire), Lewis Morris of New York (1726–98, whose great-grandfather was from Monmouthshire), Robert Morris of Pennsylvania (1734–1806), Stephen Hopkins of Rhode Island (1707–85), William Williams of Connecticut (1731–1811), and George Read of Delaware (1733–98, Welsh through his mother, Mary Howell, from Glamorgan).

1776–1783: The Revolutionary War / War of Independence in America. Many Welshmen are sympathetic to the American cause. Fourteen generals of Welsh descent fight alongside the colonists, such as Daniel Morgan of South Carolina (1736–1802), John Cadwalader of Pennsylvania, and Abraham Owen of Kentucky (from Dolgellau, Merionethshire). On the other hand, Welsh soldiers in the British army (i.e. the Royal Welch Fusiliers) participate in every campaign of the war.

1778: The naturalist Thomas Pennant (1726–98) from Flintshire publishes the first volume of his 'Tours in Wales' (under the title *A Journey in Snowdonia*), illustrated by Moses Griffith. It is followed in 1781 by the publication of a second volume.

1779: Edmund Jones of Pontypool (1702–93), an Independent minister, writes his *Historical Account of the Parish of Aberystruth* (in Monmouthshire).[9]

o February: A Welsh naval surgeon and poet, David Samwell (1751–98), witnesses James Cook's death on the Sandwich Islands (now Hawaii) during a battle with the native Hawaiians. He writes about it in his *A Narrative of the Death of Captain James Cook* (1786).

1782: David Williams (1738–1816), a political philosopher, writes *Letters on Political Liberty*, a pamphlet supporting the American Revolution. It is translated the following year into French by the future leader of the 'Girondins', Jacques-Pierre Brissot. Born in Waenwaelod, near Caerphilly (south Wales), he is a Presbyterian minister. In the 1770s, he becomes a Deist and, with the support of his friend, Benjamin Franklin, publishes in 1776 *A Liturgy on the Universal Principles of Religion and Morality*. In 1790 he founds the Royal Literary Fund, an organization to help British writers who have financial problems. The RLF still exists (cf. **1792**).

o Sir William Jones (1746–94, cf. **1786**) writes the radical pamphlet *The Principles of Government in a Dialogue between a Scholar and a Peasant* in favour of the American Revolution.

1784: The English ironmaster Henry Cort discovers the puddling process[10] for refining iron ore. By 1827 the south Wales iron industry produces one half of Britain's iron exports.

o Penydarren ironworks (in south Wales) is founded by the Homfray brothers (Samuel, Jeremiah, and Thomas) (cf. **1859**).

1785: Samuel Ellis, born in Wrexham, gives his name to Ellis Island, where millions of immigrants enter the United States between 1892 and 1954.

1786: Sir William Jones makes a speech at the Asiatic Society in Calcutta (India) in which he claims that Sanskrit, Latin and Greek are related to one another, thus laying the foundations of Indo-European philology (P. Gooden, 2009: 141). Successive discoveries and research about the links between European languages lay the groundwork for comparative linguistics, historical linguistics and ultimately modern linguistics. His father, also called William Jones, is a famous Welsh mathematician (cf. **1706**).

1786–1823: Six editions of William Warrington's *History of Wales* are published showing growing interest in Welsh history.

1788–1792: The first Welshmen arrive in Australia from Glamorgan, Monmouth and Carmarthen.

1789: The French Revolution begins. Many Welsh intellectuals, such as philosopher Richard Price (cf. **1776**), influence their French counterparts, for instance, Condorcet, who later opposes the 'Terror'[11] led by Robespierre.

o Owain Myfyr and William Owen Pughe (1759–1835, from Llanfihangel-y-Pennant, Merionethshire) publish the work of Dafydd ap Gwilym (cf. **1316–17**).

o Thomas Charles (1755–1814), inspired by Griffith Jones and his Welsh circulating schools, opens the first Sunday school in Bala. Born near St Clears, Carmarthenshire, he is the author of *Geiriadur Ysgrythyrawl* (Scriptural Dictionary, 1805–11) and *Hyfforddwr* (Manual, 1807).

Between 1789 and 1793, many Welshmen support the French Revolution because they see it as an attempt by the French people to establish a parliamentary monarchy in France. As such, they view it as a repetition of the Glorious Revolution of 1688.

As the Revolution becomes more bloodthirsty under Robespierre's leadership, the Welsh condemn the mass decapitation of the nobility and the execution of King Louis XVI and Marie-Antoinette. During the Revolutionary Wars and the Napoleonic Wars which follow (1793–1815), most Welshmen attack the French revolutionary governments (the *Consulat*) and, later, Napoleon's Empire. They strongly support the King of Britain in these wars, as can be seen from the Welsh ballads of the period.

1789; 1802: Five Welsh families settle in Utica (Oneida County, New York) because of the poor harvests in Wales. They also improve the dairy farming techniques for the production of butter. By 1855 4,000 Welshmen live in Oneida County, mainly in Steuben and Remsen. Robert Everett (1791–1875) from Flintshire publishes an anti-slavery newspaper, *Y Cenhadwr* (The Missionary), from 1840 to 1875. He is also the pastor of two Welsh Congregationalist chapels in Steuben.

1789–1838: Christmas Evans[12] (1766–1838) is a well-known Baptist minister. He becomes a minister in Llŷn (1789–91), then Anglesey (1791–1826). Between 1826 and 1838, he preaches in Caerphilly and Caernarfonshire. He is called 'the Bunyan from Wales', and contributes to strengthening the Welsh Baptist community.

1790: Richard Pennant, 1st Baron Penrhyn, establishes Port Penrhyn (near Bangor), the first port created specifically to export slate.

1790–1791: Following the deaths of Daniel Rowland (d. 1790), John Wesley (d. 1791), and William Williams (Pantycelyn, d. 1791), Calvinistic Methodism strengthens and by 1851 21 per cent of Welsh Christians belong to this denomination (see **1851** religious census).

1790s: The antiquary William Jones (1726–95) of Llangadfan in Montgomeryshire is ahead on R. J. Derfel when he advocates the creation of a national eisteddfod and a national library. He is also a staunch supporter of the American and French Revolutions, and is inspired by the ideas of Voltaire.

1792: The first Gorsedd Beirdd Ynys Prydein (The Gorsedd of Bards of the Island of Britain) is organized by Iolo Morganwg on Primrose Hill, in London (near Regent's Park). Inspired by the Welsh example, Breton and Cornish enthusiasts found respectively 'Goursez Vreizh' and 'Gorsedh'.

o   William Owen Pughe publishes the *Heroic Elegies of Llywarch Hen*, early Welsh poetry (cf. above **AD 655** and **AD 850**).

o   The intellectual David Williams is offered honorary French citizenship for his pro-Revolutionary views and is invited by the Girondins between 1792 and early 1793 to help them draft a French constitution (cf. **1782**).

1792–1799: John Evans (of Waunfawr, near Caernarfon) emigrates to America in search of Welsh descendants of Madog ab Owain Gwynedd (cf. **1170**). In an extraordinary voyage, predating the Lewis & Clark expedition, he encounters the Mandan Indians (1796), whom he identifies as 'Welsh Indians'. The next year he reaches Saint Louis, Missouri, but is imprisoned by the Spanish authorities as a spy. He dies in New Orleans in May 1799. His map of Missouri is later used by Thomas Jefferson in 1803 to assist the Lewis & Clark expedition.

1793–1794: Morgan John Rhys (1760–1804) a Baptist minister of Llanbradach in Glamorgan, edits *Cylchgrawn Cynmraeg* (Welsh Magazine). In 1791 he travels to Paris to distribute Bibles during the French Revolution.

1793–1803: William Owen Pughe publishes *Geiriadur Cynmraeg a Saesoneg: A Welsh and English Dictionary*.

1793–1815: The Napoleonic Wars break out between France and the great monarchies of Europe. Great Britain is involved in the coalitions against France. In these wars, just as in the wars against the American revolutionaries, Wales actively supplies sailors and soldiers. Cannons are made in the Bersham and Brymbo ironworks. Iron and copper are at this time the key industries.

1794: The Glamorgan Canal is built to link the ironworks of Merthyr to Cardiff. Richard Crawshay (1739–1810) becomes the sole proprietor of the Cyfarthfa ironworks. His grandson, William Crawshay II, builds a castle nearby in 1824.

o   Morgan John Rhys (cf. **1793** above) emigrates to America where he founds the towns of Cambria, Beulah, and Ebensburg, in the Allegheny Mountains of Pennsylvania. Most of the settlers are monoglot Welsh-speakers.

1795: Thomas Evans (Tomos Glyn Cothi, 1764–1833), a Unitarian minister from Carmarthenshire, publishes *Y Drysorfa Gymmysgedig* (The Mixed Treasury, 3 issues) in which he expresses his sympathy for the French Revolution. He is also a staunch partisan of religious and political freedom.

o   More settlers arrive in Pennsylvania from Bristol, and are led by Ezekiel Hughes (1766–1849) and his cousin, Edward Bebb, both from Llanbrynmair

(Montgomeryshire). Afterwards, they move to Ohio and found the colony of Paddy's Run (now Shandon, Butler County). George Roberts, an uncle of Samuel 'S. R.' Roberts (cf. **1843**, **1850**, **1857**), is also among the settlers. He remains in Ebensburg[13] (Pennsylvania) where he becomes an Independent minister. Later, Edward Bebb's son William becomes the 19th governor of Ohio (1846–9).

1795–1796; 1799: William Owen Pughe edits the English-language magazine *Cambrian Register*.

1795–1797: The poet John Jones (Jac Glan-y-gors, 1766–1821) a native of Cerrigydrudion in Denbighshire, publishes two political essays addressed to the Welsh people: *Seren Tan Gwmmwl* (Star under a Cloud), and *Toriad y Dydd* (The Break of Day). His work is inspired by the ideas of the English radical philosopher, Thomas Paine. He is also a member of the Gwyneddigion (1790).

1797–1857: John Jones (Tal-y-sarn), a Welsh Calvinistic Methodist preacher from north Wales (Dolwyddelan, Caernarfonshire), earns a reputation as a great preacher. He works in slate quarries in Tal-y-sarn in 1822, and starts preaching in 1829.

o   David Davies (d. 1807), an Independent minister from Holywell (Flintshire), founds the political journal *Y Geirgrawn* (The Magazine, 9 issues) in which he publishes a Welsh translation of the French revolutionary hymn, 'La Marseillaise', which is still the French national anthem. Considered as radical by the English authorities, his magazine is closed down because of his political views.

o   The canal between Pontypool and Newport is opened

in Monmouthshire to carry coal (40,000 tons in 1799) and iron.

1797: Often referred to as 'the last invasion of Britain', French troops, with the support of the Irish, land in Fishguard, Pembrokeshire, during the War of the First Coalition. The invasion is led by Colonel William Tate, an Irish-American from South Carolina who takes command of the French 'Black Legion' (most are ex-convicts pressed into military service). Led by Jemima Nicholas (d. 1832), who becomes a national heroine, a large number of Welsh women, dressed in red, march towards the landing site. From a distance, Colonel Tate mistakes them for British regular troops and surrenders his forces.

Here is an extract from Thomas Francis, *Cân am y waredigaeth a gafodd y Brytaniaid o ddwylaw'r Ffrancod gwaedlyd* (A song on the deliverance that the Britons had from the hands of the bloody French):

Dewch, lân Frytaniaid o bob rhyw,
Rhown glod i Dduw yn gyson
Am ein gwaredu ni mor ddwys
O law rhai cyfrwys creulon;
Gwedi'n bygwth am ein trosedd,
Mewn barn, fe gofiodd am drugaredd,
Fel na chafodd yr holl Ffrancodd
Ddim ein difa, er eu dyfod.
I garchar cyrchwyd hwynt yn rhwydd –
I'r arglwydd rhoddwn fawr-glod;
Ond boneddigion da eu doniau
Fu'n ddiffael gan Dduw'n offerynnau,
I dawelu'r cwthwn cethin
Ddaeth he barbed y nein herbyn;
Gostegodd grym y storom gref
A throwd ein llef yn chwerthin.

Come, honest Britons of every lineage,
let us consistently give praise to God
for delivering us so profoundly
from the hand of crafty, cruel ones;
after threatening us for our transgression,
in judgement, He remembered mercy,
so that all the French were not able
to destroy us, even though they came.
they were quickly taken to gaol –
let us give great praise to the Lord;
but gentlemen of good grace
were without fail instruments of God,
to quieten the hideous storm
that came against us unsparingly;
the strength of the mighty storm subsided
and our cry was turned to laughter.

(source: F. M. Jones, 2012; poem 21, lines 65–80)

1798: Thomas Roberts from Llwynrhudol, near Pwllheli (Gwynedd), writes *Cwyn yn erbyn Gorthrymder* (A Complaint against Oppression), an attack on the payment of tithes and the church establishment. It is also a plea for the recognition of the Welsh language in the administration of justice.

o Calvinistic Methodist minister Thomas Jones of Denbigh (1756–1820) writes his pamphlet *Gair yn ei Amser* (A Word in Season) in which he sees the French Revolution as the apocalypse predicted in John's Book of Revelation. He is a close friend of Thomas Charles of Bala (cf. **1789**) and participates in his missionary movements around the world. In 1814 he writes a memoir of Thomas Charles.

1799–1800: The Combination Acts prohibiting trade unions in Britain are passed by the Parliament.

Chapter 13

The Rise of the Labour Movements

With the Industrial Revolution Wales becomes the powerhouse of coal and steel production not only outproducing other areas of the United Kingdom but also many of the major western economies. The result is a transformation in the Welsh way of life. Interestingly, Welsh remains the major language in many of the industrial centres of the nation, such as Merthyr Tydfil.

Nevertheless, despite a marked increase in the standard of living of many Welshmen (Roderick, 1975), the 19th century is characterised by increasing popular discontent among the labouring classes in Wales, a situation which eventually leads to the development of the Chartist movement and the rise of trade unions.

It is also a period during which London seeks to assimilate the Welsh into the English mainstream, both culturally and linguistically (cf. *Brad y Llyfrau Gleision*).

The massive influx of 200,000 immigrants from England and Ireland between 1850 and 1911 into south-east Wales sets the stage for the Anglicization of the mining regions. The result is a backlash to this process by intellectuals and religiously-minded Welshmen who are startled by this threat to their identity. This sparks a rise in national consciousness and sensitizes Welshmen to the richness of their threatened linguistic and cultural heritage.

1800s–1830s: The woollen industry develops in Newtown (Y

Drenewydd) and Llanidloes, both located in Montgomeryshire. They are in competition with the wool industry centres of northern England (Liverpool, Manchester, and Leeds). In the 1820s and 1830s until its decline in the 1900s, Newtown is known as the 'Leeds of Wales', thanks to its 1,200 looms, 82 workshops and 35 spinning factories, which attract many English emigrants from Yorkshire and Lancashire. As a consequence, the population of the city increases from 1,665 inhabitants in 1801 to 6,842 in 1841.

1801: An Act of Union integrates Ireland into Great Britain marking the creation of the United Kingdom.

o Mary Jones, aged 15, walks barefoot 25 miles to Bala to buy a Bible from Thomas Charles. All he had were sold or spoken for, but he was so struck by her piety that he sold her a copy already promised to someone else. This story led indirectly to the founding of the British and Foreign Bible Society in 1804. The event is commemorated by a 'Mary Jones Walk'.

1801: The first census is taken in the United Kingdom. Wales numbers 588,000 inhabitants. The population of Cardiff rises from 1,871 inhabitants in 1801 to 164,333 in 1901.

1801–1807: Owain Myfyr, Iolo Morganwg and William Owen Pughe publish three volumes of *Myvyrian Archaiology*, a collection of Welsh medieval literature. Only the elite could afford it because it was too expensive.

1802: Thomas Charles writes *The Welsh Methodists Vindicated* in which he denies the *Gentleman's Magazine*'s accusation that the Methodists were Jacobins.

1803: William Owen Pughe writes his *Grammar of the Welsh Language* (translated the same year into Welsh), and *The Cambrian Biography*, the first Welsh biographical dictionary.

1804: *The Cambrian*, Wales's first weekly newspaper, is published in Swansea by T. Jenkins. It merges with *The Herald of Wales* in 1930.

o   The steam locomotive is tested by the Cornishman Richard Trevithick (1771–1833) between Merthyr and Abercynon (near Rhondda, south Wales). A replica of the locomotive is currently on display at the National Waterfront Museum in Swansea.

1805: The construction of the Pontcysyllte Aqueduct near Llangollen in Denbighshire is completed. Built by Scottish engineer Thomas Telford and English engineer William Jessop, it is the highest navigable canal in Britain (306 m), today a UNESCO World Heritage Site.

o   The Methodist hymn-writer Ann Griffiths (1776–1805) dies and her work is published the following year under the title of *Casgliad o Hymnau* (Collection of Hymns).

Hymn XIII:

Wele'n sefyll rhwng y myrtwydd
Wrthych teilwng o fy mryd;
Er mai o ran, yr wy'n adnabod
Ei fod uwchlaw gwrthrychau'r byd:
Henffych fore
Y caf ei weled fel y mae.

Rhosyn Saron yw ei enw,
Gwyn a gwridog, teg o bryd;
Ar ddeng mil y mae'n rhagori
O wrthrychau penna'r byd:
Ffrind pechadur,
Dyma ei beilat ar y môr.

Beth sy imi mwy a wnelwyf
Ag eilunod gwael y llawr?
Tystio'r wyf nad yw eu cwmni
I'w cystadlu â Iesu mawr:

O! am aros
Yn ei gariad ddyddiau f'oes.

There he stands among the myrtles,
Worthiest object of my love;
Yet in part I know his glory
Towers all earthly things above;
One glad morning
I shall see him as he is.

He's the beauteous Rose of Sharon
White and ruddy, fair to see;
Excellent above ten thousand
Of the world's prime glories he,
Friend of sinners.
Here's their pilot on the deep.

What have I to do henceforward
With vain idols of this earth?
Nothing can I find among them
To compete with his high worth.
Be my dwelling
In his love through all my days.

(Gwefan Ann Griffiths website, 2003, Cardiff University)

1805–1809: Theophilus Jones, a local historian, writes his *History of the County of Brecknock*. He is the grandson of Theophilus Evans (cf. **1716**).

1807: The Swansea-Oystermouth railway opens. Two pro-Tory weeklies are founded: *North Wales Chronicle* (1807) and *The Carmarthen Journal* (1810).

1808: William Owen Pughe writes *Cadwedigaeth yr Iaith Gymraeg* (The Conservation of the Welsh Language) demonstrating that Welshmen are increasingly fearful of the threat to the language and culture of Wales.

1808–1840: William Williams o'r Wern (1781–1840), born near

Llanfachreth in Merionethshire, becomes a Congregational minister in Wern, near Wrexham. He founds churches in Rhos, Ruabon and Llangollen. He also preaches in Liverpool (1836–9).

1811: Calvinistic Methodists (or Welsh Presbyterian Church) break with the Anglican Church. Thomas Charles ordains the first Methodist ministers this year, including John Elias (see below).

o The new census shows that there are now 673,000 inhabitants in Wales.

o The Anglicans found the National Society to teach children of poor families how to read and write. They have more than 1,000 schools by 1870 (Pembrokeshire, Radnorshire, Montgomeryshire and Flintshire).

1811–1841: John Elias (1774–1841) is a Calvinistic Methodist preacher, born near Pwllheli (Caernarfonshire). He is known as *Y Pab o Fôn* (The Pope of Anglesey) because of his authoritarian views.

1813–1815: Gwallter Mechain (born Walter Davies, 1761–1849) publishes two volumes of a survey concerning agriculture and economy in north and south Wales. This is followed in 1815 by a report on south Wales in collaboration with Iolo Morganwg. He also publishes the poems of Huw Morys (1823) and Lewis Glyn Cothi (1837, along with those of *Ioan Tegid*[1]).

1814: The first Welsh-language weekly newspaper, *Seren Gomer* (The Star of Gomer) is founded in Swansea by Joseph Harris, a Baptist minister. It survives until 1983.

o A few months before his death, the Bible Society publishes Thomas Charles's amended version of the Welsh Bible.

o Death of Thomas Coke, a leading figure of the Wesleyan Society and the first Methodist bishop. He is a native of Brecon, south Wales. He meets John Wesley in 1776 and becomes one of his lieutenants. He travels extensively and is the first to establish Methodist missions around the world: in France (1791), Ireland and the West Indies (1786; 1788–9; 1790; 1792–3) but most notably in the United States, where he twice meets President George Washington.

o After the Anglicans create the National Society (backed by the English government), the Nonconformists found the British and Foreign School Society (cf. **1843**).

1815: Napoleon's defeat at Waterloo brings peace in Europe. However, it is a disaster for the Welsh iron industry.

o The collapse in the market for war material causes the price of iron bars to fall from £12 to £8 a ton. Nevertheless, the slate industry prospers.

o The Davy lamp is invented by Sir Humphry Davy. It is especially designed to guide coal miners in the dark.

1816: Edward Pugh (1761–1813), born in Ruthin (Denbighshire), posthumously publishes his *Cambria Depicta*, a collection of landscape paintings in north Wales.

1818: Thirty-five people from Cilcennin (Ceredigion) settle in Jackson[2] and Gallia counties, Ohio. At the end of the 19th century, it is estimated that 4,000 to 6,000 Welsh people live there. Their graves, many with epitaphs in Welsh, can still be seen to this day (Oak Hill, Ohio).

1818–1819: A Welsh colony is founded in New Cambria (near Shelburne, Nova Scotia) by 12 settlers from Cardigan and Carmarthen, and in Cardigan (in New Brunswick, Canada) by 183 settlers.

1819: The Gorsedd (cf. **1792**) is first introduced at an eisteddfod in Carmarthen.

o William Owen Pughe writes *Coll Gwynfa*, a translation into Welsh of John Milton's *Paradise Lost* (1667).

1820s–1830s: The 'Scotch Cattle' are bands of colliers in south Wales who burn the houses of colliers or physically attack those who cooperate with the mine owners during strikes.

1821: Evan Jones (1788–1872), a Welsh Baptist missionary and native speaker of Welsh from Brecknockshire, teaches the Cherokee in North Carolina to read and write in their own language. In 1838, after the forced removal of the Cherokee to Oklahoma (i.e. the 'Trail of Tears'), he follows the Indians and translates the Bible from Welsh into the Cherokee language. He remains with them until his death in 1872.

o The port of Porthmadog is founded to serve the slate industry.

1822: St David's College, Lampeter, is founded by Thomas Burgess, the Anglican Bishop of St Davids (1803–25).

1823: The Society of Cymmrodorion publishes its journal *Y Cymmrodor* until 1843. After a pause, publications reappear after 1877.

o The Calvinist Methodist or Presbyterian Church of Wales publishes its confession of faith during this year.

1824: Born in Llanarmon, Caernarfonshire, Ebenezer Thomas (Eben Fardd, 1802–63) wins the chair at the Welshpool eisteddfod for his poem *Dinystr Jerusalem* (The Destruction of Jerusalem).

1825–1826: This period is marked by a banking crisis. All the banks in Pembrokeshire fail during this period because there is no liquidity. Many farmers lose their investments.

1826: The Bersham ironworks close.

o The Menai Suspension Bridge, linking Anglesey to Gwynedd, is built by Scottish engineer Thomas Telford. The chains for its construction come from Penydarren ironworks.

o Iolo Morganwg dies during this year.

1827: Cardiff is exporting 30,000 tons of iron to the Netherlands, Turkey, Portugal and Italy, representing half of British iron exports. Because the energy needed for iron production comes from coal, the main consequence is a boost in coal production (also because of the discovery of the coal-run steam-engine).

o Robert Owen (cf. **1834**) is one of the founders of British socialism (cf. **1908**). His conception of it is very similar to that of French philosophers such as Saint Simon and Charles Fourier. He criticizes the social inequalities between the British working class and aristocracy (including landowners) during the Industrial Revolution.

1828: The Corporation Act and Test Act are abrogated by Parliament. These laws had prevented Nonconformists from participating in government (cf. **1661–5**, Clarendon Laws).

1828–1830: The quarries of Gwynedd are the greatest centre of slate production in Britain.

1829: The Catholic Emancipation Act (or Roman Catholic Relief Act) is passed by the House of Commons thanks to the efforts of Irish MP for County Clare, Daniel O'Connell. For the first time since the 17th century, Catholics can participate in the government (cf. Test Act, **1673**).

o John Jenkins (*Ifor Ceri*, b. 1770), a Welsh Anglican priest and antiquarian, dies. He plays an important role in the establishment of the eisteddfodau in Wales during the 19th century.

o Iolo Morganwg's *Cyfrinach Beirdd Ynys Prydein* (the Secret of the Bards of the Island of Britain) is published posthumously by his son, Taliesin Williams (Taliesin ab Iolo).

1830: The Prime Minister, Arthur Wellesley, 1st Duke of Wellington (1820–30; 1834), abolishes the Great Sessions (cf. Acts of Union, **1543**).

o The Beer Act is passed. There is a huge increase in the number of drinking places. For example, in 1842 Blackwood (near Caerphilly), south Wales, has one pub for every five inhabitants!

o By this time, Newport exports 450,000 tons of coal, more than four times the exports from Cardiff. Swansea starts to decline, but still guarantees the link between West Glamorgan and the ports of Penzance and St Ives, Cornwall. In exchange for tin, Cornwall receives coal from Wales. Tin is used by Llanelli factories to make cans and kitchen utensils. The nickname of this town is Tinopolis.

1831 (May–June): The Merthyr Rising. Colliers from Merthyr go on strike to protest against their low wages and unemployment. They also ask for reforms. The strike quickly spreads to other mines and the ensuing riots are quelled by the British army. Twenty-six people are arrested and more than 24 people are killed. The two ringleaders are Lewis Lewis, known as *Lewsyn yr Heliwr* (Lewsyn the Hunter) and Richard Lewis (Dic Penderyn). Lewsyn is reprieved and Dic Penderyn is sentenced to death by hanging. Others are deported to New South Wales, Australia. Thousands accompany Dic Penderyn's body to his burial in Aberavon. He is considered the first Welsh working-class martyr.

- o The toll taxes on the coal trade and also on slate are abolished. This boosts Cardiff and Newport's coal exports.

- o Three thousand colliers work in the Denbighshire and Flintshire coal mines.

1832: The Reform Act gives Wales five additional members of Parliament (27 to 32 members). The representation of the counties of Glamorgan, Carmarthen, and Denbigh is raised from one to two. A borough seat is created for Merthyr and the boroughs of Glamorgan are split into two, with one seat centred in Cardiff and the other in Swansea. Before this law one in seven property-owning British men could vote (440,000 persons). After 1832 one in five (650,000) British middle-class men can vote.

- o The UK General Election takes place. John Josiah Guest, a Welsh engineer born in Dowlais, is elected MP for Merthyr Boroughs (he does not belong to any party) until his death in 1852. He is the husband of Lady Charlotte Guest (cf. **1838–45**).

- o A worldwide cholera pandemic hits Great Britain. It kills 500 people, including 160 persons in Merthyr and 152 in Swansea.

1833: The Factory Act limits the work of 9 to 13-year-old children in the factories to eight hours a day (and 12 hours a day for those between 14 and 18). In addition, they are expected to go to school for two hours a day. Employers are forbidden to hire children under nine in the textile industry. Children under 18 must not work nights.

1834: The Poor Law Act is passed by Lord Melbourne's Whig government in order to help and protect old people. Yet the result is the creation of the workhouses which are highly unpopular with the workers, Tories and religious leaders. It also abrogates the 'poor laws' passed in 1601 under the reign of Elizabeth I.

o Robert Owen (1771–1858),[3] one of the founders of socialism (cf. **1827**), establishes the Grand National Consolidated Trades Union (GNCTU), considered to be the first trade union, but it is short-lived because of internal tensions over the tactics to adopt.

1834–1853: Eisteddfodau are organized by the Abergavenny Cymmrodorion who receive the patronage of Lady Augusta Hall, Baroness Llanover.[4]

1835: Reverend David Rees (1801–1869), a Congregational minister, founds *Y Diwygiwr* (The Reformer), a periodical in support of Chartism (cf. **1836** for more details), which lasts until 1865. It also expresses support for the Rebecca Riots, the Anti-Corn Law League, and Nonconformity. Rees's nickname is *Y Cynhyrfwr* (The Agitator), which comes from Daniel O'Connell's (cf. **1829**) famous exclamation: 'Agitate! Agitate! Agitate!'

o September: The Municipal Corporation Act (or Municipal Reform Act) is passed by the British Parliament. It establishes a system of municipal boroughs, governed by town councils (led by the mayor), and elected by taxpayers. Moreover, magistrates can establish police forces in the boroughs.

1835–1836: William Williams (*Caledfryn*, 1801–69), a Congregational minister and poet from Denbigh (north Wales), creates a periodical called *Y Seren Ogleddol* (The

Northern Star). He supports the Anti-Corn Law League, and writes articles in Pro-Liberal Party periodicals such as *Y Gwron* and *Y Gwladgarwr* (cf. **1859–68**).

1835–1857: Despite the victory of the Liberal Party in England, Tories win the majority of seats in Wales in each of the six elections during this period.

1836: The Tithe Commutation Act obliges inhabitants to pay tithes to the Anglican Church in cash, regardless of religious affiliation.

1836–1850: Chartism is a movement dedicated to ameliorating the working and living conditions of the working class. It starts in England in response to the Reform Act of 1832 and the Poor Law Act of 1834 which are both highly unpopular. The Chartists are represented in Wales by Morgan Williams of Merthyr and Dr William Price (Glamorgan), John Frost (Monmouthshire), Thomas Powell and Charles Jones (for the wool towns of Montgomeryshire) and Hugh Williams (Carmarthen) (cf. **1839**).

1837: David Thomas of Neath, south Wales, uses anthracite coal to smelt iron. Afterwards, he opens the Crane Ironworks at Catasauqua, Lehigh County, Pennsylvania, where he adapts his new method and participates in the American industrial revolution. He is called 'the father of the American anthracite iron industry'.

o   The Welsh engineer, Rhys Davies (d. 1838), founds the Tredegar Ironworks (after his home town) near Richmond, Virginia, where he constructs furnaces and rolling mills. By 1860 it is the third largest foundry of the United States. During the US Civil War most of the munitions produced for the Confederate army are made here.

1837–1901: Queen Victoria reigns over Great Britain and Ireland. From a cultural, political and economic standpoint, the Victorian era is considered to be a period of great development. Victoria is known as 'the grandmother of Europe' because she arranges the marriages of her daughters and sons to other princes and princesses of different countries of Europe. George V, Czar Nicholas of Russia and Kaiser Wilhelm of Prussia are cousins.

1838–1845: Lady Charlotte Guest, the wife of the owner of the Dowlais Iron Company, John Josiah Guest, publishes the first English translation of the *Mabinogion*. For the first time this masterpiece of Middle Welsh prose is available to English speakers. Internationally, the impact of this book is enormous and indirectly enhances the status of Welsh-language literature.

1839: Bute Dock is opened in Cardiff. Vast amounts of coal are now being produced in the south-east Wales valleys. It is the ideal fuel for the world's navies, now changing over from sail to steam power. The huge new Bute Dock leads to Cardiff's rapid expansion. It becomes the largest and most important city in Wales.

o   A general assembly of the Chartist movement meets in London. In July a first petition ('People's Charter') is presented to Parliament, bearing 1,280,000 names. Despite this, Parliament ignores their pleas. Two other petitions (in May 1842 and April 1848) are also refused by Parliament.

o   Henry Vincent, the editor of the *Western Vindicator* (published in Bristol) is gaoled. His arrest leads to the Newport Rising, when 1,000 to 5,000 men, led by Chartists leaders John Frost, Zephaniah Williams and William Jones, march on the Westgate Hotel in order to liberate fellow Chartist prisoners. Twenty-eight people are shot by the police, and around 200 Chartists are arrested.[5]

o *Caledfryn* (cf. **1835**) publishes his book *Drych Barddonol neu Draethawd ar Farddoniaeth* (An Essay on Poetry).

1839–1844: The Rebecca Riots take place in south and mid Wales (Pembrokeshire, Carmarthenshire, Cardiganshire, Glamorgan, Brecknock, and Radnorshire). Although they occur during the time of the Chartist movement, none of its leaders support the riots. These are provoked by the bad living conditions of small farmers and smallholders in south-western Wales. They destroy 293 toll-gates (or turnpikes, cf. **1753**) on the roads and are also against the payment of tithes to the Anglican Church (cf. **1836** and 'tithe war' in 1886).

1840–1842: At Lord Shaftesbury's[6] instigation, a commission is set up to examine working conditions in heavy industry. The report is published in 1842 (cf. below).

1841: A railway links Cardiff to Bristol.

1841–1861: Fleeing the potato famine, 30,000 Irish Catholics settle in south Wales (Cardiff, Swansea, Newport and Merthyr). The majority of these settlers are poor, but some are also doctors and businessmen. Their arrival causes tensions with the native Welsh, leading to the first anti-Irish riot in 1848.

1842: *Hanes Cymru* (History of Wales) is published by Thomas Price (known as *Carnhuanawc*, 1788–1848). Thanks to such publications, more and more Welshmen become familiar with their historical identity.

o Parliament prohibits females of all ages from working in the pits and extends this prohibition to boys under the age of 13. Laws are also passed to favour their access to education (cf. **1833**).[7]

1843: Two Welsh-language newspapers are founded: *Y Cronicl* by Samuel Roberts (cf. **1850**, **1857**), and *Yr Amserau* (The Times) by Gwilym Hiraethog.[8] Both are Congregational ministers.

- o Tory PM Robert Peel introduces a bill in order to establish schools for poor children that would be supervised mainly by Anglicans (i.e. the English authorities) rather than Nonconformists. Two million people sign a petition against this law, leading to its withdrawal.

- o At the time, there are 28 British (Nonconformist) schools in Wales (107 in 1847; 300 in 1870), mainly in north and west Wales. These are in the hands of Calvinistic Methodist churches. Nevertheless, many more government-sponsored Anglican schools are founded by the National Society (377 in 1847).

- o Daniel Jones of Abergele emigrates to America and in this year becomes a member of the Church of Latter Day Saints (the Mormons). He returns to Wales in 1845 and converts nearly 5,000 people in Merthyr.

1844–1856: English landscape painter David Cox (1783–1859, born in Birmingham) founds an artistic colony in Betws-y-Coed (Conwy), where he spends his summer holidays each year. He paints *Penmaen Bach* in 1852.

1844: The musician Maria Jane Williams (also known as 'Llinos') publishes Lady Llanover's collection of folk songs of Wales, *Ancient National Airs of Gwent and Morganwg*.

1845: The literary journal *Y Traethodydd* (The Essayist) is founded by Thomas Gee and Lewis Edwards, who write articles in Welsh on the works of Goethe and Kant.

1846: The Corn Laws are repealed (cf. **1835–6**).

1846–1849: Famine years in Ireland. Twenty thousand Irish-born Welshmen are registered in the 1851 census, 100,000 Irishmen in 1921.

1847: A three-volume British government report on the Welsh education system (known as *Brad y Llyfrau Gleision,* The Treachery of the Blue Books, cf. **1854**), is published. It severely criticizes the use of the Welsh language and the supposed immorality of the Welsh people: 'The Welsh language is a vast drawback in Wales and a manifold barrier to the moral progress and commercial prosperity of the people.' The objective of this report is to encourage the Anglicization of Welsh-speaking Wales. The Welsh title alludes to the Treachery of the Long Knives, an event recalling Vortigern's betrayal of the Brythonic chieftains and their murder at the hands of the Anglo-Saxons (cf. **449**)

1848: Wales's first woman historian, Jane Williams (pseudonym: *Ysgafell*, cf. **1869**), publishes a scathing satire regarding the 'Treachery of the Blue Books' and the implied immorality of Welsh women in *Artegall* (cf. Jenkins 2007: 218).

- o The Anglican college, Trinity College, Carmarthen, is founded to train teachers in Anglican primary schools.

- o Publication of Spurrell's *English-Welsh Dictionary*.

- o Revolutions in France and Germany have an influence on the Welsh as well as nationalist movements in Italy, Hungary and Ireland.

- o Steam locomotives are used for the first time on the Padarn Railway to carry slate from the Dinorwic quarry to Port Dinorwic (near Llanberis, Gwynedd).

1848–1850: Born in Llanuwchllyn, Merionethshire, Michael D. Jones is a Congregational minister in Cincinnati, Ohio.

Realizing that the Welsh settlements in America will soon be anglicized, he becomes one of the principal organizers of the emigration of Welshmen to Patagonia (cf. **1865**). Shortly after his return from the US, he becomes the Principal of Bala Congregationalist College until 1886.

1849: Sir Thomas Phillips writes a report entitled *Wales, the Language, Social Condition, Moral Character and Religious Opinions of the People, Considered in their Relation to Education*, which strongly criticizes the conclusions of the 'Treachery of the Blue Books'. He also founds Llandovery College in 1848.

- o The historian Thomas Stephens writes *The Literature of the Kymry*.

- o A cholera epidemic kills 4,564 people in Wales, mainly in Merthyr and Cardiff.

1849–1855: *Udgorn Seion* (Trumpet of Zion), the Saints's periodical is published by the Mormons, an American-based religious movement (Utah). In 1949, nearly 25,000 Mormons in the United States claim Welsh descent.

1850s: The British Navy and shipyards in Cardiff, Liverpool (hence an important Welsh community there) and Newcastle begin to use coal for the steamships.

1850: According to the British Census 750,000 people in Wales speak Welsh as a first language (out of 1,163,139 inhabitants).

- o A group of Welsh religious activists, led by Evan Evans of Nant-y-glo in south Wales, settles in the province of Rio Grande do Sul in Brazil. At the end of the year they number about 2,000. Most of them are from Rhymney, Anglesey and Denbighshire. The project fails.

- o *Eben Fardd* (1802–63) wins the bardic chair at the

Rhuddlan eisteddfod for his poem entitled *Yr Adgyfodiad* (The Resurrection). This marks the beginning of a new poetic movement, *Y Bardd Newydd* (The New Poet): J. J. Roberts[9] (*Iolo Carnarvon*, 1840–1914), Rhys. J. Huws (1862–1917), Ben Bowen (1878–1903), Ben Davies[10] (1864–1937) and John Jenkins[11] (*Gwili*, 1872–1936) are active supporters. For them the poet's role should be more that of a prophet and they have a high opinion of their religious mission, using theological figures in their poems.

o Robert Stephenson builds the Britannia Bridge, the first tubular bridge in Europe across the Menai Strait, linking the island of Anglesey to the Welsh mainland (cf. **1826**).

o The south Wales railway between Swansea and Chepstow opens.

1850–1854: Samuel Roberts (cf. **1843**, **1857**) writes his pamphlet entitled *Diosg Farm* condemning landlordism. The same theme recurs in his *Farmer Careful of Cil-haul Uchaf*, published in 1881.

1850–1870: About 60,000 Welsh settle in the United States during this period, more particularly in Pennsylvania (Cambria County and Bangor) where north Welshmen work in the slate quarries, and southern Ohio (Jackson and Gallia Counties[12] are also known as 'little Cardiganshire'). The last Welsh speakers pass away during the 1950s.[13]

1850–1930: Saint-Nazaire (Loire-Atlantique, France) starts receiving Welsh coal from Cardiff, Newport and Swansea. During these years pine from Brittany (from the forest of Gâvres and Redon) is used to construct pit-props in the Welsh mines. Coal is increasingly used for ocean-going ships, but also in sugar refineries in Nantes. According to H. Chémereau (2011), the French government in the 1930s, under the influence of the northern French mine owners lobby, vote protectionist measures which lead to the decline in commerce between Wales and Brittany.

1850–1940: Welshmen from north Wales work in slate quarries in northern Maryland (now the Whiteford-Cardiff Historic District in Maryland) and in southern Pennsylvania (Peach Bottom).

1851: The British Census shows that of the 898,442 who attend a church, 32 per cent go to the Anglican Church, 21 per cent to the Calvinistic Methodist Church, 20 per cent to the Congregationalist Church (or 'Independents'), 13 per cent to the Baptist Church, 12 per cent to the Wesleyan Church, and 2 per cent to other denominations (28 Mormon chapels, 20 Catholic churches, Quakers, 27 Unitarian chapels). The 1851 census also shows that 115,000 Welsh men and women were born in England.

o   *The New York Times* is co-founded by a Welshman, George Jones (1811–91), whose father, an immigrant from Montgomeryshire, worked in the slate quarries of Vermont.

1851–1853: With the support of Augusta Hall, Baroness Llanover (1802–96), Evan Jones (*Ieuan Gwynedd*) publishes the first Welsh-language magazine dedicated to women's interests called *Y Gymraes* (The Welshwoman).

1851–1861: The number of Welsh settlers in Ballarat in the state of Victoria, Australia, grows from 1,800 in 1851 to 9,500 in 1861. By 1900, 13,000 Welsh-born people live in Australia.

1851–1881: Production at slate quarries in north Wales rises from 45,000 to 150,000 tons of slate. The population of the parish of Blaenau Ffestiniog increases from 3,460 to 11,274.

1851–1901: The number of Welsh-born people living in Lancashire and Cheshire rises from 48,000 to 87,000. The number of Welshmen living in London rises from 18,000 to 35,000 (including 4,000 from Ceredigion).

1851–1911: Liverpool attracts around 20,000 Welsh people per decade. Four National Eisteddfodau take place on Merseyside (1884, 1900, 1917 and 1929).

1851–1911: The coal exports in the Rhondda Valley rise from 708,000 tons in 1851 to 10,000,000 tons in 1911. These exports are destined mainly for England, but also France (Saint Nazaire, Brittany).

1852: The first direct train runs from London to Cardiff.

1854: Robert Jones (R. J.) Derfel publishes *Brad y Llyfrau Gleision* (Treachery of the Blue Books, cf. **1847**). William Thomas (*Islwyn*, 1832–78) composes his poem entitled *Yr Ystorm* (The Storm).

o Thomas Gee publishes the first volume of the Welsh encyclopedia, *Y Gwyddoniadur Cymreig*. It is re-edited ten times between 1854 and 1897. Both O. M. Edwards and John Morris-Jones contribute to this work.

Islwyn, *Mae'r Oll yn Gysegredig* (All is sacred)

Pa beth yw ffynnon Jacob? Y mae delw
Un mwy na Jacob ym mhob ffrwd trwy'r byd.
Fe aeth fy nhadau dros yr afon hon
A'r holl awelon nefol lawer gwaith

A'r lloer, a llawer seren ddwyfol wawr
A'r haul, a'r daran hefyd. Mae y byd
I gyd yn gysegredig, a phob ban
Yn dwyn ei gerub a'i dragwyddol gainc.

For what is Jacob's well? The visible image
Of One greater than Jacob is in every stream
Across this river passed my sires of old,
And all the winds of heaven as they blew,
The moon, and many a star divinely hued,
The sun, the thunder. Yea the whole wide world
Is one vast shrine, and every mountain bears
Its cherub with his everlasting song.

(Source: H. I. Bell, 1955, p. 352)

1855: The Llanidloes and Newtown railway is opened and operates until it is bought by the Cambrian Railways, a company that owns most of the railway tracks in Wales.

o Foundation of Christ College, Brecon, an independent boys' school (on the site of a much older school established under Henry VIII in 1541).

1855–1858; 1859–1861: London-Welshman Sir George Cornewall Lewis is appointed Chancellor of the Exchequer, then Home Secretary.

1856: The Bessemer converter is invented. It converts cast iron into steel and revolutionizes steel production. Scotsman Andrew Carnegie implements the same techniques in his foundries in Pennsylvania in the 1860s.

o In the same year *Hen Wlad fy Nhadau* (The Land of my Fathers) is composed by Evan and James James, both natives of Pontypridd. It is declared to be the Welsh National Anthem at the eisteddfod at Bangor in 1874.[14]

Welsh National Anthem:
Hen Wlad fy Nhadau (The Land of my Fathers)

Mae hen wlad fy nhadau
Yn annwyl i mi,
Gwlad beirdd a chantorion
Enwogion o fri,
Ei gwrol ryfelwyr,
Gwladgarwyr tra mad,
Dros ryddid collasant eu gwaed.

Gwlad! Gwlad! Pleidiol wyf i'm gwlad,
Tra môr yn fur
I'r bur hoff bau,
O bydded i'r hen iaith barhau.

Hen Gymru fynyddig, paradwys y bardd,
Pob dyffryn, pob clogwyn, i'm golwg sydd hardd;
Trwy deimlad gwladgarol, mor swynol yw si
Ei nentydd, afonydd i mi.

Os treisiodd y gelyn fy ngwlad dan ei droed,
Mae hen iaith y Cymry mor fyw ag erioed,
Ni luddiwyd yr awen gan erchyll law brad,
Na thelyn berseiniol fy ngwlad.

The old land of my fathers
Is dear to me,
Famous men of renown,
Land of bards and singers,
Her brave warriors,
Very splendid patriots,
For freedom shed their blood.

Nation! Nation! I am faithful to my nation,
While seas secure
The land so pure,
O may the old language endure.

Old mountaineous Wales, paradise of the bard,
Every valley, every cliff, to my eye is beautiful;
Through patriotic feeling, so charming is the murmur
Of her streams and rivres to me.

If the enemy oppresses my land under his foot,
The old language of the Welsh is alive as ever,
The spirit is not hindered by the hideous hand of treason,
Nor silenced the harp of my country.

1858–1882: *Y Gwladgarwr* (The Patriot) is founded. It is a periodical encouraging emigration to the United States.

1859: *Yr Amserau* merges with Thomas Gee's paper *Y Faner* to become *Baner ac Amserau Cymru* (Banner and Times of Wales). It favours the Liberal Party.

o   The Penydarren Ironworks close in this year.

1859–1860: Foundation of Howell's School Denbigh and Howell's School Llandaff – independent girls' schools – thanks to a trust set up in the 16th century by Thomas Howell, a merchant draper, originally for the education of orphan girls.

1859–1868: Following the abolition of the stamp tax, known as the 'Stamp Duty', or 'Tax Knowledge', the English-language press (examples: *The Star of Gwent* and the *Cardiff Chronicle*) as well as the Welsh-language press (examples: *Seren Cymru* (The Star of Wales) and Josiah Thomas Jones's *Y Gwron* (The Hero)) thrive and are written especially for a working-class public. This coincides with the successive victories of the Liberal Party in Wales until 1910.

1859–1904: Local religious revivals occur in south Wales: Cwmafan (1866), Rhondda (1879), Carmarthen and Blaenau Ffestiniog (1887), Dowlais (1890) and Pontnewydd (1892).

1860: Fifteen of the 18 copper works in the UK are situated in Wales (in the lower Tawe Valley). John Ceiriog Hughes

(1832–87) publishes his collection of poetry, *Oriau'r Hwyr* (Evening Hours).

1861: The first National Eisteddfod takes place in Aberdare.

- o David Davies of Llandinam builds the railway that links Oswestry to Newtown.

- o John Griffith Jones (1843–64), a native of Penisarwaun (near Bangor, in Gwynedd) but whose family emigrates to Beaver Dam (Wisconsin), fights during the US Civil War in the 23rd Wisconsin Volunteer Infantry of the Union army. He is killed in battle in 1864. His letters to his family, all written in Welsh, are preserved at the National Library of Wales. Two Welshmen were generals in the Union army: General Joshua Owen (1822–87) from Carmarthen, and General William Powell from Pontypool. The first fought in the 69th Pennsylvania Infantry and the second in the 2nd Regiment of West Virginia Volunteer Cavalry.

1863: The song 'God Bless the Prince of Wales' is first played during the wedding of Queen Victoria's son, Edward Prince of Wales and Alexandra of Denmark. The lyrics are composed by John Ceiriog Hughes (cf. **1860**).

Bendith ar ei ben (God Bless the Prince of Wales)

Ar D'wysog gwlad y bryniau,
O boed i'r nefoedd wen
Roi iddo gyda choron,
Ei bendith ar ei ben!

Pan syrthia'r aur wialen,
Pan elo un i'r nef,
Y nef a ddalia i fyny
Ei law frenhinol ef!

Ei faner ef fo uchaf
Ar goedwig fyw y môr,
A'i liniau ef fo isaf
Wrth orseddfainc yr Iôr.

Drychafer gorsedd Prydain
Yng nghariad Duw a dyn,
Yn agos at orseddfainc
Y Brenin mawr ei hun.

Pan syrthia'r aur wialen,
Pan elo un i'r nef,
Y nef a ddalia i fyny
Ei law frenhinol ef!

Among our ancient mountains,
And from our lovely vales,
Oh! Let the pray'r re-echo,
God bless the Prince of Wales!

With hearts and voice awaken
Those minstrel strains of yore,
Till Britain's name and glory
Resounds from shore to shore.

Should hostile bands or danger
E'er threaten our fair Isle,
May God's strong arm protect us,
May Heav'n still on us smile!

Above the throne of Britain,
May fortune's star long shine,
And round its sacred bulwarks,
The olive branches twine!

With hearts and voice awaken
Those minstrel strains of yore,
Till Britain's name and glory
Resounds from shore to shore.

(Lyrics translated by George Linley)

1863: The first Welsh-language eisteddfod in Australia is held in Victoria.

1864: R. J. Derfel publishes his book *Traethodau ac Areithiau* (Essays and Speeches), in which he advocates a national university for Wales, a daily Welsh-language newspaper, a national museum of Wales and a national library of Wales (cf. Owain Glyndŵr's 'Pennal Letter' of **1406** in which he requests the creation of two Welsh universities).

1864–1866: The Cambrian Railway reaches Aberystwyth and Tenby.

1865: General Election: 18 Liberals and 14 Conservatives are elected.

o   The first Welsh-language periodical, *Yr Ymgeisydd* (The Endeavourer), is published in Australia, followed in 1866 by *Yr Australydd* (The Australian). It is published monthly by William Meirion Evans[15] until 1872.

o   Mount Everest is named after Sir George Everest (1790–1866), born in Crickhowell, Powys. He is an explorer, geographer and surveyor-general of India between 1830 and 1843.

o   Michael D. Jones, a Congregational minister from Bala, emigrates to Argentina with 153 fellow Welshmen and they found a Welsh colony in the Chubut Province. Fearful of the ongoing Anglicization of Wales, the objective of the settlement is to create an entirely Welsh-speaking, Nonconformist community. This is accomplished thanks to the efforts of Lewis Jones and Captain Love Jones-Parry who in 1862 negotiate with Argentinean Interior Minister Guillermo Rawson. The Welsh settle in the new towns of Puerto Madryn and Rawson. Currently, about 50,000 Argentinians claim Welsh descent and about 5,000 can still speak Welsh. Spanish is now the official language for all.[16] The Patagonian settlement is known as Y Wladfa (The Colony).

1865–1866: Matthew Arnold (1822–88),[17] professor of poetry at Oxford University, gives four lectures on 'The Study of Celtic Literature'. This has a profound effect in stimulating international interest in Celtic studies worldwide. Arnold is clearly inspired by Ernest Renan's[18] influential essay, *La poésie des Races Celtiques,* written in 1854.

1866: Henry Richard, a Congregational minister, writes his *Letters on the Social and Political Condition of Wales* (second edition in 1884).

1867: Reform Act is passed. The measure allows 59,000 new working-class electors in Britain the right to vote, the vast majority of them in the boroughs (cf. suffrage law of **1832**).

1868: The General Election is held. Welsh Liberal Party members gain 21 seats in Parliament.

o Landore Steel Company (Glandŵr, near Swansea) is the first to experiment with 'open hearth furnaces' or the 'Siemens process', named after Carl Wilhelm Siemens, a German engineer.

o William Gladstone is elected Prime Minister until 1874. He is married to Lady Catherine Glynne from Hawarden in Flintshire whose castle still belongs to his descendants.

o Henry Richard is elected Liberal MP for Merthyr Tydfil until 1888.

o In Argentina, six issues of *Y Brut* (The Chronicle) are published.

1869: The AAM (Amalgamated Association of Mineworkers) is founded in Lancashire by Thomas Halliday. It counts 45,000 Welsh members in 1873 (especially from Aberdare and the Rhondda Valleys).

o Jane Williams (*Ysgafell*, 1806–85) publishes *A History of Wales derived from Authentic Sources*. She comes from a Welsh family that migrated to London. She also publishes a collection of poems in 1824 (cf. **1848**).

o John Hughes (1814–89) of Merthyr emigrates to the Ukraine (Donetsk Basin, near the Azov Sea) where he founds the town of Yuzovka. He forms the *New Russia Company* and most of his ironworkers come from Merthyr, Dowlais, and Rhymney.

o Joseph Jenkins, a farmer from Tregaron (Ceredigion) abandons his family and emigrates to Melbourne (Victoria State, Australia) where he becomes a 'swagman' (or tramp). His experience is widely known, thanks to his diaries which are preserved at the National Library of Wales (for his Welsh period from 1839 to 1868, and 1895 to his death in 1898) and the State Library of Victoria (for the Australian period from 1869 to 1894).

1870: Elementary Education Act (or Forster's Education Act[19]). All children in England and Wales are required to attend school between the ages of five and 12. School boards are founded whose task is to create new schools and provide subsidies for poor children between the ages of five and 13. One of the major consequences is the teaching of standard English to children whose families speak dialects of English (throughout England and the anglicized regions of Wales). In Celtic-speaking regions, such as Wales and Scotland, it is often in the schools that children are exposed to English for the first time.

1870–1889: Joshua Hughes (Anglican) is appointed Bishop of St Asaph by Prime Minister William Gladstone. His appointment is greeted with enthusiasm as he is the first native Welsh speaker since John Wynne (1714–1727) to occupy this position.

1871: Lewis Jones (1836–1904), a native of Caernarfon, is appointed governor of the province of Chubut in Argentina. He is one of the original founders of the Welsh settlement in Patagonia.

1871–1872: Henry Morton Stanley, born John Rowlands (1841–1904) in Denbigh, is hired by the *New York Herald* to find the explorer David Livingstone in Africa. When Stanley meets him in Ujiji (in modern-day Tanzania), Livingstone is ill. It is Stanley who utters the famous line: 'Doctor Livingstone, I presume.'[20]

1872: Aberystwyth University College is opened thanks to the donations of thousands of Welshmen, thus realizing R. J. Derfel's (and Owain Glyndŵr's) dream. Thomas Charles Edwards (son of Lewis Edwards) is its first Principal. Women are not admitted until 1884. They have to wait until 1885 to obtain financial assistance.

1874: The North Wales Quarrymen's Union is founded by William J. Parry (1842–1927).

o   Cardiff Arms Park hosts its first rugby game.

o   *Yr Australydd* (The Australian) is replaced by the newspaper *Yr Ymwelydd* (The Visitor), published every month until December 1876 by W. M. Evans.

1875: The famous whisky distillery, Jack Daniel's, is founded in Lynchburg, Tennessee, by Jack Daniel (1846–1911), whose grandfather, Joseph 'Job' Daniel, was from Ceredigion (Wales).

1877: A Chair of Celtic is created at Jesus College (Oxford) and John Rhŷs is the first to occupy the position until his death in 1915 (cf. **1571**).

o   William Abraham (1842–1922), known as 'Mabon' to his fellow miners (a bardic name in reference to a figure of Welsh mythology[21]), is appointed head of the Cambrian Miners' Association in the Rhondda Valleys. He is MP for Rhondda (1885–1918) and for Rhondda West (1918–20). In 1910 he leaves the Liberal Party for Labour and chairs the Joint Sliding Scale Association which determines the pay of the colliers (1875–1903).

o   The 'Basic process' is discovered by Sidney Gilchrist Thomas (1850–1885) and his cousin, the chemist Percy Gilchrist. It consists in eliminating phosphorus from molten iron. It is tested the same year in the Blaenavon ironworks. Five other ironworks adopt his converter: Dowlais, Cyfarthfa, Ebbw Vale, Rhymney, and Tredegar. It has a revolutionary effect on the production of iron and steel.

1878: Lewis Jones publishes six issues of *Ein Breiniad* (Our Privilege) in Patagonia.

1879: The Battle of Rorke's Drift is fought (22–23 January) in South Africa between 150 British soldiers of the 24th Regiment (or South Wales Borderers, based in Brecon) and 3,000–4,000 Zulu warriors. Eleven soldiers are awarded the Victoria Cross, among whom are seven members of the 24th Regiment. Two of them were born in Wales: Privates Robert Jones (Penrhos, near Raglan, Monmouthshire) and John Williams (Abergavenny, Monmouthshire).

1879–1889: Sarah Jane Rees (*Cranogwen*, d. 1916) becomes the editor of *Y Frythones* (The Brython Woman), an independent Welsh-language magazine for women.

Figure 22: Photograph of Sarah Jane Rees (Cranogwen), by John Thomas (c. 1879–1889)

1880: 32 per cent of the coal exported from Britain comes from Wales. Cardiff is the most important coal port in the world (handling 72 per cent of Welsh exports).

o   UK General Election. William Gladstone is re-elected Prime Minister of the UK. Liberals in Wales win 29 of the 33 seats.

1881: For religious reasons and in an attempt to fight alcohol abuse, the Welsh Sunday Closing Act obliges pubs to close on Sundays. It is the first piece of Wales-only legislation since 1542.

o   Henry Austin Bruce, 1st Lord Aberdare, is appointed by William Gladstone to lead a committee on the education system in Wales. Many Welshmen, including John Rhŷs, are members of the committee. They issue a report which leads to the creation of universities at Cardiff (cf. **1883**) and Bangor (cf. **1884**), and the Welsh Intermediate Education Act (cf. **1889**).

o   Based in north Wales (Plas Mawr, Conwy), the Royal Cambrian Academy of Art[22] is founded by Welsh and English painters led by Henry Clarence Whaite, a landscape painter influenced by William Turner. Born in 1828 in Manchester, he died in 1912 in the Conwy valley (Llangelynnin, north Wales). His most famous paintings are: *A Welsh Funeral* (1865) and *Snowdon* (1911).

1881–1894: Four of Daniel Owen's novels are published: *Y Dreflan* (1881), *Rhys Lewis*, an autobiography of Rhys Lewis, a minister of Bethel (1885), *Enoc Huws* (1891), in which he discusses religion in Wales, and *Gwen Tomos* (1894), in which he describes rural life in Flintshire. Born in Mold (Yr Wyddgrug), Flintshire in 1836 (d. 1895), he studies at Bala theological college in 1865 in order to become a Methodist minister but he finally abandons this route. He works as a tailor between 1867 and 1876 in Mold.

1881–1911: The number of Englishmen who emigrate to Glamorgan rises from 70,711 to 194,041. This has a powerful impact on the anglicization of south Wales.

1883: Christians of all denominations, philanthropists and ordinary citizens make donations permitting the foundation of universities at Cardiff and Aberystwyth.

1883–1888; 1890–1893: Sir Samuel Griffith, a native of Merthyr Tydfil, becomes Prime Minister of the state of Queensland (the north-eastern part of Australia, whose capital is Brisbane). He is also one of the two authors of the constitution of Australia.

1884: The University College of North Wales is founded at Bangor. The same year, a Chair of Celtic Studies is founded at Cardiff University. The Representation Act of 1884 gives 60 per cent of British men the right to vote (cf. suffrage laws in **1832** and **1867**).

1885: Redistribution of the Seats Act passed by Parliament. As a result, the constituencies of Denbighshire, Glamorganshire and Monmouthshire are among those suppressed.

- o General Election: for the first time, the Liberals gain 30 seats out of a total of 34; the Conservatives retain only four seats.

- o Dan Isaac Davies (1839–1887), a schools inspector from Glamorgan, founds the Cymdeithas yr Iaith Gymraeg (Welsh Language Society), with the support of MP Henry Richard. It is designed to defend the Welsh language and teach it in primary schools. It also requests that the British Government recognize the Welsh language as a subject to be taught in primary schools. There is a strong religious motivation associated with this endeavour.[23]

1886: Gladstone's Irish Home Rule Bill is defeated in the House of Commons (343 to 313). This political defeat leads to the foundation of Cymru Fydd (Young Wales, 1886–95) by T. E. Ellis,[24] David Alfred 'D. A.' Thomas,[25] Owen M. Edwards and David Lloyd George. They are in favour of a Welsh Home Rule Bill, in order to have more autonomy with regard to Westminster.

o During the summer of this year farmers with small holdings in Denbighshire (mainly Nonconformists) rebel against Anglican tithe collectors and auctioneers. The farmers are supported by the Liberal Party which criticizes social injustices. This event is known as the 'Tithe War' and lasts until 1888. This leads indirectly to the disestablishment of the Anglican Church in 1920.

o Edward Hughes founds the North Wales Miners' Association which is one of the first to join the Miners' Federation of Great Britain a few years later (cf. **1889**). They count 2,732 as members in 1898.

o UK General Election: Wales sends 25 Liberals to Westminster out of a total of 34 seats. The Conservatives retain six seats and Liberal-Unionists[26] only one (William Cornwallis-West, MP for Denbighshire West, 1885–92).

1888: The colliers of the Cambrian Colliery are granted a holiday every first Monday of each month (Mabon's Day), negotiated between Mabon and the owners of the mine.

o The Local Government Act is passed by Parliament. Wales is divided into 12 counties: Anglesey, Brecknockshire, Caernarfonshire, Ceredigion, Carmarthenshire,

Denbighshire, Flintshire, Glamorgan, Merionethshire, Montgomeryshire, Pembrokeshire, and Radnorshire. The new divisions come into effect on 1 April 1889.

o In this year, Thomas Edward Lawrence is born in Tremadog, Gwynedd. He is best known as Lawrence of Arabia (d. 1935). He serves in Egypt in the British intelligence services during the First World War and has a leading role in organizing the Arab Revolt against the Ottoman Empire.

o A new Welsh settlement, Trevelin (Cwm Hyfryd, Pleasant Valley) is founded in Argentina.

1889: The Miners' Federation of Great Britain is founded in Newport, Monmouthshire, and includes Welsh and English trade unions. Led by William Brace, it counts 6,000 members by 1893, mainly north Welsh miners. The Miners' Federation is opposed to the sliding scale (the system by which miners are paid per ton of coal), and is in favour of the eight-hour working day (see **1899**).

o Establishment of the County Councils replaces the office of Justice of the Peace (cf. **1536**).

o The Welsh Intermediate Education Act allows the creation of 95 state-financed secondary schools, between 1889 and 1905, which are attended by 8,000 Welsh working- and middle-class pupils.

1890: The McKinley Tariffs, imposed by the United States government on all imported tinplate, nearly ruin the tinplate industry in Wales (the annual value of exports from Britain drops from £7.2 million in 1891 to £2.7 million in 1898). More than a third of tinplate workers move to Pennsylvania (3,000 natives of Wales move to Pittsburgh, Scranton Wilkes-Barre) and Baltimore (Maryland).

Figure 23: Photograph of David Lloyd George, by John Thomas (*c.* 1890)

o For the first time, David Lloyd George is elected MP for Caernarfon Boroughs (1890–1945).

1890–1900: The US Census shows that, during this decade, 100,000 Welshmen become citizens of the United States (compared with 29,868 in the 1850 census).

1890s: South Wales's ironworks produce nearly all the rails for the world's railways which originally are made out of cast iron. The switch to steel rails deals a severe blow to the Welsh ironworks.

1891: The 'Newcastle programme' is the Liberal Party's political programme for the 1892 general election. Its main subject is Irish Home Rule, but it also concerns Welsh and Scottish religious disestablishment and other social reforms (land reform, reform of the House of Lords, and the abolition of plural voting).[27]

o The Dowlais Company (south Wales) transfers its steel production to East Moors in Cardiff thus strengthening Cyfarthfa, the industrial giant (cf. **1765**, **1794**, **1921**).

o First census recording the number of Welsh speakers is taken. One million people (54.4 per cent of the population) can speak Welsh fluently, most as a first language.

o Publication of the first volume of Owen M. Edwards's *Cymru'r Plant* (Children's Wales). It is followed by its English-language version, *Wales*, in 1894.

o The Welsh-language newspaper *Y Dravod* (The Discussion) is founded in Argentina by Lewis Jones and is published weekly until 1961. His daughter, Eluned Morgan, becomes its editor in 1893.

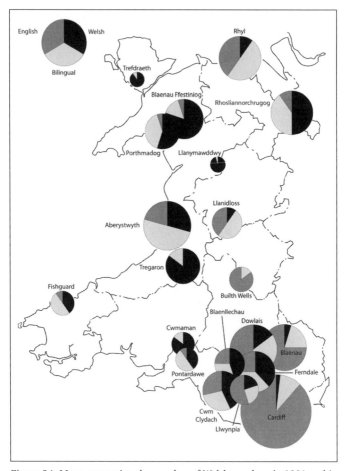

Figure 24: Maps comparing the number of Welsh speakers in 1891 and in 2011 (inspired by G. Jenkins, 2007)

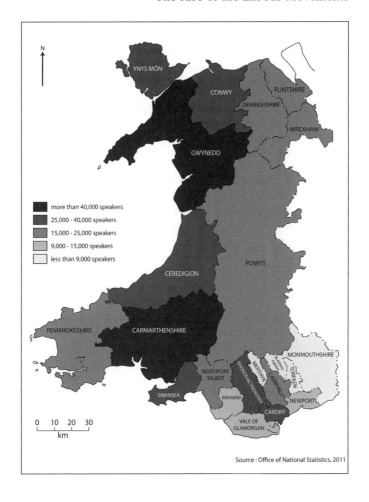

1892: General Election: The Liberal Party gains 31 seats in Parliament for Wales.

o Publication of the first volume of the *Welsh Review* (published annually).

1893: A royal charter marks the foundation of the University of Wales, federating the three university colleges of Aberystwyth, Cardiff and Bangor.

o Foundation of the Independent Labour Party (ILP) and its newspaper *The Labour Leader* by the Scot Keir Hardie (1856–1915). In 1898, it numbers 1,704 members in south Wales and 31 branches (27 in 1905). Originally from Scotland, Hardie started his career at eight years of age as a trapper in the pits in Ayrshire. In 1898 he comes to Wales to cover the miners' strike in south Wales for the party's newspaper.

o Of the 120,000 colliers of south Wales, 6,000 belong to the Miners' Federation of Great Britain and 45,000 to other pro-Mabon unions. As many as 72,000 do not belong to a union.

o An eisteddfod takes place at the World's Columbian Exposition, in Chicago.

1894–1899: T. E. Ellis enters the British government as Chief Whip, an MP whose role is to check that all MPs should attend the voting sessions at the House of Commons and respect the instructions given by the party leader.

1895: In the UK General election, the Liberals are defeated by the Conservatives. Lord Salisbury (Tory) is elected Prime Minister of Great Britain. In Wales, 25 Liberals and nine Conservatives are elected.

1896: The Central Welsh Board for Intermediate Education is founded by the Welsh Local Authorities. Arthur Humphreys-Owen (MP for Montgomeryshire) is its first chairman. Its mission is to supervise Welsh Intermediate Schools and co-ordinate the exams and inspectors.

o John Summers, whose father comes from Cheshire, establishes iron and steel works in Shotton, near Queensferry (Flintshire). By 1914 3,500 people work in these plants. Their production increases from 4,500 tons of steel in 1896 to 500,000 tons during the First World War. There are close ties between the industrial communities of Wales, industrial Lancashire and north-eastern England.

o Griffith Park and Griffith Observatory are established in Los Angeles, California. They bear the name of Griffith J. Griffith, born in Bettws, Glamorganshire in 1850. He moves to Pennsylvania in 1865, then to California in 1873. His fortune derives from the mining industry during the Gold Rush.

1896–1906: This period is termed the 'Welsh Revolt' by Welsh historian Kenneth Morgan (1963) and is characterized by the opposition of the Welsh to the Boer War and to the Education Act of 1902.

1898: The first strike in south Wales to remove the sliding scale fails. It shows the limits of the sliding scale system which ends in 1903. With Mabon as its president, the South Wales Miners' Federation is established (also known as 'The Fed'). By the end of 1899 104,000 miners join it. 'Mabon's Day' (cf. **1888**) is suppressed by the owners of the Cambrian Colliery.

Chapter 14

The World Wars and the Rise of Welsh National Consciousness

On the eve of the 20th century Europe was the world's foremost centre of affluence, power as well as scientific and cultural development. The First World War puts an end to this and brings traumatic changes to Wales and Europe as a whole. In this section the events leading up to this conflict are presented, as well as the disastrous consequences.

The inter-war years are characterized by relative industrial decline and large-scale immigration to England, the US and the Commonwealth nations. One of the consequences is the rapid decline of Welsh as a community language in the industrial areas, particularly the eastern and southern regions of Wales.

1899: 'The Fed' (Mabon's South Wales Miners' Federation) joins the Miners' Federation of Great Britain.

1899–1902: The South African War (or Boer War) divides the Liberal Party. D. A. Thomas is against it, whereas Pritchard Morgan[1] supports it.

1900: The General Election: the Liberals win 28 of the 34 seats in Wales. Keir Hardie is the first MP for the Independent Labour Party (a party affiliated with the Labour Party) in Merthyr Tydfil.

- o Many Welshmen fight at the battles of Paardeberg and the River Tugela, South Africa.

o Only ten per cent of the iron produced in Britain is now produced in south Wales.

o John Rhŷs and David Brynmor Jones (Liberal MP for Swansea District, 1895–1914), publish a Welsh history in English entitled *The Welsh People*. It signals the beginning of a revival of Welsh identity.

1900–1903: The Penrhyn Quarry Strike occurs in reaction to an attempt to diminish the influence of the North Wales Quarrymen's Union. E. A. Young, director of the Penrhyn Quarry (Bethesda, Gwynedd), refuses to pay the syndicated quarrymen. Following this, 2,800 of their fellow workers go on strike. The strike turns into a riot in June 1901 in which the houses of the 400 men who accept a return to work are destroyed. The strike ends in November 1903 after the Chief Constable of Caernarfonshire sends in troops to quell the disturbances. This also marks the beginning of the decline of the slate industry.

1900–1914: The Welsh rugby team wins the Triple Crown six times (1900, 1902, 1905, 1908, 1909, and 1911) in twelve years, and defeats New Zealand in December 1905.

1900–1920: This is the golden age of Welsh boxing: Freddie Welsh (lightweight), Jim Driscoll (featherweight) and Jimmy Wilde (flyweight) are world champions.

1901: The 1901 census shows that 929,828 Welshmen (49.9 per cent of the population) can speak Welsh. Regions where Welsh speakers are most numerous are the coal-mining counties: Merthyr Tydfil (57.5 per cent), Margam (62 per cent), Rhondda (64.5 per cent), Rhymney (69 per cent), Maesteg and Aberdare (72 per cent each), and Neath Valley (75 per cent). This disproves the often repeated allegation that Welsh is a 'rural language'.

o Edward VII is crowned King of Great Britain and Ireland.

o Sarah Jane Rees founds Undeb Dirwestol Merched De Cymru (The South Wales Women's Temperance Union).

o Alf Morgans, born in Machen, Monmouthshire, is elected Prime Minister of Western Australia, the capital of which is Perth.

1901–1911: 63 per cent of those arriving in Glamorgan come from south-western and western England. This has a profound effect on the development of Welsh-English spoken in that area.[2]

1902: The Education Act is passed by the Conservative government. The main consequence is the creation of the Local Education Authorities (LEA) and the suppression of school boards (cf. **1870**). The Nonconformists and the Labour Party, as well as some members of the Liberal Party, are against this. This law is a major issue in the local elections of 1906.

o Sir Alfred Moritz Mond from Lancashire opens the Mond nickelworks at Clydach near Swansea, the largest in Europe at the time.

1904–1905: A great religious revival starts in Ceredigion under the leadership of preacher Evan Roberts (a former collier) and other preachers, such as Joseph Jenkins (of New Quay, Cardiganshire) and Nantlais Williams (of Ammanford, Carmarthenshire). Welsh is still the primary language of religious worship. Many Welsh believers consider English to be the secular language of 'the world' and thus not suited for prayer (cf. also **1716**).[3]

1905: Cardiff (128,000 inhabitants) is granted the status of a city by King Edward VII.

1905–1909: Thomas Price from Brymbo, Denbighshire, is elected Prime Minister of South Australia.

1906: General Election: the Liberal Party, allied to the Labour Party, wins 33 of the 34 seats in Wales. The Conservatives win 36 per cent of the Welsh vote.

- o Robert Ambrose Jones (Emrys ap Iwan, b. 1848) dies. He is considered to be one of the fathers of modern Welsh nationalism. Born in Abergele, Denbighshire, he is a literary critic and writer on politics and religion. In 1874, he teaches English in Lausanne (Switzerland), Bonn and Giesen (Germany) and learns German and French at the same time. After returning to Wales he is ordained minister in 1884 and serves in Denbighshire until his death. He is an advocate of the Welsh language and Welsh self-government.

- o *Y Brython* (The Briton), a Welsh-language newspaper, is founded in Liverpool and published until 1939.

- o Charles Stewart Rolls co-founds the Rolls Royce automobile, with Frederick Henry Royce. Born in London, he is the son of John Rolls, MP for Monmouthshire (1880–92) and Baron Llangattock. From 1767 to 1987 his family owned a property known as The Hendre in Monmouthshire.

1907: A royal charter creates the National Library of Wales (Llyfrgell Genedlaethol Cymru, opens on its present site in 1916) in Aberystwyth and the National Museum of Wales[4] in Cardiff (Amgueddfa Cymru, which opens in 1927). Sir John Williams (1840–1926, born in Gwynfe, Carmarthenshire) is considered to be the founder of the National Library of Wales because he gives his private library and his manuscripts (including the Peniarth manuscripts) (cf. also R. J. Derfel **1864**). Son of a Congregational minister, he was a benefactor and surgeon to Queen Victoria. One of his descendants accused him in 2005 of being 'Jack the Ripper'.

o   Adran Gymreig y Bwrdd Addysg (The Welsh Department of the Board of Education) is created in this year and is a significant step towards devolution. Owen M. Edwards is the chief inspector of schools (1907–20).

1907–1910: Charles Evans Hughes, the son of a Welsh minister from Tredegar, becomes governor of the state of New York. He is then appointed associate justice of the United States Supreme Court (1910–16), Secretary of State (1921–5), Chief Justice of the United States Supreme Court (1930–41).

1908: Gwendoline (1882–1951) and Margaret Davies (1884–1963)[5] begin their collection of French and English impressionist and post-impressionist paintings by artists such as Corot, Millet, Turner and Monet. During the First World War the Davies sisters work as volunteers for the Red Cross, and in 1920 purchase Gregynog Hall near Newtown, Powys which becomes a centre for music and the arts. It hosts the Gregynog Music Festival each summer between 1933 and 1938. Between 1951 and 1963 Gwendoline and Margaret Davies donate their art collection to the National Museum of Wales.

o   'The Fed' is affiliated to the Labour Party.

o   The Old Age Pensions Act is passed by Parliament under the Liberal Government (1906–14) and is considered a key measure for the social welfare programme. Every person over 70 years old receives five shillings per week.

o   William Henry 'W. H.' Davies (1871–1940, a native of

Newport, Monmouthshire) publishes his autobiography entitled *Autobiography of a Super-Tramp*. He deals essentially with the lifestyle of tramps in England and in the United States.

o Sidney Curnow Vosper (1866–1942) paints *Salem*, possibly the most famous painting associated with Wales – a woman in Welsh costume arriving at the small Baptist chapel near Harlech for the morning service.

o The Coal Mines Regulation Act (or Eight Hours Act) is introduced by the House of Commons in order to limit the workday to eight-hour shifts.

1908–1910: The Welshman Thomas L. Lewis, heads the UMWA (United Mine Workers of America). Born in Pennsylvania of Welsh parents from Dowlais, he is described in 1909 by the *Cardiff Weekly Mail* as the 'Mabon of American Miners'. His oldest brother William, born in Dowlais, south Wales, is a member of the Knights of Labor. Another brother, Isaac Lewis is the mayor of Martins Ferry, a coal mining town in Ohio (1909–11).

1908–1914: Branches of the ILP are set up in north-west Wales (Caernarfonshire Labour Council, 1912; North Wales Labour Council, 1914). David Thomas publishes *Y Dinesydd Cymreig* (The Welsh Citizen), the Labour Party newspaper in north Wales, until 1929. Every week, it publishes articles on Welsh literature, politics and religion (for more information on socialism, cf. **1827**).

1908–1915: David Lloyd George is Chancellor of the Exchequer.

1910: George V becomes King of England.

o Two general elections (January and December) lead

to the victory of the Liberal Party. In Wales, although Labour is defeated (including Vernon Hartshorn, one of the main leaders of the South Wales Miners' Federation), Keir Hardie is re-elected, along with four collier colleagues.

o A strike begins at the Cambrian Colliery in Tonypandy, Rhondda, in August. This leads in November to the Tonypandy Riots (also known as the Cambrian Combine Dispute, in reference to the company which regulated the wages of the miners). Violent fighting between the colliers and the police ensues. In response Winston Churchill, the British Home Secretary, sends troops to support the chief constable of Glamorgan. Several colliers are shot but none are killed. The strike officially ends in August 1911.

o Robert Williams Parry (1884–1956) wins the chair at the National Eisteddfod in Colwyn Bay, Gwynedd, for his poem *Yr Haf* (The Summer). He is a native of Tal-y-sarn, Gwynedd (cf. **1952**).

1911: The 1911 census: 43.5 per cent of the Welsh people speak Welsh, the majority in the coal-mining counties of Glamorgan, Monmouthshire and Carmarthen, which count 556,000 people (57 per cent of all the speakers). G. Jenkins (2007: 232) points out that during this time two-thirds of the 2,420,921 inhabitants of Wales are concentrated in Monmouthshire and Glamorgan which is one of the reasons why the Welsh language is widely spoken in these counties.

o The House of Commons passes a law that ends the right of the House of Lords to block legislation.

o Christopher Williams (1873–1940, born in Maesteg,

Glamorgan) paints *Deffroad Cymru* (The Welsh Awakening) to commemorate the investiture of Edward (future King of England, Edward VIII), Prince of Wales, in Caernarfon.

o J. E. Lloyd (1861–1947, born in Liverpool) publishes his two-volume *A History of Wales to the Edwardian Conquest*. The approach is nationalistic. He is also a member of Cymru Fydd (cf. **1886**).

o The National Insurance Act is passed by the House of Commons, based on the German system. For the first time, this law gives the working class protection against illness and unemployment.

o During the summer of this year strikes are organized by the dockers in Cardiff, and in August are extended to the railway workers of Llanelli, Carmarthenshire, and the Bargoed, Ebbw Vale and Tredegar collieries. They all degenerate into riots. Troops are sent to quell the violence. Two rioters are shot dead.

o Born in Swansea, the artist Evan Walters (1893–1951) paints *Cefn Cyfelach Colliery*. With other painters, such as Vincent Evans and Archie Rhys Griffiths, he represents the working class of south Wales. Another of his famous paintings is *The Welsh Collier* (1931), and the following year, the more political *The Communist*.

o The Glynn Vivian Art Gallery opens in Swansea. It bears the name of Richard Glynn Vivian (1835–1910), the son of the Cornishman John Henry Vivian, owner of the largest copper works in Swansea. Around this time fewer than 4,000 people work in copperworks in south Wales.

1911–13: Augustus John[6] (1878–1961) and James Dickson 'J. D.' Innes[7] (1887–1914) participate in the Camden Town Group, in London. It is a group of British post-impressionist artists. In 1913 they also attend the Armory Show, an international modern art exhibition in New York City.

1912: Six branches of the ILP[8] (Independent Labour Party) are active in the south Wales coalfields.

o   Noah Ablett (a native of Porth, Rhondda) publishes his pamphlet calling for a minimum wage for workers. It is entitled *The Miners' Next Step*.

o   Thomas Herbert Parry-Williams (1887–1975), a cousin of Robert Williams Parry, wins the chair and crown at the National Eisteddfod in Wrexham for his poems, *Y Mynydd* (The Mountain) and *Gerallt Gymro*, and also in Bangor in 1915 for his poems, *Eryri* and *Y Ddinas* (The City). He is professor of Welsh at the University of Wales in Aberystwyth (1920–52).

o   Thomas Mardy Rees (1871–1953) from Neath (Glamorgan) writes a dictionary of Welsh artists, entitled *Welsh painters, engravers, and sculptors (1527–1911)*. He also writes books on the Welsh Nonconformists and on Welsh art history (cf. P. Lord, 2009: 205).

1913: John Morris-Jones publishes his classic work *A Welsh Grammar, Historical, and Comparative*. He is professor of Welsh at the University College of North Wales, Bangor from 1895 to his death in 1929.

o   439 men are killed in a gas explosion in the Senghennydd colliery (near Caerphilly, south Wales). This is the worst mining disaster in the UK.

o   The Railway, Transport and Miners Unions form the

'triple alliance' (see **1921**) and promise to support one another if there is a strike.

o Reverend W. F. Phillips, a Calvinistic Methodist minister and member of the Newport branch of the ILP, publishes an anti-socialist tract, *Y Ddraig Goch ynte'r Faner Goch?* (The Red Dragon or the Red Flag?).

1914: The First World War is declared: 40,000 Welshmen are killed between 1914 and 1918 (out of a total of 700,000 British fatalities).[9]

o Ramsay MacDonald resigns as leader of the Labour Party to protest against Great Britain's involvement in the First World War. He is succeeded by Arthur Henderson (1914–17) as party leader.

o Thomas Jones and David Davies of Llandinam (cf. **1861**) found an English-language monthly periodical entitled *Welsh Outlook*, published until 1933. It deals with topics such as Welsh politics, nationalism and society. Both men lead a campaign against tuberculosis (also called the white plague), which is responsible for ten per cent of the fatalities in some areas in Wales.

o Edward Thomas John, Liberal MP for East Denbighshire (1910–18), introduces a Welsh Home Rule Bill in the English Parliament. After a four-year campaign, his attempt ends in failure.

o 233,000 colliers work in south Wales producing 56.8 million tons per year.

o Union membership in Britain rises from four million in 1914 to 6.5 million in 1918.

o Dylan Thomas, the English-language poet, is born in Swansea.[10]

1915: King George V creates the Welsh Guards Regiment,[11] one of five regiments that constitute the Royal Foot Guards.

o 9–15 August: During the Gallipoli or Dardanelles campaign the 53rd Welsh Division participates in the landing at Suvla Bay, along with eight other British divisions. The campaign ends in the defeat of British and French forces.

o Herbert Stanley Jevons, the son of English economist William Stanley Jevons, publishes *The British Coal Trade*, an 800-page book in which he studies the reserves of British coal and its supply. He warns the public of the progressive exhaustion of the nation's coal reserves.

o Caradoc Evans writes *My People*. Using a peculiar form of Welsh-influenced English invented by the author, the book portrays life in rural, Nonconformist west Wales in a particularly negative light. Because it seems to confirm many English stereotypes about the Welsh, Evans is viewed as a traitor by many Welshmen.

1915–1923: Born in London of Welsh parents, William Morris Hughes is elected Prime Minister of Australia. His father William Hughes is a Baptist deacon from Holyhead, Anglesey, and his mother Jane Morris is from Llansantffraid, Montgomeryshire. He is also one of the signatories of the Treaty of Versailles in 1919.

1916 (7 December): David Lloyd George is elected Prime Minister.

o July to December: 420,000 British soldiers are killed during the Battle of the Somme. The 38th (Welsh) division, under the command of General Watts (15th corps) and General Rawlinson (4th army), suffers heavy losses during this battle at Mametz Wood where a memorial has been erected.

o During the First World War Sir Robert Jones, the nephew of Welsh surgeon Hugh Owen Thomas (from Anglesey, 1834–91), introduces his uncle's invention. Commonly called the 'Thomas splint', it reduces the death rate due to bone fractures from 80 per cent in 1916 to less than eight per cent in 1918, saving tens of thousands of lives.

o The Ministry of Pensions is created to help wounded soldiers and widows.

o William Brace (MP for South Glamorgan, 1906–18 and MP for Abertillery, 1918–20) becomes Under-Secretary of State for the Home Department (1916–19).

o Born in Llandaff to Norwegian parents, Roald Dahl (1916–90) is the author of many short stories (*Umbrella Man*) and novels (*Charlie and the Chocolate Factory*, *Matilda*, *James and the Giant Peach*, *Fantastic Mr Fox*).

1916–1918: The 53rd Welsh Division participates in the Palestine campaign supporting the Arab revolt against the Turkish army (cf. **1888** T. E. Lawrence). It participates in General Edmund Allenby's capture of Jerusalem from the Turks (December 1917). In 1918 (September–October) it fights in the Battle of Megiddo, also in Palestine.

1917: From July to September, between 200,000 and 300,000 British soldiers are killed in the Third Battle of Ypres (Belgium). Many Welshmen fall there, particularly at Hill 52.

o At Pilkem Ridge poet Ellis Humphrey Evans[12] (better known as *Hedd Wyn*, meaning 'blessed peace'), Royal

Welsh Fusiliers, is killed on 31 July. He posthumously wins the chair at the Birkenhead eisteddfod (Merseyside, England), where Prime Minister David Lloyd George is present, for his poem, *Yr Arwr* (The Hero).

o In addition to Pilkem Ridge (31 July – 2 August), the 38th Welsh Infantry Division participates in the battles of Langemarck (16–18 August) and the Menin Road Ridge (20–25 September), all part of the Battle of Passchendaele (Belgium).

Y Blotyn Du by Hedd Wyn
(The Black Spot, English translation by Jim Finnis)

Nid oes gennym hawl ar y sêr,
Na'r lleuad hiraethus chwaith,
Na'r cwmwl o aur a ymylch
Yng nghanol y glesni maith.

Nid oes gennym hawl ar ddim byd,
Ond ar yr hen ddaear wyw;
A honno sy'n anhrefn i gyd
Yng nghanol gogoniant Duw.

We have no right to the stars,
Nor the homesick moon,
Nor the clouds edged with gold
In the centre of the long blueness.

We have no right to anything
But the old and withered earth
That is all in chaos
At the centre of God's glory.

(Source: http://www.firstworldwar.com/poetsandprose/wyn.htm)

o February to October: The Russian Revolution breaks out and Tsar Nicholas II (Kaiser Wilhelm and George V's cousin) is overthrown by the Bolshevik Revolution led by Vladimir Ilyich Ulyanov, better known as

Lenin (1870–1924). This event inspires socialists and communists around the world.

1917–1918: David Alfred 'D. A.' Thomas (cf. **1886**, **1899**) from Ysguborwen, near Aberdare (south Wales) is appointed Minister for Food Control.

1918: First World War ends on 11 November.

- o A collection of Hedd Wyn's poems, *Cerddi'r Bugail* (Poems of the Shepherd), is published.

- o Education Act (Fisher's Act[13]). Children must attend school until the age of 14.

- o Representation of the People Act: all men of 21 and over and women over 30 are given the right to vote (cf. suffrage laws in **1832**, **1867**, and **1884**).

- o General Election. Victory for the Conservatives.

1918–1919: Ten thousand Welsh people die of Spanish Flu.

1918–1939: During the inter-war decades the population declines sharply. Infant mortality (mainly because of tuberculosis) in the coal-mining areas (mainly in south Wales) is one reason. Another is the financial pressure by landowners and a rise in the unemployment rate during the Great Depression, which leads 500,000 people to emigrate to England, Australia, the US and Canada. Many of these are Welsh speakers.

1919: The Ministry of Health is created. Christopher Addison is appointed to this office until 1921. Judge John Sankey, Viscount Sankey (his father comes from Moreton, Gloucestershire) leads the Royal Commission on Coal and recommends the nationalization of the coal industry.

1920: Anglicanism ceases to be the official religion of Wales. After a conflict lasting 13 centuries, the Church in Wales is no longer dependent on Canterbury and has its own archbishop. This ends the conflict that began in 597 when Augustine was appointed first Archbishop of Canterbury by Pope Gregory I. Two new dioceses are added (Monmouth in 1921; Swansea and Brecon in 1923).

o 13,000 Welshmen emigrate to the United States during the 1920s. The US Censuses in 1920 and 1930 show that 73 per cent of the Welsh immigrants become American citizens.

o John Llywelyn Lewis becomes the leader of the UMWA (United Mine Workers of America) from 1920 to 1960 and is the founder-president of the CIO (Congress of Industrial Organization[14]) between 1938 and 1942. These are two of the largest unions in the United States. He was born in Lucas, Iowa, of Welsh parents from south Wales and was himself a former collier. He is also the second Welshman to head the UMWA (cf. **1908**).

o The British Communist Party is founded by Arthur Horner.[15]

o The Unemployment Insurance Act is passed by Parliament. It extends unemployment benefits to most manual workers and lower-paid non-manual workers from the age of 16.

o The University College of Swansea is founded.

1920–1922: The Labour Party wins all six by-elections in the Welsh mining constituencies.

1921: The 1921 British Census: 37.1 per cent of the population speaks Welsh, a six per cent fall since 1911 (977,366 to 922,092). The decline in the number of native Welsh speakers between 1911 and 1921 is partly due to the death of young Welsh soldiers on the battlefields of France during the First World War and especially to emigration.

o Another important factor in the decline of the Welsh language is the 'Welsh Not', an interdiction, since the 1847 report, prohibiting young children from speaking Welsh in primary schools, a policy that lasts well into the 20th century. If a child speaks Welsh (s)he is denounced by other schoolmates and must carry a wooden plate around the neck with the inscription 'WN'. The same type of policy is practised in France to prohibit the use of Breton.

o Black Friday (15 April). Miners strike in protest at the decision of the government to give back the mines to the owners. The strikers are defeated because they are not supported by the rail and transport unions. It also ends the alliance between the rail, transport and miners' unions (called 'triple alliance', cf. **1913**).

o The Cyfarthfa Ironworks close during this year (cf. **1765**, **1794**, **1895**).

1922: David Lloyd George resigns after the Conservative Party leaves the coalition. He is replaced as Prime Minister by the Conservative Andrew Bonar Law.

o Foundation of Urdd Gobaith Cymru (Welsh League of Youth) by the son of Owen M. Edwards, Sir Ifan ab Owen Edwards (1895–1970). Its purpose is to promote and encourage the Welsh language. Today this organisation has 50,000 members.

1922–1955: The literary review *Y Llenor* (The Writer) is founded by the editor William John 'W. J.' Gruffydd (1881–1954) (cf. **1943–1950**). It publishes the work of Welsh-language authors such as Robert Williams Parry, Saunders Lewis and Kate Roberts. Moreover, its aim is to make Welsh literature accessible to all generations. In 1909 W. J. Gruffydd wins the crown at the National Eisteddfod in London for his poem *Yr Arglwydd Rhys* (the Welsh name for Lord Rhys).

The Rise of Welsh Political Consciousness

1925: Plaid Genedlaethol Cymru (The Welsh Nationalist Party) is founded by Lewis Valentine, Saunders Lewis and others. Lewis takes over the leadership of the party the following year.

o   The Dawes Plan allows Germany to re-enter the international coal market by exporting 'free coal' to France and Italy as part of the reparations for the First World War. The result is a fall in coal prices in Wales.

o   Red Friday (31 July), led by Herbert Smith and Arthur James 'A. J.' Cook, secretary of the Miners' Federation of Great Britain (a trade union). The miners consider this a victory. The Tory government (led by Stanley Baldwin) agrees to establish a royal commission, led by Sir Herbert Samuel, to study the problems of the coal industry over a nine-month period. The government uses this as a pretext to prepare a plan against the miners which consists in using the Emergency Powers Act of 1920 to place the south Wales coalfields under the control of Dominions House (Cardiff). North Wales's coalfields are under the authority of Liverpool.

1925–1939: 390,000 Welshmen leave Wales for the Midlands and the south-east of England. The most disastrous effects of the Great Depression are on heavy industry.

1926–1939: Saunders Lewis is the president of Plaid Cymru.

1926: The General Strike is organized by the Trades Union Congress (TUC) in order to stop the government from lowering wages and worsening working conditions for colliers. One of the main consequences of this strike is that the government passes the Trade Disputes and Trade Union Act of 1927 (Section 3) forbidding future industrial strikes and declaring that 'mass picketing'[16] is 'unlawful'. The General Strike is particularly serious in south Wales. It lasts only 12 days for most workers, but the miners and consequently the south Wales ports do not resume work until November.

o   Born in Allt-wen near Swansea, *Gwenallt* (David James Jones, 1899–1968) wins the chair at the National Eisteddfod in Swansea, for his poem *Y Mynach* (The monk). He wins the chair a second time at Bangor in 1931. He edits the magazine *Taliesin* from 1961 to 1965, for the Academi Gymreig (Welsh Academy, cf. **1959**).

1927: Cardiff City wins the FA Cup (or Football Association Challenger Cup), defeating Arsenal in Wembley Stadium, London.

1928: Women over 21 are granted the right to vote in Great Britain (cf. suffrage laws **1832**, **1867**, **1884** and **1918**).

1929 (30 May): Megan Lloyd George (1902–66), MP for Anglesey, becomes the first woman to represent a Welsh constituency. Reverend Lewis Valentine, Plaid Cymru's first Parliamentary candidate, obtains 609 votes in Caernarfon (nicknamed 'the gallant six hundred'). Aneurin Bevan (Labour Party) is elected MP for Ebbw Vale (until his death in 1960).

o   24 October marks the beginning of the Great Depression after the stock market crashes on Wall Street, New York City.

1931: The census shows that 36.8 per cent (909,261) of the inhabitants of Wales claim to be able to speak Welsh, a 13.1 per cent drop since 1901.

o UK General Election. Labour wins all the coalmining constituencies.

1934: A gas explosion occurs at Gresford Colliery in Denbighshire, killing 266 colliers.

1935–1938: Sir Ifor Williams[17] publishes his landmark studies on the *Hengerdd* (Early Welsh Poetry), *Canu Aneirin* (Poetry of Aneirin cf. **541**, **1265**) and *Canu Llywarch Hen* (Poetry of Llywarch the Old cf. **655**, **850**).

o BBC Radio agrees to broadcast programmes in the Welsh language from the studios in Bangor (Gwynedd).

1936: Edward VIII becomes King of Great Britain and Ireland. He abdicates because of his relationship with a divorced American woman, Wallis Simpson. George VI succeeds him as King.

o Saunders Lewis, Lewis Valentine and D. J. Williams burn a building at the RAF bombing station in Penrhos on the Llŷn Peninsula, in Gwynedd, in protest against the construction of RAF bases by Stanley Baldwin's government.

o Kate Roberts publishes *Traed Mewn Cyffion* (Feet in Chains, 1936). She is known as 'Brenhines ein Llên' (Queen of our Literature). Born in Rhosgadfan, Gwynedd in 1891 where her father Owen Roberts works in the slate quarries. She is also a member of Plaid Cymru where she meets her future husband, Morris Williams, an editor who works for the party, in 1928. She dies in 1985. *Traed Mewn Cyffion*, like most of her novels and stories, is directly inspired by her childhood in Gwynedd.

1936–1939: The Spanish Civil War rages. 174 Welshmen are among 2,000 British men who fight against Franco in the International Brigade. 33 of them lose their lives. Many of them belong to the Communist Party of Great Britain.

1937: Trade union leader Lewis Jones[18] publishes *Cwmardy*, a book on the ordeals of Welsh miners during the early 20th century. The dialogues are written in the Welsh-English of the Valleys, later called Wenglish by John Edwards in his book *Talk Tidy* in the 1980s. The fictional name Cwmardy may have been inspired by Maerdy, a mining village in the Rhondda referred to at the time as 'Little Moscow'.

- o The Welsh Region of BBC Radio is established on a separate wavelength from Washford (Somerset).

- o Kate Roberts publishes *Ffair Gaeaf a Storiau Eraill* (Winter Fair and Other Stories).

- o Heavyweight champion Tommy Farr from Clydach Vale, nicknamed the 'Tonypandy Terror', fights the legendary American boxer Joe Louis at the Yankee Stadium in New York City but narrowly loses the 15-round fight by a split decision.

1938: Geraint Goodwin (1903–41) publishes his novel, *Watch for the Morning*; and *The White Farm*, a collection of English-language short stories. He was born in Newtown (Montgomeryshire).

- o Idris Davies (1905–53) publishes the poem 'Bells of Rhymney', a ballad about the Depression, in his book *Gwalia Deserta*. Pete Seeger, the American folk singer, makes the poem popular in North America during the 1960s.

1939: The Second World War breaks out in September of this year; 15,000 Welshmen lose their lives during this conflict (out of a total of 388,000 British fatalities).

o   Richard Llewellyn publishes his international bestseller, *How Green was my Valley,* about the Welsh mining communities in south Wales (150,000 copies are sold).

o   Lewis Jones's novel, *We Live*, a sequel to *Cwmardy*, is published posthumously.

o   Pwyllgor Amddiffyn Diwylliant Cymru (Committee for the Defence of the Culture of Wales) is founded.

1940: Winston Churchill (Conservative) is elected Prime Minister in May of this year.

o   John Ford makes a Hollywood film out of Richard Llewellyn's *How Green was my Valley*, starring Walter Pidgeon and Maureen O'Hara. It is an international success, presenting an idealized vision of life in the Welsh coalfields.

1940–1943: Nazi Germany launches 44 raids on towns in Wales; 369 people are killed, including 230 who die during the three-night blitz on Swansea, 19–21 February 1941. Cardiff is also bombed and Llandaff Cathedral seriously damaged.

1941: Formerly known as Pwyllgor Amddiffyn Diwylliant Cymru (Committee for the Defence of the Culture of Wales, cf. **1939**), the cultural association is merged with Undeb Cenedlaethol y Cymdeithasau Cymreig (The National Union of Welsh Associations) and renamed Undeb Cymru Fydd (The Union of Wales to be). It is led by Thomas Iorwerth Ellis (1899–1970), the son of politician Thomas Edward Ellis (cf. **1886**). One of its first initiatives is to lead a campaign against the War Office's plan to requisition Mynydd Epynt and transform it into a firing range. The attempt fails. Undeb Cymru Fydd also asks the British government to vote measures in favour of the Welsh language in domains such as education and radio.

1942: The coal industry is placed under the control of the Ministry of Fuel and Power.

    o   The Welsh Courts Act is passed by Parliament, allowing Welshmen to use the Welsh language in courts (cf. Acts of Union **1536**).

1943: A ceremony is held in Cardiff to celebrate the 25th anniversary of the Soviet Red Army.

1943–1947: Thomas Rowland Hughes (1903–49) publishes five novels in consecutive years: *O Law i Law* (From Hand to Hand, 1943), *William Jones* (1944),[19] *Yr Ogof* (The Cave, 1945), *Chwalfa*[20] (Upheaval, 1946), *Y Cychwyn* (The Beginning, 1947). He was born in Llanberis, Gwynedd, and his father worked in a slate quarry. He studies at the University of Bangor and Jesus College, Oxford, and wins the chair of the National Eisteddfod on two occasions: Machynlleth in 1937 for his poem *Y Ffin* (The Boundary), and Aberpennar in 1940 for his poem *Pererinion* (Pilgrims).

1943–1950: W. J. Gruffydd (cf. **1922–55**) is MP for the University of Wales. He is best known for his work on Welsh literature and his articles published in the review *Y Llenor*. He comes from Bethel, Caernarfonshire.

1944: The Education Act (or Butler Education Act) is passed. One consequence is the creation of the Welsh Joint Education Committee in 1949. It replaces the Central Welsh Board and introduces the 'tripartite system': Grammar Schools, Secondary Modern Schools, Technical Schools, as well as the 11-plus exam. Secondary education becomes free for all and the school-leaving age is raised from 14 (in 1918) to 15.

o 100,000 Welsh miners go on strike to protest against the wage differences between skilled and unskilled colliers.

o Thomas Parry publishes his *Hanes Llenyddiaeth Gymraeg* (The History of Welsh Literature). It is translated into English in 1955 by H. Idris Bell.

1944–1955: Polish painter Josef Herman (1911–2000) stays in Ystradgynlais, near Swansea. His paintings are mostly inspired by the Welsh mining communities.

1945: Germany surrenders unconditionally on 8 May, ending the war in Europe. Japan surrenders on 14/15 August.

o Clement Attlee is elected Prime Minister (Labour). Some Welsh MPs are included in his government: Aneurin Bevan[21] (Minister for Health), Tom Williams (Minister for Agriculture) and James Griffiths[22] (Minister for National Insurance).

o The Miners' Federation of Great Britain is renamed the National Union of Mineworkers (NUM).

1945–1981: Gwynfor Evans (1912–2005) is appointed president of Plaid Cymru.

Chapter 15

The Post-War Period and the Struggle for Civil Rights (1946–1997)

The United Kingdom comes out of the Second World War militarily victorious, but the result of the enormous war effort is unparalleled economic decline. Another consequence of the war is the rise of a new world order, dominated by the United States and the Soviet Union. It is a period during which Britain and the other major European nations lose their colonies and hence their imperial pretensions. Between 1947 and 1964 most of the colonies worldwide request and achieve independence, although many remain active partners in the British Commonwealth of Nations.

Non-state nations such as Wales and Scotland, as well as ethnic minorities living in Britain itself, also claim their civil rights in what Bud Khlief (1978) calls 'Ethnic Awakening in the First World'. In this context many Welshmen see Wales not as a participant in British colonial expansion but rather as a victim of it, a process having its ultimate origins in the arrival of the English in the 5th century. According to this long-term view, Wales itself is an internal colony (cf. Michael Hechter, *Internal Colonialism*) within the British state. Whether one accepts this view, however, is a matter for debate. This chapter outlines some of the concessions that the British government was forced to make during this period in order to provide the Welsh with a greater voice in their own affairs.

It is during the decade following the Second World War that

Welsh national identity is reinforced by such concrete acts as the recognition of Cardiff as the capital city of Wales, the officialization of the Welsh national flag and other similar measures.

1946: Cwmni Opera Cenedlaethol Cymru (The Welsh National Opera Company) is founded in Cardiff. It performs in Wales (Cardiff, Llandudno and Swansea) but also in England (Bristol, Birmingham, Liverpool, Plymouth, Southampton and Oxford).

o Cerddorfa Genedlaethol Gymreig y BBC (the BBC National Orchestra of Wales has borne this name since 1993) is created.

1946–1949: The first wave of nationalizations of the coal, iron and steel industries occurs. From 1947 to 1950, 34 pits are closed because people start switching from coal to oil heaters.

1947: The National Coal Board is created. By this time 700,000 colliers work in over 1,500 coal mines. In 1987 it is renamed British CC (Coal Corporation).

1948: Until its abolition in 1966, the Council of Wales and Monmouthshire is created to advise the government on matters relating to Wales. Huw T. Edwards is its first president (1948–58).[1]

o Under the leadership of Aneurin Bevan the National Health Service (NHS) is created. This is a direct result of the National Insurance Act passed the same year. Bevan explains that he is inspired by experiences during his youth in Tredegar (Blaenau Gwent, south Wales), his hometown. The measure receives a warm welcome in Wales.

o Founding of St Fagans Folk Museum (now National History Museum) by Iorwerth Peate, one of Europe's finest open-air museums.

o The sprinter Ken Jones from Blaenavon wins a silver medal during the Olympic Games in London.

o Glamorgan's cricketers win the county championship this year (and also in 1969 and 1997).

1949: The *Anglo-Welsh Review* (first called *Dock Leaves*, 1949–1957) is founded by Raymond Garlick (editor from 1949 to 1960) and Roland Mathias (editor between 1961 and 1976). This review allows English-speaking Welshmen to have an identifiable literary voice in Wales.

o The Central Welsh Board (cf. **1896**) is replaced by the Cyd-Bwyllgor Addysg Cymreig (Welsh Joint Education Committee), based in Cardiff. It is in charge of the Local Education Authorities (cf. **1902**) and organizes national examinations (examples: Entry Level Certificate, GCSE and A Level) for all pupils in primary and secondary schools in Wales.

o Fifty members of Plaid Cymru leave the party to found the Mudiad Gweriniaethol Cymru (Welsh Republican Movement).

o T. H. Parry-Williams publishes *Ugain o Gerddi* (Twenty Poems, 1949).

o Gwyn Jones and Thomas Jones produce a masterly translation of the *Mabinogion*.

o The Welsh are authorized to celebrate civilian marriages in the Welsh language, but official acts still must be written in English.

1950: This year marks the beginning of the 'Parliament for Wales Campaign'. It is led notably by Megan Lloyd George and Stephen Owen 'S. O.' Davies (MP for Merthyr, 1934–72).

o The philosopher Bertrand Russell (1872–1970) receives the Nobel Prize for Literature. Born to an aristocratic family in Trellech, Monmouthshire, he is considered by many to be one of the three masters of language philosophy, along with his student, Ludwig Wittgenstein. Noam Chomsky (the father of Generative-Transformational Linguistics, MIT) was also inspired by his theories.

1951: Winston Churchill's government creates the Office of Minister for Welsh Affairs under the leadership of the Home Secretary.

o 1951 census: the percentage of Welsh speakers drops from 36.8 per cent (909, 261) in 1931 to 28.9 per cent (714, 686).

o The General Certificate of Education (GCE), composed of the A-level and O-level exams, is introduced in secondary schools. These replace the School Certificate and Higher School Certificate.

o The first Welsh National Park is founded in Snowdonia, Gwynedd. Welsh National Parks currently occupy 20 per cent of the surface area of Wales. The Pembrokeshire Coast National Park and the Brecon Beacons National Park are founded in 1952 and 1957.

1952: Robert Williams Parry is described by J. M. Edwards as the greatest 'folk poet of our century'. An example of his free verse is his tribute to an elderly minister who is symbolized by *Gaeaf* (Winter). The following is an extract (cf. **1910**).

Gaeaf

Ti wyddost fel mae'r llanciau
Mewn hiraeth am un iau;
Ti wyddost am ystranciau
Hynafgwyr, un neu ddau;
A gwyddost ti, mor drist, mor drist,
Yw diwedd oes dan groes dy Grist.

Rhag dirmyg amlwg llanciau
Mewn hiraeth am un iau,
Rhag blin dristâd ystranciau
Hynafgwyr, un neu ddau,
Rhodded ei Feistr, o'i fawr ras
Ei dirion nodded i'r hen was.

Winter

You know the wish of youngsters
'A younger one' than you;
You know the subtle scheming
Of elders, one or two,
And you know too, how sad, how sad,
At journey's end the cross you've had.

But when the youth are longing
For one more young than you,
And when you hear the scheming
Of elders, one or two,
I pray the Master will uphold
In grace, his servant, now grown old.

(Gwasg Gee, poem translated by W. Rhys Nicholas, 1978, p. 43)

1953: Dylan Thomas (cf. **1914**) dies in New York City. Bob Dylan (born Robert Zimmerman), a great admirer of his poetry, adopts his name.

o   A report entitled 'The Place of Welsh and English in the Schools of Wales' is published by the British Minister of Education in which it proposes teaching Welsh and English to all pupils in primary and secondary schools.

o D. J. Williams writes two autobiographies between 1953 and 1959: *Hen Dŷ Ffarm* (The Old Farmhouse,[2] 1953) and *Yn Chwech ar Hugain Oed* (Twenty-Six Years Old, 1959).

1954: Under the patronage of the Welsh Joint Education Committee, the Welsh Joint Scheme is set up to prepare educational materials for Welsh-medium schools.

1954–1957: Gwilym Lloyd George, the son of former Prime Minister David Lloyd George, is Home Secretary in the cabinet of Sir Winston Churchill and Sir Anthony Eden.

1955: Cardiff is recognized as the capital of Wales.

1956: Waldo Williams (1904–71) publishes his volume of poetry entitled *Dail Pren* (Tree Leaves). Born in Haverfordwest, Pembrokeshire, his father is a Welsh speaker and a teacher. He is remembered as a committed anti-war poet and Welsh nationalist. An extract of his work follows:

Waldo Williams, *Cofio* (Remembrance)

Un funud fach cyn elo'r haul o'r wybren,
Un funud fwyn cyn delo'r hwyr i'w hynt,
I gofio am y pethau anghofiedig
Ar goll yn awr yn llwch yr amser gynt.

Fel ewyn ton a dyr ar draethell unig,
Fel cân y gwynt lle nid oes glust a glyw,
Mi wn eu bod yn galw'n ofer arnom –
Hen bethau anghofiedig dynol ryw.

One fleeting moment as the sun is setting,
One gentle moment as the night falls fast,
To bring to mind the things that are forgotten,
Now scattered in the dust of ages past.

Like white-foamed waves that break on lonely beaches,
Like the wind's song where no one hears the wind,
They beckon us, I know, but to no purpose –
The old forgotten things of humankind.

(Gomer & Cymdeithas Waldo Williams, poem translated by Alan Llwyd)

o W. J. Edwards, a socialist theoretician, publishes his autobiography, *From the Valley I Came*.

o Goronwy Roberts (Labour), MP for Caernarfon, presents a petition to the House of Commons signed by 240,000 people in favour of a Welsh Parliament. The petition is ignored.

o Kate Roberts publishes *Y Byw sy'n Cysgu* (The Living Sleep).

1957: T. H. Parry-Williams (cf. **1912**, **1949**, **1966**) publishes a book of poetry entitled *Myfyrdodau* (Meditations).

o John Charles, perhaps Wales's greatest footballer ever, is transferred to the Italian club Juventus Turin for a record fee. He helps Juventus to win the Italian championship three times and the Italian Cup twice.

1957–1964: The National Coal Board closes 50 pits in the south Wales coalfield.

1958: Welsh boxer Howard Winstone from Merthyr Tydfil wins a gold medal at the British Empire and Commonwealth games. He is managed by a former Welsh boxer, Eddie Thomas, also from Merthyr Tydfil.

1958–1964: The British government invests £260 million in the Welsh economy by installing companies such as Prestcold (refrigerators) in Swansea, Rover in Cardiff, and Hoover in Merthyr.

1959: The red dragon flag is officially recognized by the British Crown as the national flag of Wales.

o Kate Roberts publishes *Te yn y Grug* (Tea in the Heather).

o Yr Academi Gymreig (The Welsh Academy) is founded by Bobi Jones and Waldo Williams (cf. **1956**) to promote the Welsh language and also English-language literature in Wales. On 1 April 2011 it merges with Tŷ Newydd (the National Centre for Writing in Wales, based in Llanystumdwy, near Criccieth, Gwynedd) and changes its name to Literature Wales (Llenyddiaeth Cymru).

o In its political programme for the 1959 elections the Labour Party proposes the creation of a Welsh Office under the direction of a Secretary of State for Wales. This idea is put into practice in 1964 by Harold Wilson's government.

1960: Kate Roberts publishes her autobiography, *Y Lôn Wen* (The White Lane).

1961: Cyngor Llyfrau Cymraeg (The Welsh Books Council) is established to encourage the interest of children and adults in Welsh-language books. Nowadays it is financed by the Welsh Assembly Government.

o The 1961 census: 26 per cent of the inhabitants of Wales (656,002) speak Welsh.

o The Sunday Closing Act of 1881 is repealed this year, though eight counties vote to remain 'dry'.

o Richard Booth opens his first bookshop in Hay-on-Wye, Powys, the future 'Town of Books'.

o Born in Bethesda, Gwynedd, Caradog Prichard (1904–

80) publishes his novel, *Un Nos Ola' Leuad* (One Moonlit Night). He wins the crown at the National Eisteddfod three times (1927, 1928 and 1929), and the chair in 1962 in Llanelli for his poem *Llef un yn Llefain* (The Voice of him that Crieth).

1962: Following Saunders Lewis's lecture on BBC radio entitled *Tynged yr Iaith* (The Fate of the Language), Cymdeithas yr Iaith Gymraeg (The Welsh Language Society) is founded by a group of nationalists belonging to Plaid Cymru. Their goal is to defend and promote the Welsh language. In the 1960s they also launch a campaign for bilingual road signs and daub them with green and 'Cymraeg'. Gradually all signs for public information became bilingual.

o Ceri Richards, a Welsh painter (1903–71, born in Dunvant, near Swansea), represents Wales at the Venice Biennale[3] where he wins the Einaudi[4] Painting Prize. Many of his paintings are exhibited in the Tate Gallery (London) and the National Museum in Cardiff.

o Atlantic College (World College of the Atlantic), the international sixth-form college, is founded at St Donats, Glamorgan.

1963: Actor Richard Burton (1925–84, born Richard Walter Jenkins in Pontrhydyfen, near Port Talbot) plays Julius Caesar in the blockbuster hit *Cleopatra* alongside his future wife, Elizabeth Taylor, who is also his partner in *Who's afraid of Virginia Woolf* (1966).

1964: BBC Wales is launched and is based in Llandaff, near Cardiff.

o The post of Minister for Welsh Affairs is abolished. The Welsh Office, under the leadership of a Secretary of State for Wales, is created to replace it. Between

Figure 25: Photograph of Saunders Lewis (*c.*1962)

1968 and 1993 the British Government progressively transfers responsibilities to the Welsh Office in domains such as health, tourism (1968), primary and secondary education (1970), childcare and water sanitation (1971), industry (1975), higher education (but this does not yet concern the universities) and agriculture (1978).

o The athlete Lynn Davies from Bridgend, wins a gold medal during the Olympic Games in Tokyo for his performance in the long jump.

1964–1967: James Griffiths (Labour), MP for Llanelli, becomes the first Secretary of State for Wales.

1964–1969: Goronwy Daniel becomes the permanent secretary of the Welsh Office.

1964–1970: Harold Wilson (Labour) is elected Prime Minister (first term). At the same time, 40 pits in the south Wales coalfield close with another four in north Wales.

1964–1979: Rugby legends Gareth Edwards and Barry John lead the Welsh rugby team to win the Triple Crown seven times (1965, 1969, 1971, 1976, 1977, 1978 and 1979).

o Dame Shirley Bassey, born in Cardiff, sings the theme song of three 007 movies: *Goldfinger* (1964), *Diamonds are Forever* (1971), and *Moonraker* (1979).

1965: Singer Tom Jones (from Treforest, near Pontypridd) releases his first international hit single, 'It's not unusual'. Shortly afterwards, he hosts a weekly variety show on ABC Channel in the United States, *This is Tom Jones* (1969–71). He ends each show with a phrase in Welsh.

o Around this time, Mary Quant, born near London of Welsh parents, is a famous fashion designer and a pioneer of the miniskirt. She is also well known in the US and in Europe.

1965–1973: Meic Stephens[5] founds and edits the review entitled *Poetry Wales*.

1966–1970; 1974–1979: Gwynfor Evans, President of Plaid Cymru, is elected MP for Carmarthen. This marks a breakthrough for the party.

1966: The Severn Bridge is opened in the presence of Queen Elizabeth II. It links South Gloucestershire (south-west England) to Monmouthshire (south Wales).

- o The Aberfan tragedy (21 October): 144 people (116 children and 28 adults) are killed when a coal tip buries the local primary school.

- o The Council of Wales is dissolved (see **1948**).

- o T. H. Parry-Williams publishes *Pensynnu* (Daydreaming).

1967: The Welsh Language Act is passed. For the first time since the Act of Union (cf. **1536**) Welsh can be used in official documents.

- o The Gittins Report (named after Charles Gittins, vice-principal of University College Swansea, 1967–70) is published by the Central Council for Education. It encourages Welsh children to learn the Welsh language in primary school.

- o Publication of the volume I of *Geiriadur Prifysgol Cymru* (The University of Wales Dictionary), on which work had started in 1921. The other volumes appear in 1987, 1998 and 2002.

1968: Glyn Jones (1905–95) publishes *The Dragon has Two Tongues*, an autobiography in which he discusses Welsh

Figure 26: Photograph of Gwynfor Evans (*c.*1966)

society between the two world wars and their impact on his generation. Born into a Welsh-speaking family in Merthyr Tydfil, Glamorgan, he is an author and poet.

1968–1969: Welsh militants of the Free Wales Army set off about a dozen bombs in Wales causing considerable consternation among the general public and the authorities.

1969: In the presence of his mother Queen Elizabeth, Prince Charles is invested as Prince of Wales at Caernarfon castle on 1 July. As part of the ceremony he reads a short passage in Welsh. It is attended by 4,000 people. It is a worldwide event broadcast on television to an audience of 500 million, including 19 million British people. Gerallt Lloyd Owen composes a scathing condemnation of the event in his poem, *I'r Farwolaeth* (To the Death). Here is an extract:

> Awn heb yr hoen i barhau
> I'r nos na ŵyr ein heisiau,
> Awn i gyd yn fodlon gaeth
> Efo'r hil i farwolaeth.
>
> *We will go without the vigour to continue*
> *To the night which does not miss us,*
> *We will all go happily enslaved*
> *With the race to Death.*

(T. G. Hunter, 1998:119–20)

o   Dafydd Iwan (cf. **2003**) writes and sings 'Carlo', a satirical song ridiculing the investiture of Prince Charles. Born in 1943 in Brynaman, Carmarthenshire, he studied architecture. He was firstly a singer, then a Welsh-language activist in the 1960s, and later founder of Sain, one of the main Welsh music labels.

o   The South Wales Borderers (cf. Rorke's Drift, **1879**) and the Welch Regiment merge to form the Royal Regiment of Wales (RRW, cf. **2006**).

1969–1973: The Kilbrandon Commission (or Royal Commission on the Constitution) is created by Lord Crowther, followed by Lord Kilbrandon, to study devolution in Wales and Scotland and the formation of an elected assembly. Their conclusions pave the way for the referenda on devolution which are held in 1979 and 1997.

1970: Tory Party leader Edward Heath is elected Prime Minister.

o   The Welsh Office moves from London to Cardiff.

o   Ned Thomas founds the magazine *Planet*. He later publishes *The Welsh Extremist* in 1973.

o   Meic Stephens (cf. **1965–73**) begins the publication of the *Writers of Wales* series to provide a better understanding of Welsh-language literature for English speakers, but also Anglo-Welsh literature.

1971: The British Census shows that 20.9 per cent (542,425) of the population can speak Welsh. Most of these people are still native speakers who learnt Welsh in their households and communities.

1972: The Local Government Act is passed. It reorganizes the administrative divisions of Wales into eight counties: Gwent, South Glamorgan, Mid Glamorgan, West Glamorgan, Dyfed, Powys, Gwynedd and Clwyd. It comes into force on 1 April 1974.

1973: Great Britain is accepted into the European Economic Community on 1 January.

o   The school-leaving age is raised from 15 (since 1944) to 16.

1974: Laura Ashley (née Mountney, born in Dowlais, 1925–85), a Welsh designer, opens stores in Paris and San Francisco.

o The Wales TUC (Trade Union Congress) is created in April of this year. Dai Francis becomes its chairman during the first congress in Aberystwyth, until 1976.

o The Welsh painter Sir Kyffin Williams (born in Llangefni, Anglesey, 1918) is elected a member of the Royal Academy of Arts. He is a landscape painter who is influenced by Vincent Van Gogh. Most of his oil paintings are landscapes of the Menai Straits and Snowdonia.

1974–1976: Harold Wilson is re-elected Prime Minister for a second term. There are two elections during 1974 (February and October).

1975: A referendum is organized to keep the UK in the EEC. Every one of the eight counties in Wales records a majority in favour of continued membership (64.8 per cent answer 'yes') showing Wales's pro-European stance. Moreover, the Welsh disagree with the anti-European stance of the Labour Party which declared in April of this year that it wanted to leave the EEC. Given that Wales is in the middle of de-industrialization, it is possible that the public felt that trade with Europe would help develop the Welsh economy. Since the 1980s Wales has strengthened its economic ties with the EU (see **1988**).

o Around this time Ulpan courses (Wlpan in Welsh) are set up, based on the Israeli model of total immersion courses, to assist Welsh learners.

1976: Awdurdod Datblygu Cymru (The Welsh Development Agency) is created in order to encourage investment in Wales. James Callaghan, MP for Cardiff, becomes Prime Minister, after having been Chancellor of the Exchequer, Home Secretary and

Foreign Secretary. George Thomas (later Viscount Tonypandy) is elected Speaker of the House of Commons.

1977: Inspired by the *Survey of English Dialects* (University of Leeds, 1950–61), David Parry, Professor of English at the University of Wales, Swansea, publishes the first volume of the SAWD (*Survey of Anglo-Welsh Dialects*: south-east).

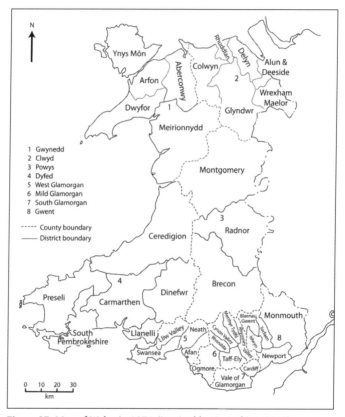

Figure 27: Map of Wales in 1974 (inspired by G. Jenkins, 2007)

o   Radio Cymru, the first entirely Welsh-language radio station, is founded.

o   Roy Jenkins, member of the Labour Party and a native of Abersychan (Monmouthshire), is elected president of the European Commission until 1981.

o   The DBRW (Development Board for Rural Wales) is created to encourage the economic development of rural Wales.

1977–1978: The 'Lib-Lab Pact' is signed between the Liberal Party and the Labour Party.

1978: The Welsh CBI (Confederation of British Industry) is founded – a trade union which defends employers.

1978–1979: 'The Winter of Discontent', an expression taken from Shakespeare's play *Richard III*, is used to refer to a period of strikes involving the private sector (Ford motor company) and also the public sector (grave-diggers, NHS employees). This favours Margaret Thatcher's Conservative Party victory in the May 1979 general election.

1979: On 1 March the St David's Day referendum on devolution is heavily defeated (46.5 per cent of the electorate answer 'No', 12 per cent 'Yes'). The opposition comes mainly from Labour (the 'Gang of Six'[6]). The Conservative Party also stands beside them against the referendum, as well as the Welsh CBI. However, critics of the process point out that those who did not vote at all are counted as 'no votes'. The strongest supporters of the initiative are Plaid Cymru, certain members of the Labour Party (Elystan Morgan, former MP for Cardiganshire, 1966–74; Barry Jones, MP for East Flintshire, 1970–83; and Phylipp Rosser) who are part of the WAC (Wales for the Assembly Campaign), as well as Wales TUC and the Liberals.

o David Parry publishes the second volume of the SAWD (*Survey of Anglo-Welsh Dialects*: South-West).

o First arson attacks on English-owned holiday homes in the Welsh heartland carried out by Meibion Glyndŵr, 'the Sons of Glyndŵr'. There were other groups but this was the most prominent. 220 homes were attacked over the following ten years. The problem resulted from English buyers prepared to pay exaggeratedly high prices for cottages, only occupied for part of the year, effectively pricing potential young Welsh buyers out of the market – and reducing considerably the number of Welsh speakers. Between the 1960s and 1990s hundreds of protesters are imprisoned for various offences.

o The UK General Election results in a victory for Margaret Thatcher and the Conservative Party. Eleven Welsh MPs are elected: 32.2 per cent of the Welsh vote for the Conservaties, 48.6 per cent for Labour. Two Welshmen serve in the cabinet: Geoffrey Howe (born in Port Talbot) as Chancellor of the Exchequer between 1979 and 1983, and Michael Heseltine (born in Swansea), Secretary of State for Defence (1983–6) and also Environment (1979–83, 1990–2).

o 7 June: European Union elections: three Welsh Labourites (Ann Clwyd, Win Griffiths, and Allan Rogers) and one Conservative (Beata Brookes) are elected to the European Parliament.

o The Welsh Affairs Select Committee is founded. It is composed of 11 MPs who control expenses as well as the policy of the Welsh Office. Since 1998 it has handled relations with the National Assembly for Wales.

1979; 1992: Two European directives complement one another.

The Directive on the Conservation of the Wild Birds (Birds Directive, 1979) and the Directive on the Conservation of Natural Habitats and of Wild Fauna and Flora (Habitats Directive, 1992) establish Special Protection Areas and Special Areas of Conservation, to protect bird species as well as fauna. There are respectively 17 and 85 of these areas in Wales that are part of the European network, Natura 2000. Sites of Special Scientific Interest (SSSIs) also have the same role.[7] Moreover, other reserves in Wales are created after the application of the RAMSAR Convention (1971)[8] to protect wetlands.

1980: The Welsh Language Society starts a campaign of civil disobedience to protest against the Conservative government's decision to refuse the creation of a Welsh television channel. Gwynfor Evans, the president of Plaid Cymru, threatens to go on a hunger strike.

o The Big Pit (National Coal Museum) opens in Blaenavon, Gwent. It was a working mine from 1860 to 1980 and is now a World Heritage Site.

1981: The British Census indicates that 18.9 per cent (508,207) of the population speak Welsh.

o Another Welsh fashion designer, David Emanuel (born in 1952 in Bridgend) rises to fame as the creator of the wedding dress of Diana, Princess of Wales (1961–97).

1981–1984: Dafydd Wigley, MP for Caernarfon, is elected president of Plaid Cymru.

1982: In November, S4C (Sianel Pedwar Cymru), the fourth Welsh TV Channel is launched (after BBC1, ITV, and BBC 2). One of its most successful programmes is the Welsh-language soap opera *Pobol y Cwm* (People of the Valley) which has been broadcast since 1974 on BBC Wales, and since 1982 on S4C. It is still shown to this day.

o During the Falklands War against Argentina, 55 soldiers of the Welsh Guards regiment are killed and many others wounded when the RFA *Sir Galahad* is bombed by the Argentine Air Force.

o The abandoned village of Nant Gwrtheyrn, on the northern coast of the Llŷn peninsula, opens as a centre for intensive courses in the Welsh language for adults.

o The opening of St David's Hall, Cardiff, gives Wales a world-class concert hall.

1983: A UK General Election is held (9 June) and Margaret Thatcher is re-elected Prime Minister. In Wales, 37.5 per cent of the voters support Labour and 31 per cent the Conservatives.

o Foundation of Diversions (renamed the National Dance Company of Wales in 2009) by the Scots, Roy Campbell-Moore and Ann Sholem.

1983–1992: Neil Kinnock, a native of Tredegar (Blaenau Gwent), leads the Labour Party until his resignation following his defeat against Conservative John Major after the 1992 General Election. Afterwards, he occupies the position of Vice-President of the European Commission (1999–2004) under the presidency of former Italian Prime Minister, Romano Prodi.

1984: The European Union elections are held in which three Welsh Labourites (Win Griffiths, David Morris, Llew Smith), and one Conservative (Beata Brookes) are elected to the European Parliament.

1984–1985: A colliers' strike is organized by the leader of the National Union of Mineworkers, Arthur Scargill, to protest against the closure of pits: 21,000 colliers from south Wales and 1,000 from north Wales participate.

1984–1991: Dafydd Elis-Thomas is elected president of Plaid Cymru.

Figure 28: Photograph of the miners' strike in the 1980s (*c.*1984–5)

1985: The Centre for Advanced Welsh and Celtic Studies in Aberystwyth is founded by the University of Wales. Its first director is R. Geraint Gruffydd, until 1993, followed by Geraint H. Jenkins, until 2008. Dafydd Johnston is the current director.

1986: In April of this year a nuclear plant in Chernobyl, Ukraine, explodes. As a consequence many countries in Europe, including Wales, are contaminated by radiation. 10,000 farms in the United Kingdom are affected, including 334 in north Wales. Until 2012 farmers are ordered by the FSA (Food Standard Agency) to monitor the level of Caesium-137 before they sell their sheep, to prevent the spread of contamination.[9]

1987: The Campaign for a Welsh Assembly (CWA) is founded. It is a lobby group in favour of a Welsh Assembly and is led by the Labour MP for Cardiff Central, Jon Owen Jones. It becomes known as a Campaign for a Welsh Parliament in 1993.

o On 11 June a UK General Election is held in which Margaret Thatcher is elected Prime Minister for a third time; 45.1 per cent of the Welsh vote Labour and 29.5 per cent Conservative.

o Wales finishes in third place in the Rugby Union World Cup, behind Australia and New Zealand.

1988: The Education Reform Act is passed by Parliament. Later, President George W. Bush takes it as a model for his 'No Child Left Behind' Act, signed by the US Congress in 2001. The National Curriculum (NC) and Key Stages[10] (KS) are introduced. The General Certificate of Secondary Education (GCSE) replaces the O-level and the Certificate of Secondary Education (CSE).

o In order to allow the European regions to participate in the establishment of the Treaty of Maastricht (1992), the 'Four Motors of Europe', an association of four European regions (Catalonia in Spain, Baden-Würtemberg in Germany, Rhône-Alpes in France and Lombardia in Italy) sign an agreement in September of this year to co-operate in fields such as scientific research, education and environment. The following year, Wales becomes an associate member of the group. This shows Wales's interest in developing relations with the European Union.

o The athlete Colin Jackson (born in Cardiff) wins a silver medal for the 110m hurdles at the Olympic Games in Seoul (South Korea). He wins ten gold medals and five silver medals in the European and World Championships in the 1990s–2000s.

1989 (15–18 June): European Union elections: Plaid Cymru decides to distance itself from the EEC. Four Labourites

(Wayne David, David Morris, Joe Wilson and Llew Smith) are elected to the European Parliament.

1990s–2000s: Welsh rock 'n' roll groups gain success on the international stage, such as the Manic Street Preachers (from Blackwood, Caerphilly), Stereophonics (from Cwmaman, near Aberdare, mid-Glamorgan) and Catatonia (from Cardiff). Furthermore, Welsh actors are very successful in Hollywood movies, such as Sir Anthony Hopkins (from Port Talbot), Michael Sheen (from Newport), Catherine Zeta-Jones (from Swansea), Ioan Gruffudd (from Llwydcoed, near Aberdare), Rhys Ifans (from Haverfordwest), and Matthew Rhys (from Cardiff). Bryn Terfel (b. 1965, a farmer's son from Pant Glas, Caernarfon), is a world-famous bass-baritone.

1990: The poet R. S. Thomas (1913–2000) calls for a campaign to deface English-owned houses.

1991: The British Census shows that the percentage of Welsh speakers is 18.9 per cent (508,207), the same as in 1981. This implies that the efforts by the language movement to counter the decline of the number of Welsh speakers are beginning to pay off. However, sceptics claim that the figures are artificial and that older native speakers are being replaced by learners.

o Dafydd Wigley is elected president of Plaid Cymru for the second time. He resigns in 2000 because of health problems.

1992: A UK General Election (9 April) is held in which John Major is elected Prime Minister. Fifty per cent of the Welsh vote goes to Labour, 28.6 per cent to the Conservatives.

1993: The Welsh Language Act is passed by the House of Commons. For the first time, Welsh is granted official and equal status alongside the English language (cf. **1536** and

1967). The Welsh Language Board is created to promote the Welsh language throughout Wales. It is abolished in 2012 and replaced by a Welsh Language Commissioner (Comisiynydd y Gymraeg), the first of whom is Meri Huws.

    o Plaid Cymru votes in the House of Commons in favour of the ratification of the Maastricht Treaty.

1993–1997: Dr John Savage, a native of Newport, Monmouthshire, is elected Prime Minister of Nova Scotia, Canada.

1993–2009: Joe Calzaghe, a Welsh middleweight and world champion boxer, nicknamed the 'Pride of Wales', wins 46 fights and remains undefeated. He was born in London of a Welsh mother and a Sardinian father.

Figure 29: A Cymdeithas yr Iaith demonstration for a Welsh Language Act in Central London (*c.*1993)

1994 (9–12 June): European Union elections are held in which five Labourites (Wayne David, Eluned Morgan, David Morris, Joe Wilson, and Glenys Kinnock) are elected to the European Parliament.

o The Local Government Act is passed by the House of Commons and creates 22 unitary authorities. It comes into effect in April 1996.

o Cyngor Celfyddydau Cymru (The Arts Council of Wales) is created by royal charter to develop the arts in Wales. Since July 1999 it has been sponsored by the National Assembly for Wales.

1994–2013: Wales wins the Five Nations[11] Rugby championship (1994, 2005, 2008, 2012 and 2013). The key players of this era are: Ieuan Evans (1987–98), Neil Jenkins (1991–2003), Stephen Jones (1998–2011), Shane Williams (2000–11) and Ryan Jones (since 2004).

1996 (28 June): Tony Blair announces that referenda will be held concerning devolution in Scotland and Wales. The new Severn Bridge is inaugurated this year.

1997 (1 May): The UK General Election. Tony Blair (Labour) is elected Prime Minister. Four female Labour MPs are elected in Wales: Julie Morgan, MP for Cardiff North (1997–2010); Ann Clwyd, MEP (1979–84), MP for Cynon Valley (since 1984); Betty Williams, MP for Conwy (1997–2010); Jackie Lawrence, MP for Preseli Pembrokeshire (1997–2005).

o For the first time Wales is the special guest at the *Festival Interceltique* of Lorient,[12] Brittany.

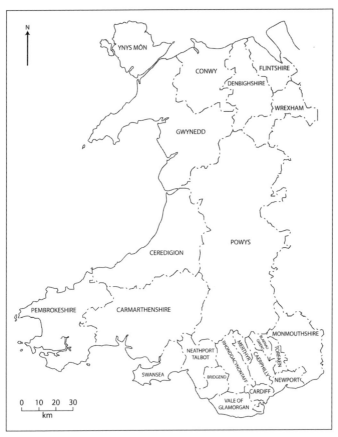

Figure 30: Map of Wales in 1996 (inspired by G. Jenkins, 2007)

Chapter 16

Wales since Devolution

In his book *Land of my Fathers*, Gwynfor Evans writes that the Welsh bards were mistaken when they identified the sovereignty of Wales with the crown of London. In his view Wales has been a nation for over three millennia and for this reason the centre of Welsh political power and identity should instead have been located in Wales itself. This point of view was shared by many Welsh nationalists like him.

In 1955 Cardiff is named capital of Wales. In 1959 the red dragon is officially recognized as the national Welsh flag. These are among a number of small but important symbolic steps which develop an increased sense of Welshness that leads to the votes on devolution in 1979 and again in 1997.

Since 1998, and for the first time in its history, Wales has had its own National Assembly and institutions. This is a development which many Welshmen hope may eventually lead to the creation of a Welsh Parliament. If so, Owain Glyndŵr's dream may yet be realized. In this section some of the achievements accomplished since the referendum on Welsh devolution are outlined.

1997 (18 September): The referendum on devolution in Wales: 50.3 per cent of the Welsh answer positively to the following question: 'I agree that there should be a Welsh Assembly.' The motion is supported by the Labour Party, the Liberal Democrats, and Plaid Cymru. On the other hand, the Conservative Party is against it.

1998 (31 July): The Government of Wales Act 1998 is passed.

It establishes Cynulliad Cenedlaethol Cymru (The National Assembly for Wales). It opens in June 1999 and is based in Tŷ Hywel,[1] Cardiff, and the Senedd (Senate) in Cardiff Bay (south of Cardiff). Llywodraeth Cynulliad Cymru (The Welsh Assembly Government), based at Cathays Park, Cardiff, is its executive body until 2007. Most of the powers of the Welsh Office and the Secretary of State for Wales are transferred to the Assembly.

1999 (6 May): The first Assembly Elections are won by the Labour Party (which wins 28 seats, Plaid Cymru wins a record 17 seats, the Conservatives nine seats, the Liberal Democrats six seats). Alun Michael becomes the First Secretary for Wales, and Lord Dafydd Elis-Thomas (Plaid Cymru) is Speaker of the National Assembly for Wales. One of the main consequences of the establishment of the National Assembly for Wales is the rise of the number of Welsh women representatives, from 2.5 per cent in 1992 to 40 per cent[2] in 1999. Around the world, only Sweden has as many women representing the nation, with 42.7 per cent of women.

- o June: Opening of the Cardiff Millennium Stadium in Cardiff. It replaces the iconic Cardiff Arms Park.

- o 10–13 June: EU elections. Two Labourites (Glenys Kinnock, Eluned Morgan), one Conservative (Jonathan Evans), two members of Plaid Cymru (Jill Evans and Eurig Wyn) are elected to the European Parliament.

- o 1 July: The Welsh Office is dissolved and its powers are transferred to the National Assembly for Wales.

2000 (9 February): The First Secretary of Wales, Alun Michael, resigns. Rhodri Morgan succeeds him. The title changes from First Secretary to First Minister of Wales.

- o This year marks the beginning of the coalition between

Labour and Liberal Democrats. Michael German (Liberal Democrat born in Cardiff) becomes Deputy First Minister until 2001 and also from 2002 to 2003. In 2007 he becomes the leader of the Liberal Democrats, until 2008.

o Neil Kinnock inaugurates the Welsh Assembly's bureau at the European Commission.

o 'Learning to live differently': the Welsh Assembly launches a project concerning sustainable development.[3] Moreover, Wales is the first to include in its constitution an article (Article 121[4] of the Government of Wales Act 1998) about sustainable development. In 2004 France follows by including an 'environmental charter' in its constitution.

o The National Botanic Gardens of Wales open for the first time in the Towy Valley (Carmarthenshire). They are built on the Middleton Estate (belonging to the Middleton family of Oswestry).

o The artist Sue Williams wins a gold medal for fine arts at the National Eisteddfod in Llanelli.

2000–2003: Ieuan Wyn Jones[5] is the President of Plaid Cymru and leader of his party in the Welsh Assembly (2000–12).

2001: According to the Welsh Language Board, 20.8 per cent of the Welsh population now speaks Welsh, a rise of two per cent in the number of speakers compared to the preceding census. This is the first increase in the number of Welsh speakers since 1891.

o According to the 2001 Canadian Census, 60,000 Canadians living in Alberta claim to be of Welsh descent. The main communities are in Edmonton, Calgary, and Lethbridge.

o Between February and November of this year, British and European farmers are hit by Foot and Mouth Disease (FMD). The Welsh Government decides to slaughter more than one million animals and bury infected animals in the Epynt Mountains in Powys, which greatly upsets farmers. Public footpaths in the countryside are closed as a result. The latter decision harms the tourist industry, mainly in Powys, Anglesey and Monmouthshire; £1 billion in compensation is given to the farmers for their losses.[6]

o After the Al-Qaeda attacks on the New York Twin Towers and the Pentagon on 11 September (9/11), the world community participates in UN-sanctioned military operations in Afghanistan. Under the auspices of NATO the British army contributes the second largest number of combat troops. Several Welsh regiments (cf. **2003**) take part in the fighting for nearly a decade: The Welsh Guards, The Royal Welch Fusiliers and the Royal Regiment of Wales. Some of these same regiments fight in Iraq two years later (cf. **2003**).

o 27 May: The British government ratifies the European Charter for Regional or Minority Languages. France is the only European nation which does not, citing the 'French exception'.

o 7 June: A UK General Election is held in which Tony Blair is elected for the second time. 34 Labour MPs, four Plaid Cymru members and two Liberal Democrats are elected in Wales, but no Conservatives.

o Born in Merthyr Tydfil, Julien Macdonald is a famous designer who succeeds Alexander McQueen at the head of Givenchy. The same year, he is named British Fashion Designer of the Year.

2002–2004: The Richard Commission, led by Ivor Richard,[7] presents a report to Westminster suggesting that the Welsh Assembly should have more powers by 2011 (for example: the power to vote on laws), more representatives (60 to 80), and separate the executive and legislative powers. Most of these measures are adopted in the Government of Wales Act 2006.

2002: For the second time Wales is the special guest of the *Festival Interceltique* of Lorient, Brittany. Seven Welsh artists, including Iwan Bala,[8] Mary Lloyd Jones,[9] and Tim Pugh, participate in the *Ystyr y Tir* (Meaning of the Land) exhibition, funded by the *Festival Interceltique* of Lorient and the Welsh Assembly.

2003: The Labour Party wins the Assembly Elections: 30 seats for Labour, 12 seats for Plaid Cymru, 11 seats for the Conservatives and six seats for the Liberal Democrats. Fifty per cent[10] of the Welsh AMs are women (and also in 2007).

o   Ieuan Wyn Jones, the President of Plaid Cymru, resigns. Dafydd Iwan (cf. **1969**) succeeds him.

o   Wales has its own pavilion at the Venice Biennale where artists exhibit their work. Cerith Wyn Evans represents Wales with his painting *Cleave 03 (Transmission, Visions of the Sleeping Poet)*, inspired by Ellis Wynne's masterpiece (cf. **1703**). (I. Bala, 'Re:maging Wales, Wales-Art-World', 2009: 197).

o   In defiance of a UN decision, and amid domestic and international calls against an invasion of Iraq, the United States and United Kingdom overthrow Saddam Hussein's government in Iraq in 2003. This leads to a long conflict in which several Welsh regiments fight alongside the Americans.

2003–2005: Michael Howard is the leader of the Conservative Party. Born in Gorseinon, near Swansea, he is Home Secretary from 1993 to 1997.

2004: European Union elections. Two seats for the Labour Party (Glenys Kinnock and Eluned Morgan), one for the Conservative Party (Jonathan Evans), one for Plaid Cymru (Jill Evans).

- o Canolfan Mileniwm Cymru (Wales Millennium Centre) opens. It is an art centre in Cardiff, which hosts notably: the Welsh Academy (cf. **1959**), the National Dance Company Wales (cf. **1983**), the Welsh League of Youth (cf. **1922**), the Welsh National Opera (cf. **1946**), and the BBC National Orchestra of Wales (cf. **1946**).

2005: In response to the Richard Commission, the UK Government publishes its White Paper,[11] 'Better Governance for Wales', which criticizes some of the Commission's proposals.

- o A UK General Election is held in which Tony Blair is re-elected for the third and last time until he resigns and is succeeded by the Chancellor of the Exchequer, Gordon Brown, in 2008. Three Conservatives, 29 Labourites, four Liberal Democrats and four members of Plaid Cymru are elected in Wales.

- o Photographic artist Peter Finnemore (born in 1963 in Llanelli) represents Wales at the Venice Biennale. He wins the gold medal for fine arts at the National Eisteddfod at Vaynol/Y Faenol, Gwynedd in the same year.

- o Relaunch of the *Dr Who* series by BBC Wales. Scenes are often shot in Wales.

2006: The Government of Wales Act 2006 comes into force giving the Assembly more powers to pass laws, known as 'Assembly Measures'. Also, from 2007 onwards, The Welsh Government and The National Assembly become separate bodies.

- o 1 March: The famous Welsh Regiment of Fusiliers, created in 1689, is dissolved and becomes the 1st Battalion of the Royal Welsh (Y Cymru Brenhinol). The Royal Regiment of Wales (RRW, see **1969**) becomes the 2nd Battalion.

- o According to the Australian Census, 25,317 of its citizens were born in Wales, and 113, 242 claim Welsh ancestry.

- o According to the Canadian Census, 440,965 people claim Welsh ancestry (including 27,115 who identify themselves as only Welsh).

2007: The third Assembly elections are won by Labour (26 seats) with 15 for Plaid Cymru, 12 for the Conservatives, six for the Liberal Democrats.

- o A coalition is formed between Labour and Plaid Cymru. Ieuan Wyn Jones becomes Deputy First Minister for Wales, and also Minister for Economy and Transport. The coalition government signs 'One Wales: a Progressive Agenda for the Government of Wales'.

2008: The 'One Wales' plan begins. It is a three-year plan (until 2011) passed by the Welsh Assembly. According to the Welsh Government website: '... it set more than 200 specific commitments to be delivered by the One Wales government to improve the quality of life of people in all of Wales's communities.' One of these commitments is the establishment of a Welsh language commissioner who replaces the Welsh Language Board in 2012 (cf. **1993**).

- o Featuring the Welsh bands Carreg Lafar and Sibrydion, Wales is the special guest of the *Festival Interceltique* in Lorient, Brittany, for the third time.

- o The Holtham Commission (or Independent Commission on Funding and Finance for Wales) begins studying how the Welsh Assembly government is funded. Moreover, it seeks to replace the Barnett Formula (in use since 1978) which was used to calculate the budgets of the Welsh Office and (since 1999) the Welsh Assembly. In its July 2010 report, the commission proposes that the National Assembly should receive more powers to raise taxes on personal property, second homes and on corporate profits. It also proposes the reform of local taxes.

- o According to the 2008 US Community Survey, two million Americans claim to be of Welsh descent; 3.8 per cent of the US population bear Welsh names, mainly in the southern states.

- o Welsh cyclist Nicole Cooke, from Swansea, wins a gold medal for her performance in the women's road race at the Summer Olympics in Beijing. Cyclist Geraint Thomas from Cardiff also wins a gold medal (and in 2012) for his performance in the men's team pursuit.

2009: European Union Elections: one Conservative (Kay Swinburne), one Labourite (Derek Vaughan), one member of Plaid Cymru (Jill Evans) and one UK Independence Party member (John Bufton) are elected to the European Parliament.

- o August to November: All Wales Convention is chaired

by Sir Emrys Jones Parry. Its report recommends that a referendum should be held in 2011 requesting more powers.

o December: Rhodri Morgan, First Minister of the Welsh Assembly, retires. Carwyn Jones succeeds him and is also leader of the Welsh Labour Party.

o John Cale (born in 1942 in Ammanford, Carmarthenshire), the former guitarist of the Velvet Underground, represents Wales at the Venice Biennale.

o Wales is invited to the Smithsonian Folklife Festival in Washington DC. It is a great success, with a million people visiting the exhibition. The National Slate Museum of Llanberis (in Gwynedd) and the Slate Valley Museum of New York State are among the partnerships developed. This event is covered notably by *USA Today*, *The Washington Post*, and *Ninnau* (a Welsh-American newspaper).

2010: The Welsh Assembly passes the Legislative Competence Order on the Welsh language. From now on the Assembly can legislate on issues concerning the Welsh language. Also the 'Proposed Welsh Language Measure' is published by the Heritage Minister. It bases itself on commitments made by the 'One Wales' coalition (2007): more rights for Welsh speakers, the creation of a commissioner for the Welsh language in the Assembly, and more equality between English and Welsh.

o MEP Jill Evans is elected president of Plaid Cymru.

o The UK General Election is held on 6 May: Conservative David Cameron becomes Prime Minister. In Wales, the Labour Party wins 26 seats, the Conservatives eight, Plaid Cymru and the Liberal Democrats three each.

- o 8 May: A detachment from the 1st Battalion of the Welsh Guards marches alongside Russian, French and American soldiers on Red Square in Moscow to celebrate the 65th anniversary of the victory over Nazism.

- o 24 June: Julia Gillard, born in Barry, Vale of Glamorgan, is the first woman to become Prime Minister of Australia. She is defeated in 2013.

2010–2012: Cheryl Gillan, a native of Cardiff, is appointed Secretary of State for Wales in David Cameron's Conservative government and is also the first woman to occupy the post.

2011: A referendum is held in Wales to allow the National Assembly for Wales to vote laws without the authorization of the UK Parliament in 'devolved areas such as health, education, social services, local government and environment'.

- o 21 out of the 22 local authorities (excepting Monmouthshire) answer positively to the following question: 'Do you want the Assembly now to be able to make laws on all matters in the 20 subject areas it has powers for?' 63.49 per cent of the Welsh population answer 'yes' and 36.51 per cent 'no'. First Minister Carwyn Jones declares at the Assembly that 'today an old nation came of age', and Secretary of State for Wales, Cheryl Gillan, that this is 'a good day for Wales'.

- o National Assembly Elections are held on 5 May: Carwyn Jones is elected as First Minister of Wales. The Labour Party ends its coalition with Plaid Cymru and gains 30 seats, the Conservatives win 14 seats, Plaid Cymru 11 and the Liberal Democrats five. 25 women are elected (41.7 per cent of all AMs).

- o The United Kingdom Alternative Vote referendum is

held on 13 May. Its purpose is to replace the FPTP[12] (First Past the Post) system with the Alternative Vote[13] (AV) in the Westminster elections. It is rejected by 67.9 per cent of the British (65.45 per cent in Wales).

o   Artist Tim Davies[14] (born in Pembrokeshire) represents Wales at the Venice Biennale. He also wins the Artes Mundi prize in 2004. He is part of Beca, a group of Welsh artists created in the 1970s by the Davies brothers (Paul and Peter). They are joined later by Iwan Bala, David Garner (*Pockets of Resistance*), John Meirion Morris, Carwyn Evans and Peter Finnemore.

o   AmeriCymru, a Welsh-American association, organizes a festival dedicated to the celebration of Welsh poetry and arts in Los Angeles, California. The festival is first founded in 2009 in Portland, Oregon, under the name Left Coast Eisteddfod. Afterwards it is renamed West Coast Eisteddfod.

o   The Welsh-Australian Cadell Evans wins the Tour de France.

o   The young Welsh rugby team thrills fans around the world by its performance in the Rugby World Cup in New Zealand. Wales comes in fourth place after being narrowly defeated by France and Australia.

2012 (15 March): The AM (Assembly Member) for South West Central, Leanne Wood (from Llwynpia), succeeds Ieuan Wyn Jones as the leader of Plaid Cymru in the National Assembly for Wales.

o   February: A report entitled 'Statistical overview of the Welsh Language' is published by Hywel Jones, the Welsh language commissioner's statistician. According to this, Wales lost 2,000 to 3,000 fluent native Welsh speakers per year between 1991 and 2001, and this process is continuing. Moreover, four Welsh-speaking counties (Anglesey, Gwynedd, Ceredigion and Carmarthenshire) represent 56 per cent of all Welsh speakers in Wales. From the 2011 Schools Census, it was calculated that 62 per cent of primary school pupils whose parents said they could speak Welsh fluently lived in these four counties. According to this same report, in 2004 only 58 per cent of those who claimed to speak Welsh considered that they speak the language fluently. The conclusion seems to be that as older native speakers pass away, they are not being replaced by a new generation of native speakers but rather by younger learners with various levels of fluency.

o David Jones, MP for Clwyd West, is the new Secretary of State for Wales. He was born in London of Welsh parents.

2013: Welsh footballer Gareth Bale (born in Cardiff) is transferred from Tottenham Hotspur to the Spanish club Real Madrid. Another of his compatriots, Ryan Giggs (also from Cardiff), plays at Manchester United from 1992 to 2014. In 2014, the new manager of Manchester United, Louis Van Gaal, names Giggs as his assistant.

o Fire causes damage to the roof at the National Library of Wales in Aberystwyth.

2013–2014: Cymdeithas yr Iaith writes to First Minister Carwyn Jones, asking him to give a statement in six policy fields by 1 February, 2014. Judging the response insufficient, they now plan to launch a period of civil disobedience.

Endnotes

Chapter 1: Prehistoric Wales, Britain and Western Europe

[1] According to archaeology site http://www.archaeology.co.uk/the-timeline-of-britain/boxgrove.htm

[2] The term 'Acheulean' comes from Saint-Acheul, a French eponymous site near Amiens.

[3] The term 'Mousterian' comes from the cave of Le Moustier in Dordogne (France).

Chapter 2: Prehistoric Population Movements and the Roots of proto-Celtic Culture

[1] The Severn Sea is also called the Bristol Channel and separates Wales and south-west England.

[2] This is a well-known Welsh tale about the flooding of an entire region of Wales which has parallels around the world including the Breton legend of *Ker Ys* (the city of Ys), the Atlantis tale, the Biblical story of Noah's Ark as well as the epic of Gilgamesh.

[3] Herbert John Fleure (b. 1877, Guernsey – d. 1969, Surrey), was an English zoologist and geographer. He taught at the University of Wales, Aberystwyth.

[4] Gordon Childe (1892–1957): an Australian archaeologist and prehistory specialist.

[5] John T. Koch is an American linguist specializing in Celtic Studies (pre-Roman period until the 5th and 6th centuries) at the University of Wales' CAWCS (Centre for Advanced Welsh and Celtic Studies, Aberystwyth).

[6] Not to be confused with the Anglo-Saxon Kingdom of Wessex.

[7] Stuart Piggott (1910–96) was a British archaeologist who specialized in this prehistoric culture. He participated in excavations at Avebury and Sutton Hoo in the 1930s.

[8] 'Tartessos' is mentioned in Greek and Roman sources, for instance Herodotus, Pytheas, Strabo and Pliny the Elder. Also, some archaeologists identify it as 'Tarshish', often mentioned in the Old Testament (cf. Philip Freeman, 2010).

[9] Excavations between 1846 and 1862 by Georg Ramsauer at Hallstatt (Salzkammergut, Austria), near Salzburg.

[10] Excavations in 1858 at La Tène, near the lake of Neufchâtel (Switzerland).

[11] Livy, *History of Rome*, V, 34–49 (Brennus is probably related to Breton *Bren* and Welsh *Bryn*, meaning 'hill').

[12] His book was probably burnt in the fire of the library of Alexandria in AD 48 but classical authors of the first century AD, such as Strabo (*Geography*), Polybius (*The Histories*) and Pliny the elder (*Natural History*) but also Ptolemy give us some

extracts (a Roman-Greek geographer who calls Britain 'Albion', one of the sons of Poseidon (or Neptune in Roman mythology), the god of the sea).

13 Professor Leslie Alcock (University of Glasgow) led excavations at Dinas Powys (1954–8).

14 'Sledgehammer fighters'.

15 Caesar, *De Bello Gallico*, 4.

16 The *Catuvellauni* are also known as the *Catalauni* in Gaul, in the region of Châlons-en-Champagne. The name survived in the form of personal names giving *Catuualon* in Old Breton (*Cadoalen* in Modern Breton) and *Cadwallawn* in Middle Welsh.

17 This Gaulish tribe gave its name to Auvergne. Most major Breton and French cities take their names from Gallic tribes: Vannes (< *Veneti*, *Gwened* in Breton), Nantes (< *Namnetes*, *Naoned* in Breton), Rennes/Redon (< *Redones*, *Roazhon* in Breton), Chartres (< *Carnutes*), Bourges (< *Bituriges*), Tours (< *Turones*), Paris (< *Parisii*), etc.

Chapter 3: Celtic Britain and the Roman Empire
(AD 30 – AD 405)

1 Shakespeare's *Cymbeline* (c.1610).

2 The *Parisii* settled in what is modern South Yorkshire.

3 *Camulos*, the Roman god of war, is the equivalent of *Cumhal* in Irish mythology.

4 In his history of Wales, *Land of my Fathers*, Gwynfor Evans, president of *Plaid Cymru* (1945–81), stresses that the Welsh people are direct descendants of those Celtic tribes who fought the Romans: 'It can be claimed that the majority of the Welsh of this generation are descended from the people who inhabited the country when Ostorius and his legions came here in AD 47.'

5 The English archaeologist, Cyril Fox (1882–1967), divided the British Isles into two geographical regions: the highland zone (Wales, northern England and Scotland) and the lowland zone (the south and east of the British Isles). He did several excavations on prehistoric sites in Wales and was the Director of the National Museum of Wales (1926–48).

6 For more information concerning the Roman campaigns against the *Silures*, read Tacitus, *Annals* (chapters 12 and 14) and *Agricola* (chapter 17).

7 Efrawg has the same etymological origins as Evry and Ivry, both near Paris (tree: yew).

8 Julius Frontinus is also well known as a military author (*Strategematon libri III*), and for his treatise on the aqueducts.

9 The etymology of Chester is Latin *castrum* 'legionary fort or camp'. Latin *Castella* is a diminutive form of *castrum* which was borrowed in Welsh as *Castell* and Breton as *Kastell* as well as in Old French *Castell*. The English word, *castle*, is first attested in the 12th century and appears to have been taken directly from French.

¹⁰　The name of the *Caledonii* may be related to the modern Welsh, Cornish and Breton word, *caled, kaled* meaning 'hard' or 'tough'. They are the ancestors of the Picts according to historian Peter Salway. Tacitus (*Life of Agricola*) and Ptolemy also give us accounts of the Roman campaigns against the *Caledonians*.

¹¹　*Civitas* is the Latin word for the main town of a tribe.

¹²　Carawn is mentioned in Geoffrey of Monmouth's *History of the Kings of Britain*.

¹³　Known as *Frisiavones* by the Romans, they originate from north-western Germany, the Netherlands and Denmark.

¹⁴　In fact, Emperor Galerius ended them in 311 because he thought his illness was a punishment sent by God.

¹⁵　Leslie Alcock (1971, 1983) affirms that there are two more sons: Osmail and Enniaun Girt (grandfather of Maelgwn Gwynedd and Cinglas).

¹⁶　In the Mabinogion, Maximus is the main character of the story *The Dream of Maxen Wledig* (*Breuddwyd Maxen Wledig*). He falls in love with Elen, and goes to *Segontium* (Caernarfon) to ask her hand in marriage but in the meantime he loses his empire. To conquer it back, he is assisted by Kynan (Conan Meriadog) who later founds the Brythonic colony in *Llydaw* (Brittany).

¹⁷　The Irish name O'Neill comes from Niall.

¹⁸　The name Brycheiniog (modern Breconshire) takes its name from an Irish Prince, Brychan Brycheiniog. He is the son of Marchell (the daughter of Tewdrig) and Amlech (son of the Irish king, Coronac), who settles in the region of Brycheiniog.

Chapter 4: Wales during the Dark Ages

¹　This is the origin of the author's own name. The greatest concentration of the 'German' family name is to be found in the region of Caernarfon.

²　It is possible that the Agitius mentioned by Gildas is Flavius Aetius (assassinated in 454), the Roman consul in 432, 437, and 446 who is also called the 'last of the Romans'. He has the title of *dux* which means he defends the empire against the Burgundians and Visigoths, and defeats Attila the Hun in 451 at the Battle of the Catalaunian Plains (the Battle of Châlons).

³　According to Léon Fleuriot, Ambrosius Aurelianus (*c.*450–*c.*485) and Riothamos were one and the same. Aside from the fact that Ambosius and Riothamos are nearly contemporaneous figures, another argument in favour of this analysis is the existence of an Irish document which describes Ambrosius as 'King of the Britons of Armorica and of the Franks' ('o niurt Ambrois ri Frangc 7 Bretan Letha'). According to Gildas, it is Ambrosius who defeats the Anglo-Saxons at the key battle of Mount Badon. Sidonius Apollinaris also describes him as *the last of the Romans*.

⁴　According to the 'Triads of Britain', Emrys Wledig was the brother of Uther Pendragon. The latter was said to be the father of King Arthur.

⁵　Owain's character could be inspired by the figure of Owain mab Urien, the son of Urien, King of Rheged. In the Arthurian legend, he is married to Arthur's sister,

Morgan, whereas in some of the Welsh triads, his wife is named Penarwan, the sister of Esyllt (Iseult). Yvain is a Breton form of the name. It is still a common family name in Brittany: Yvain, Yvin, Ewen.

6   The capital of the Kingdom of Strathclyde (*Ystrad Clud* in Brythonic) is Dumbarton ('The fort of the Britons') until 870 when the Vikings plunder the region (source: *Annales Cambriae*) thus marking a decline of Strathclyde.

7   In Old English, the tonic accent fell on the first syllable: Brythonic Ceredig pronounced as an Old English name was probably Ceredig > Cerdig > Cerdic. According to early Welsh tradition, one of Cunedda's sons also bore this name and gave his name to the territory of Ceredigion, cf. **383**.

8   Their language was Brythonic, a fact which is proven by the placenames of lowland Scotland, which are often of Brythonic rather than of Gaelic origin: Edinburgh (< *Din Eidyn*), Dunbarton (< *Dun Brython*, 'Fort of the Britons'), Glasgow (< *Glasgu*), etc.

9   Saint Tysilio (or Sulio) is a Welsh bishop who establishes a monastery in Saint-Suliac (near Saint Malo), where he is buried. This town bears his name.

10 The term 'Old North' (*Yr Hen Ogledd*) is used to designate the regions where the Brythonic language is spoken, in the north of England and the south of Scotland, including Rheged, Strathclyde, Elmet and Gododdin.

11 The oldest mention of Merlin (Myrddin) is in *Armes Prydein* (c.930): 'Myrddin foretells that they will meet in Aber Peryddon, the stewards of the Great King (i.e Athelstan).'

12 John Richard Green (*Short History of the English People*, 1874); William Stubbs (*Constitutional History of England*, 1874–78) and E. A. Freeman (*History of the Norman Conquest*, 1867–76).

13 Although we do not know where it is, some believe Degsastan is at Dawstane in Liddesdale (cf. Bede, Book I, Chapter 34).

14 The ancient tribal name of the 'Votadini' is an early form of the name 'Gododdin' (cf. entry for **541**).

15 Cynddylan is the son of Cyndrwyn (d. 642), and a ruler of Pengwern. He lived during the 7th century and is described as the ruler of Dogfeiling (kingdom part of Gwynedd) in a poem, *Marwnad Cynddylan* (Elegy for Cynddylan).

16 Many historians continue to use the terms 'Briton' (i.e. 'ancient Briton') in place of 'Brython' and 'British' in place of 'Brythonic' (or 'Brittonic'). In this book, I use the latter to avoid any confusion with the modern terminology.

17 Kenneth Jackson (1909–91) was a linguist specializing in Celtic languages. In 1969 he translated the *Gododdin* into English.

Chapter 5: The Viking Age (789–1066)

1   Modern English place-names ending in -by 'a farmstead' (Derby, Helsby), -thorpe 'village' (Weaverthorpe, Bishopthorpe, Copmanthorpe), and -thwaite 'clearing'

(Langthwaite, in Yorkshire) are originally Scandinavian settlements. The English and Norman-French place-names, respectively -thwaite / -toft (Langtoft, Lincolnshire) and -tuit / -tot (Vautuit and Yvetot, Normandy), all have Scandinavian origins.

[2] Gruffudd ap Llywelyn's mother Angharad marries Cynfyn ap Gwerstan. He is the half-brother of Bleddyn ap Cynfyn and Rhiwallon ap Cynfyn.

Chapter 6: Wales and the Anglo-Normans (1086–1485)

[1] William Fitzosbern, Earl of Hereford from 1067 to 1071.

[2] Roger of Montgomery, Earl of Shrewsbury from 1071 to 1094.

[3] Hugh of Avranches, Earl of Chester from 1071 to 1101.

[4] Arthur I of Brittany is followed by two other Breton dukes of the same name. Conscious of the great symbolic value of the name, which was enhanced by Geoffrey of Monmouth's work and increasing popularity of the Arthurian Cycle, Henry VII (i.e. Henry Tudor) also names his first son Arthur (cf. **1489–1502**).

[5] Hubert de Burgh (1180–1243) is first Earl of Kent, Justiciar of England and Ireland during the reigns of John I and Henry III.

[6] Not to be confused with his son, Gilbert de Clare (cf. **1314**)

[7] The Mortimer family is of Anglo-Norman origin. Its name comes from the town of Mortemer (Normandy).

Chapter 7: The Political Assimilation of Wales by the Anglo-Normans (1284–1400)

[1] Gruffudd Llwyd is the great-grandson of Ednyfed Fychan, Seneschal of Gwynedd (1216–1246) who serves Llywelyn I (Fawr) and his son, Dafydd, and also the cousin of Goronwy ap Tudur.

[2] Ifor Bach (also known as Ifor the Short, or Ifor ap Meurig). He is a Welsh leader at Senghennydd (Caerphilly) in south Wales.

[3] The 'Black Prince' is the name that was used posthumously after the 1530s and 1540s. During his lifetime, he was better known as Edward of Woodstock. He was never crowned king of England.

[4] Born to a family from Eifionydd (Llŷn Peninsula), he is knighted and becomes an *uchelwr* in 1355. He is the constable of Criccieth from 1359 to his death in 1381. He earns his nickname 'of the axe' for his exploits at the Battle of Poitiers.

[5] A descendant of Ednyfed Fychan, he fights alongside the English army at Crécy and is killed at the Battle of Poitiers in 1356. He owned lands in south Wales (Carmarthenshire and Ceredigion) and participated in the recruitment of soldiers in west Wales.

[6] John of Gaunt's third wife, Katherine Swynford, is sister to Chaucer's wife, Philippa de Roet.

[7] He is not the Gruffudd Llwyd mentioned in **1322**.

[8] Mentioned in John Foxe's *Book of Martyrs* (published in 1563 by the Protestant John Day).

Chapter 8: The Revolt of Owain Glyndŵr (1400–1413)

[1] Hotspur is the son of Henry Percy, Earl of Northumberland (cf. **1405**). The father is killed at the Battle of Bramham Moor (February 1408).

[2] The letter is preserved in the French National Archives but a copy can be seen at the National Library of Wales and the Parliament House in Machynlleth.

[3] These extracts from the Pennal Letter were translated by Matthews (1910): http://www.canolfanglyndwr.org/pennal-letter.php

Chapter 9: The Second Half of the Hundred Years' War and the Wars of the Roses (1413–1485)

[1] He also receives the honorific title of Lord of Pembroke (1414), Justice of Chester (1427), and Justice of the South (1440).

[2] In 1452, Edmund is given the title of Earl of Richmond and marries Margaret Beaufort (great-granddaughter of John of Gaunt). He is asked to re-assert the power of the crown in west Wales. After capturing Gruffudd ap Nicolas's castle, he dies in Carmarthen in 1456. He leaves a son, Henry Tudor, the future king of England, Henry VII.

[3] Member of the British garrison in Carentan in Normandy in 1431.

[4] Thomas Stanley, 1st Earl of Derby (1485–1504). His brother, William Stanley (d. 1495), who originally supports the Yorkists, changes sides at the last moment and fights alongside Henry Tudor at the battle of Bosworth Field.

Chapter 10: Wales and the Tudors (1485–1603)

[1] Jones (< John's son), Evans (Ieuan's [John's] son), Davies (David's son), Williams (Guillaume's son), Humphreys (Onfroi's son), etc. The use of the possessive case (-s) corresponds to the use of Welsh *ap* (son of): ap John, ap William… The name Humphreys comes from the Norman town *Onfroi*.

[2] Thomas Cromwell is an ancestor of Oliver Cromwell. Thomas's sister, Katherine, married Morgan Williams of Llanishen, in Glamorgan, and was the owner of the abbey of Neath.

[3] Born around 1520 in the parish of Llansannan, Conwy, he studies ancient languages (Greek, Latin and Hebrew) at Oxford University, and also the texts written by Martin Luther and William Tyndale, forbidden under Catholic Queen Mary I.

[4] *Ban wedi ei dynnu air yng ngair allan o hen Gyfraith Hywel Dda* (a case extracted word for word out of the ancient law of Hywel Dda).

[5] Richard Davies (1505–81). He studies at New Inn Hall, Oxford, and during the reign of Mary flees to Geneva (1553–8), and returns to England when Elizabeth is

crowned queen. He is consecrated bishop of St Asaph in 1560 and St Davids in 1561 until his death in 1581.

6   It could be a translation of *De Doctrina Christiana* by Ioannes Polanco (1517–74), a Spaniard and first General Secretary of the Society of Jesus.

7   http://www.jesus.ox.ac.uk/about/the-welsh-college

8   He writes his masterpiece *Anglica Historia*, published four times: 1512–13, 1534, 1546, and 1555.

9   William Morgan (1545–1604). He studies at Cambridge. He is the vicar of Llanrhaeadr-ym-Mochnant, in Powys; Bishop of Llandaff (1595–1601) and St Asaph (1601–4).

10 The Marprelate controversy (1588–9) is a war of pamphlets in England and Wales between a Puritan writer, 'Martin Marprelate', and defenders of the Established (Anglican) Church.

11 He is raised near Lamphey (Pembrokeshire). He serves alongside Robert Devereux, 2nd Earl of Essex, during the Anglo-Spanish War (Portugal, 1589; Cádiz, 1596; the Azores, 1597) and in Ireland (1599–1600). After they are disgraced by Queen Elizabeth, he organizes a rebellion with Devereux and rallies to his cause his family network in south Wales and also former Welsh soldiers who fought with them.

Chapter 11: Wales and the Stuarts (1603–1714)

1   Born in Trefela, near Llangwm, Monmouthshire.

2   For more information: http://www.british-civil-wars.co.uk/

3   Son of Robert Devereux, Earl of Essex (d. 1601).

4   John Jones (1597–1660). He is Oliver Cromwell's brother-in-law (he marries his sister, Catherine) and is executed in 1660. He becomes in 1647 a military commissioner in Ireland but opposes the protectorate.

5   Thomas Wogan serves under Colonel Horton at the battle of St Fagans in May 1648. He is appointed governor of Aberystwyth castle. After Oliver Cromwell's death in 1658 and the beginning of Charles II's reign, he is held prisoner at York castle from 1660 to 1664, but then escapes to the Netherlands.

6   The Fifth Monarchists, or Millenarians, such as Vavasor Powell and Thomas Harrison, believe in the return of Jesus Christ to earth and his 1,000-year rule.

7   Born in Knucklas, Radnorshire, Vavasor Powell (1617–70) preaches the gospel in Wales from 1650 to 1653 as part of 'The Act for the Better Propagation of the Gospel in Wales'.

8   The Baptist community follows the example of John the Baptist by which only adults can be baptized.

9   Philip Jones (1618–74). He retires to his lands at Fonmon in the Vale of Glamorgan. He becomes High Sheriff in 1671 until his death in 1674.

10 Or 'faith unfeigned', borrowed from 1 Tim. 1:5.

11 He is an ancestor of the American Revolutionary War hero, Daniel Morgan, commander of frontier riflemen.

12 The Welsh Trust is an organization which founds schools to teach Welsh children to read and write in English.

13 Bryn Mawr is the place where Rowland Ellis, a Quaker from Dolgellau, settled in 1686. Also, it is the home of Bryn Mawr's women's college, founded in 1885.

14 John Bunyan (1628–88) is one of the greatest English authors of the 17th century. He writes his masterpiece *Pilgrim's Progress* in 1678.

15 The museum of the Royal Welch Fusiliers is located in Caernarfon castle where 14 Victorian Crosses, won by soldiers throughout the campaigns, are exhibited. The poets Siegfried Sassoon, David Jones and *Hedd Wyn* (cf. 1917) served in this regiment and wrote about it in their poems as did Frank Richards, the author of *Old Soldiers Never Die* (1933), who also served in this regiment during the First World War. The title of this book was quoted by American General Douglas McArthur when he was forced to resign in 1951 by President Truman: 'Old soldiers never die, they just fade away.'

16 Sir Rowland Gwynne (1660–1726) was born in Builth Wells, in Radnorshire. He is a Whig MP for Radnorshire (1679–98). He is knighted by King Charles II in 1680, and holds an office under King William III.

Chapter 12: Wales during the Age of Enlightenment

1 He corresponds with the brothers John and Charles Wesley (founders of the Methodist Church, cf. below), and George Whitefield, one of the foremost leaders of the First Great Awakening in the English colonies of America during the 1730s and '40s.

2 Paul-Yves Pezron, *Antiquité de la Nation et de la Langue des Celtes* (1703). It is translated into English in 1706 under the title *The Antiquities of Nations more particularly of the Celtae or Gauls*.

3 Called *Utgorn y Diwygiad* or 'The Trumpet of the Revival'.

4 Along with Cornell (New York), Harvard (Massachusetts), Yale (Connecticut), University of Pennsylvania, Princeton (New Jersey), Columbia (at Ithaca, New York), and Dartmouth (New Hampshire), Brown is nowadays part of the Ivy League.

5 Not to be confused with another poet also known as Ieuan Prydydd Hir (around 1450).

6 William Turner tours Wales in the 1790s.

7 Joshua Reynolds (the founder of the Royal Academy of Arts in 1768) paints one portrait of Sir Watkin Williams Wynn and his first wife, Henrietta Somerset (d. 1770, cf. painting), and another painting around 1778 of his second wife (Charlotte Grenville, the daughter of former Prime Minister George Grenville, 1763–5) and his children.

8 Joseph Banks (1743–1820) is an English botanist and a naturalist who serves as

chief scientist on James Cook's first around-the-world voyage (1768–71). He is said to have introduced eucalyptus, acacia and mimosa to Western Europe.

9 Not to be confused with Aberystwyth, in Ceredigion.

10 'The operation or business of making wrought iron from pig iron in a puddling furnace' (*Funk & Wagnalls Standard College Dictionary*).

11 The 'Terror' (1793–4) is a dictatorship led by Robespierre (leader of the Jacobins). It is characterized by mass executions of his opponents, the Girondins, and the members of the French royal family, such as Queen Marie-Antoinette.

12 Born in Llandysul (Ceredigion), his father, Samuel Evans, is a shoemaker. In 1783 David Davis, a Presbyterian minister, teaches him to write English and Welsh.

13 Ebensburg was named after Eben Lloyd, the son of Congregationalist minister Rheese Lloyd, who died in childhood.

Chapter 13: The Rise of the Labour Movements

1 Ioan Tegid was John Jones, a clergyman born in Bala in 1792, and also a scholar associated with Lady Charlotte Guest.

2 The first Eisteddfod in Oak Hill, Jackson County, Ohio, occurs in 1875 and in Jackson in 1922. For more information: http://ohio.llgc.org.uk/co-jacksongallia.php (Wales-Ohio Project) and http://www.jacksonEisteddfod.com/

3 Born in Newtown (Montgomeryshire), Robert Owen is also known as being the co-founder of the Utopian town of New Harmony, Indiana, in 1825.

4 Augusta Hall, Baroness Llanover (1802–96). She helps to found the first Welsh-language periodical for women, *Y Gymraes* (The Welshwoman, cf. **1851–3**). Also, as the patron of the Welsh Manuscripts Society, she buys the manuscripts of Taliesin Williams (Taliesin ab Iolo) and the collection of Iolo Morganwg, now all in the National Library of Wales in Aberystwyth.

5 In 1840, John Frost, Zephaniah Williams and William Jones are sent to Van Diemen's Land (now Tasmania), Australia. In 1854 and 1856 they are each pardoned. Zephaniah Williams chooses to stay in Australia and his family leave Wales to join him. William Jones decides to do the same, but John Frost returns to Britain.

6 Lord Shaftesbury, born Anthony Ashley-Cooper, 7th Earl of Shaftesbury, was a celebrated social reformer.

7 These laws seem to have inspired other governments around the world to follow suit. For instance, a similar report is published by Dr Villermé in 1841 describing the working conditions of children in French factories.

8 Gwilym Hiraethog (born William Rees) is minister to a Welsh Congregation in Liverpool from 1843 to 1875.

9 He wins the Crown at the National Eisteddfod twice (Bangor, 1890; Rhyl, 1892).

10 He wins the Crown twice (Pontypridd, 1893; Caernarfon, 1894) and the Chair at Llandudno in 1896.

11 He wins the Crown at the National Eisteddfod at Merthyr Tydfil in 1901.

12 The Madog Center for Welsh Studies is part of the University of Rio Grande (Gallia County, Ohio).

13 The Welsh-language epitaphs on the local gravestones show that many of the original inhabitants were from Cilcennin, Ceredigion (cf. **1818**).

14 The Welsh National Anthem is translated into Breton during the 19th century under the title of *Bro Gozh ma Zadoú* (The Land of my Fathers) and also becomes the 'national' anthem of Brittany in an attempt to encourage pan-Celticism.

15 William Meirion Evans (1826–83) is native of Caernarfonshire and a minister who also works in the copper and gold mines of South Australia.

16 For more information, a website was created in 2005 (www.glaniad.com) as a result of a partnership between Patagonian and Welsh organisations (National Library of Wales/the University of Bangor) and supported by the Welsh Assembly Government. In Welsh, *glaniad* means 'landing'.

17 Matthew Arnold (1822–88) teaches poetry at Oxford from 1857 until his retirement in 1886.

18 Ernest Renan is a Breton philosopher from Breton-speaking Trégor (Tréguier, Côtes-d'Armor).

19 William Forster (1818–86): MP for Bradford (1861–85) and vice-president of the Committee on Education (1868–74).

20 In 1859 he leaves Wales and goes to New Orleans where he fights in the Confederate Army during the US Civil War. After the war he becomes a journalist.

21 In Celtic Mythology, Mabon is the son of Modron ('divine mother', related to Gaulish goddess Matrona who gave her name to the River 'Marne', France).

22 Two famous presidents are: Augustus John (1934 to 1939) and landscape painter Sir Kyffin Williams from 1969 to 1976 and again from 1992 until his death in 2006.

23 In Washington DC the Washington Memorial is inaugurated by US President Chester Arthur. Inside the memorial, a surprising inscription is to be found in Welsh, inscribed perhaps by one of the builders: *Fy iaith, fy ngwlad, fy nghenedl Cymru – Cymru am byth* (My language, my land, my nation of Wales – Wales for ever).

24 Thomas Edward Ellis (1859–99). Born near Bala, he is MP for Merionethshire for the Liberal Party (1886–99). In 1892 he joins the government as 'second whip' and also publishes the first volume of the poems of Morgan Llwyd, which is completed after his death in 1899 by his brother-in-law, J. H. Davies.

25 David Alfred Thomas (1856–1918), MP for the Liberal Party for Merthyr Tydfil (1888–1910) and Cardiff (1910).

26 In 1886 the Liberal Unionist Party, created by Joseph Chamberlain and Lord Hartington, splits from the Liberal Party, because they do not agree with Gladstone's policy concerning Irish Home Rule. In 1912 it merges with the Conservative Party.

27 The term 'plural voting' refers to when one person is permitted to vote several times. The Representation of the People Act 1948 puts an end to this illegal practice.

Chapter 14: The World Wars and the Rise of Welsh National Consciousness

1. William Pritchard Morgan is a Member for Merthyr Tydfil (1888–1900).

2. For more, cf. David Parry's *A Survey of Anglo-Welsh Dialects*, the South-east, 1977 and South-west, 1979.

3. This belief has its origins in the 18th century (cf. Theophilus Evans, **1716**). A myth circulated that the Bible had been translated into Welsh (i.e. British Celtic) during the time of Joseph of Arithmathea who would have visited Britain shortly after the crucifixion of Christ. Joseph of Arimathea was to have collected the last drops of Christ's blood in a chalice while he was still on the cross. This legend is also associated with the Arthurian stories surrounding the quest for the 'holy grail', such as *Perceval le Gallois* by Chrétien de Troyes and Peredur ab Efrawg (Mabinogion).

4. The National Museum of Wales (Amgueddfa Cymru) now includes eight museums: the National Museum (Cardiff); St Fagans National History Museum (Cardiff); Big Pit National Coal Museum (Blaenafon); National Woollen Museum (Dre-fach Felindre, near Llandysul); National Slate Museum, Llanberis; National Roman Legionary Museum (Caerleon); National Waterfront Museum (Swansea); Turner House Gallery (Penarth).

5. The Davies sisters are the granddaughters of David Davies (1818–90), a railway and coal entrepreneur from Llandinam, near Newtown, Powys. He was also MP for Cardigan (1874–85), and Cardiganshire (1885–6).

6. Born in Tenby (Pembrokeshire), most of his portraits are exhibited at the National Portrait Gallery in London, such as his two portraits of Lawrence of Arabia (1919, 1929) and one of Lady Ottoline Morrell, an English patron of the arts. His sister Gwen John (1876–1939) is also a painter and sculptor and Auguste Rodin's model.

7. Born in Llanelli (Carmarthenshire), he is a close friend of Augustus John with whom he spends some time in Marseille between 1909 and 1913. He admires the work of William Turner (1775–1851) and John Constable (1776–1837). His famous paintings are *The Seine at Caudebec* (1908) and *The Cathedral at Elne* (1911). He dies of tuberculosis in 1914.

8. The ILP (Independent Labour Party) was founded in 1893. It is affiliated to the Labour Party between 1906 and 1932, before it decides to leave completely.

9. There seems to be no basis for the common claim that the British Army placed troops from the Celtic countries in particularly difficult combat areas in order to spare the lives of English troops.

10. Main works: *Eighteen poems* (1934), *Twenty-Five Poems* (1936), *The Map of Love* (1939), *Portrait of the Artist as a Young Dog* (1940), *Country Sleep* (1952), and *Under Milk Wood* (published posthumously in 1954).

11. The Welsh Guards participate in the First World War (La Somme, Arras, Ypres); Second World War (defence of Arras and Boulogne, 1940; North Africa, 1943; and Italy, 1944–5); and the Falkland Islands (1982).

12 He was born in Trawsfynydd, Merionethshire in 1887.

13 Herbert Fisher is the President of the Board of Education (1916–22).

14 The Congress of Industrial Organization (CIO) merges with the American Federation of Labour (AFL) in 1955 and becomes AFL-CIO, the most powerful trade union of the United States.

15 Arthur Horner is the President of the South Wales Miners' Federation (1936–46) and General Secretary of the National Union of Mineworkers (NUM, 1946–59). He is one of the founders of the British Communist Party and leads the Welsh section.

16 'Mass picketing' means that the strikers (or picketers) occupy the factory, thus blocking production.

17 Sir Ifor Williams (1881–1965) is a renowned Welsh scholar and one of the foremost specialists in Old Welsh poetry. He edited the *Bulletin of the Board of Celtic Studies*, 1937–48. He was knighted for his work in 1947.

18 Lewis Jones (1897–1939) was a committed author and trade-unionist, born in Clydach Vale (Rhondda). He was a member of the Communist Party of Great Britain between 1923 and 1925 while studying in London. He participated in the General Strike of 1926 and supported the Spanish Republicans during the Civil War (1937–9).

19 *William Jones* (1944) is about a man who decides to leave Gwynedd in order to find work as a collier in south Wales.

20 *Chwalfa* (1946) is inspired by the strike at Penrhyn Quarry, Gwynedd (cf. **1900–3**).

21 Aneurin Bevan (1897–1960), MP for Ebbw Vale (1929–60), Minister of Health (1945–51), Deputy Leader of the Labour Party (1959–60).

22 James Griffiths (1890–1975), President of the South Wales Miners' Federation (1934–6), MP for Llanelli (1936–70), Minister for National Insurance (1945–50), Secretary of State for the Colonies (1950–1), Deputy Leader of the Labour Party (1955–9).

Chapter 15: The Post-War Period and the Struggle for Civil Rights (1946–1997)

1 Huw T. Edwards resigns in 1958 because he is against the influence of Whitehall over Welsh affairs. He is a member of *Plaid Cymru* from 1959 to 1965.

2 *Hen Dŷ Ffarm* is translated into English by Waldo Williams in 1961, under the title 'The Old Farmhouse'.

3 The Venice Biennale is an international art festival founded in 1895, but also extends to music, cinema, and architecture. Another festival where Welsh artists assert themselves is 'Artes Mundi' at the National Museum of Cardiff.

4 This prize is named after Giulio Einaudi, an Italian publisher and son of an Italian president, Luigi Einaudi (1948–55).

5 Meic Stephens is literature director of the Welsh Arts Council from 1967 to 1990.

He publishes an invaluable *Companion to the Literature of Wales* (1986) and *New Companion to the Literature of Wales* (1998).

6   There are six Labour MPs: Leo Abse, MP for Torfaen (1958–87); Neil Kinnock, MP for Bedwellty (1970–83); Donald Anderson, MP for Swansea East (1974–2005); Alfred Evans, MP for Caerphilly (1968–79); Ifor Davies, MP for Gower (1959–82), and Ioan Evans, MP for Birmingham Yardley (1964–70), Aberdare (1974–83) and Cynon Valley (1983–4).

7   There are currently over 1,000 of these sites and they cover 12 per cent of the territory.

8   Ramsar is the name of a city in Iran where an international convention was signed in 1971 (and ratified by the UK Government in 1973) to protect wetlands (eight sites in Wales).

9   'Chernobyl sheep controls lifted in Wales and Cumbria' (BBC Wales, 22 March 2012), http://www.bbc.co.uk/news/uk-wales-17472698 accessed 18 February 2015

10   Key stages are conceived as part of the National Curriculum. They are divided according to pupils' ages: KS1 (5–7 years), KS2 (7–11 years), KS3 (11–14 years), KS4 (14–16 years).

11   After Italy joins the competition in 2000, it becomes known as the Six Nations Championship.

12   The *Festival Interceltique* of Lorient has been held every year since 1971. Singers come from Celtic countries (Scotland, Wales, Brittany, Ireland, the Isle of Man), but also the United States (Eileen Ivers, Gaelic Storm, Clandestine, and Lily Neill), Canada (Dominique Dupuis, Loreena McKennitt), Galicia (an autonomous community of Spain where Carlos Nuŷez comes from), and Corsica (I Muvrini).

Chapter 16: Wales since Devolution

1   The building is named after Hywel Dda (cf. **945**).

2   Fifteen Labourites out of 28 (53.5 per cent); six Plaid Cymru out of 17 (35.3 per cent); no Conservatives; and three Liberal Democrats out of six (50 per cent).

3   Wales also actively participates in some networks, such as NRG4SD (or Network of Regional Governments for Sustainable Development), created in 2005 during the Johannesburg summit by a group of regions committed to a policy of sustainable development; reunited in Cardiff in March 2004.

4   'The Assembly shall make a scheme setting out how it proposes, in the exercise of its function, to promote sustainable development.'

5   He is MP for Anglesey in the UK Parliament (1987–2001), and AM in the Welsh Assembly (since 1999).

6   Article by Iolo ap Dafydd, 'Foot and mouth fears in Wales 10 years on from outbreak,' on BBC (19 February, 2011).

7   Ivor Richard: MP for Barons Court (1964–74), British Ambassador to the United

Nations (1974–9), EU Commissioner for Employment and Social Affairs (1981–5), Lord Privy Seal and Leader of the House of Lords (1997–8). He was born in Carmarthenshire in 1932.

8   Iwan Bala was born in 1956 in Bala and has won numerous prizes, nationally and internationally, for his art. In 1997 he won the gold medal for fine art at the National Eisteddfod in Bala, Gwynedd.

9   She is a Welsh artist born in 1934 in Pontarfynach, Ceredigion.

10 19 out of 30 Labourites (63 per cent), six out of 12 Plaid Cymru, three out of six Liberal Democrats, and two out of 11 Conservatives (18 per cent).

11 A White Paper is a pilot study of a law in order to anticipate the reaction of the political parties. It may be preceeded by a Green Paper which is for discussion only.

12 The candidate who wins most of the votes gets elected.

13 The voter votes for candidates according to their preference.

14 His famous paintings include *Capel Celyn* (1997) and *Postcards Series, Welsh Lady* (2003).

Who's Who in Welsh History

Aedan Mac Gabrain, King of Dal Riada (574–609) **603**

Aethelbald, King of Mercia (716–757) **716–757**

Aethelbert, King of Kent (d. 616) **597, 601, 602, 616**

Aethelfrith, King of Bernicia, and later Northumbria (593–616) **593, 603, 616**

Agitius, legendary king **446**

Alan II 'Wrybeard', Duke of Brittany (938–952) **937**

Alfred the Great, King of Wessex (871–899) **871–99, 880, 924–939**

Allectus, Roman usurper (293–296) **286–293, 296–305**

Athelred II the Unready, King of England (978–1013, 1014–16) **1042–1066**

Ambrosius Aurelianus, King of the Brythons (Welsh: *Emrys Wledig*) **446, 469, 496**

Amminius, son of Cunobelinus **AD 40**

Anarawd ap Rhodri, King of Gwynedd (878–916) **878–916, 879, 881, 894, 895**

Angharad, wife of Rhodri Mawr **856**

Angharad, daughter of Maredudd ab Owain **1039**

Anthemius, Roman emperor (467–472) **469**

Antoninus Pius, Roman emperor (138–161) **142**

Arthur, legendary king **383–388, 470–540, 496, 515–530**

Arthur I, Duke of Brittany (1201–3) **1199, 1202**

Arthur III, Duke of Brittany (1457–8) **1429**

Athelstan, King of Wessex (924–39) **924–939, 929, 935, 937**

Aulus Plautius, 1st Roman Governor of Britain (43–7) **AD 43**

Bernard de Neufmarché, Norman lord **1088–1095, 1093**

Bleddyn ap Cynfyn, King of Powys and Gwynedd (1063–75) **1039, 1063–1075**

Boudicca, Queen of the *Iceni* (killed in 61) **61**

Brennus (1), Celtic leader **279–278 BC**

Brennus (2), Celtic leader **390 BC**

Brochfael Ysgithrog, King of Powys (c.540–c.560) **560–630**

Cadell ap Rhodri, King of Seisyllwg (878–909) **895, 904–905**

Cadfan ap Iago, King of Gwynedd (616–25) **625, 640**

Cadwaladr ap Cadwallon, King of Gwynedd (655–82) **655–682**

Cadwaladr ap Gruffudd, third son of Gruffudd ap Cynan (d. 1172) **1136**

Cadwallon ap Cadfan, King of Gwynedd (625–34) **625, 632–633, 634**

Cadwallon Llawhir, King of Gwynedd (c.470–534) **470**

Cadwgan ap Bleddyn, King of Powys (1075–1111) **1075–1111, 1094–1100**

Canute (or Cnut) of Denmark, King of England (1016–35) and Denmark (1018–35) **1018–1035**

Caracalla, Roman emperor (211–17) **214**

Caradog ap Gruffudd, King of Gwent (1075–81) **1072, 1078, 1081**

Caratacus (Welsh: *Caradog*, Breton: *Caradec*), King of *Catuvellauni* **AD 40, 47–52**

Carausius (Welsh: *Carawn*), Roman usurper (286–93) **286–293**

Cartimandua, Queen of the *Brigantes* (43– 69) **AD 51, 68–69**

Catherine II, Russian empress (1762–96) **1737**

Cerdic, first King of Wessex (519–34) **495, 508**

Ceredig ap Gwallog, King of Elmet (precise dates unknown) **617**

Charles I, King of England (1625–49) **1625, 1646, 1647, 1649**

Charles II, King of England (1660–85) **1660, 1661–1665, 1678–1681, 1685**

Charles II 'the bald', King of France (843–77) and Holy Roman Emperor (875–7) **856**

Charles IV, King of France (1322–8) **1322, 1325**

Charles the simple, King of France (898–922) **911**

Charles V, King of France (1364–80) **1337**

Charles VI, King of France (1380–1422) **1404, 1406**

Charles VII, King of France (1429–61)

Charles, Prince of Wales (since 1969) 1969 **1429**

Clodius Albinus, Roman Governor of Britain (191–7) and rival of Septimus Severus **193–197**

Coel Hen, Brythonic king (precise dates unknown) **850**

Constantine I, Roman emperor (306–37) **306, 306–324**

Constantine II, King of *Alba* (900–43) **937**

Constantine III, Roman usurper (406–11) **406, 411**

Constantius Chlorus, *Caesar* (293–306) of Gaul, Spain and Britain **296–305, 306**

Constantius II , Roman emperor (337–61) of the Western Roman Empire **350–353**

Cunedda, leader from the Brythonic *Votadini* tribe **383, 470, 490–570**

Cunobelinus (Welsh: *Cynfelyn*), King of the *Catuvellauni* **AD 30**

Cyndyllan, King of Powys (precise dates unknown) **642, 655**

Cyngen ap Cadell, King of Powys (808–55) **808–855**

Dafydd I (Dafydd ab Owain Gwynedd), King of Gwynedd (1170–95, dies in exile in 1203) **1170–1195, 1174, 1194, 1197, 1201**

Dafydd II (Dafydd ap Llywelyn), King of Gwynedd (1240–45) **1220, 1226, 1229, 1240, 1241**

Dafydd III (born Dafydd ap Gruffudd), Prince of Wales (1282–3) **1255, 1274, 1282**

Dermot Mac Murrough, Irish King of Leinster (1126–71) **1169–1171**

Diocletian, Roman emperor (284–305) **293–311, 300, 303–311**

Eadbald, King of Kent (616–40) **616**

Eanfrith, King of Bernicia (633–4) **632–633, 634**

Edmund Mortimer, Lord Mortimer of Wigmore (1282–1304) **1282**

Edmund Mortimer, son-in-law of Owain Glyndŵr **1405, 1406**

Edmund Tudor, 1st Earl of Richmond (1452–6) **1431**

Edward 'the Black Prince', Prince of Wales (1343–76) **1343–1376, 1356, 1377**

Edward Bruce, 'High King' of Ireland (1315–18) **1315–1318**

Edward I, King of England (1272–1307) **1272, 1275, 1277, 1282, 1284, 1286, 1287–1288, 1297, 1307, 1757**

Edward II, King of England (1307–27) **cf. 1307, 1314, 1315–1318, 1316–1317, 1321–1322, 1325, 1326, 1327**

Edward III, King of England (1330–77) **1327–1330, 1343–1376, 1347, 1362, 1377**

Edward IV, King of England (1461–70, 1471–83) **1461–1470**

Edward the Confessor, King of Wessex (1042–66) **1042–1066, 1066**

Edward V, King of England (1483) **1470, 1483**

Edward VI, King of England (1547–53) **1547, 1553**

Edward VII, King of England (1901–10) **1862, 1901**

Edward VIII, King of England (1936) **1936**

Edwin, King of Northumbria (616–33) **616, 617, 626, 632–633**

Edwin ap Hywel Dda, King of Deheubarth (950–4) **950, 951, 952**

Egbert, king of Wessex (802-839) **829, 871–99**

Einion ap Owain (dies in 984) **960**

Eleanor of Aquitaine, queen of England (1152-1189) **1173, 1174, 1189**

Elisedd ap Gwylog (d. c.755) **808–855**

Elizabeth I, Queen of England (1558–1603) **1558, 1559, 1570, 1577, 1586, 1588, 1601**

Elizabeth II, Queen of the United Kingdom (since 1952) **1966, 1969**

Elizabeth Woodville, Queen of England (1464 until her death in 1483) **1461–1470**

Francis II (1433–88), Duke of Brittany (1458–88) **1485**

Galba, Roman emperor (68–9) **68–69**

Galerius, Roman emperor of Illyria (307–11) **293–311**

Geoffrey II, Duke of Brittany (1181–6) **1199**

George I of Hanover, King of Great Britain (1714–27) **1714**

George V, King of United Kingdom (1910–36) **1910, 1915, 1917,**

George VI, King of the United Kingdom (1936–52) **1936**

Gerontius (Welsh: *Gereint*), Constantine III's right-hand general **406, 411**

Gilbert de Clare, Lord of Glamorgan (1263–95) **1267–1271**

Gilbert de Clare, Lord of Glamorgan (1307–14) **1314**

Godwin, Earl of Wessex (1020–53) **1063**

Gruffudd ap Cynan, King of Gwynedd (1081–1137) **1075–1081, 1081, 1094–1100**

Gruffudd ap Gwenwynwyn, Prince of Powys Wenwynwyn (1241–87) **1274, 1286**

Gruffudd ap Llywelyn, King of Powys and Gwynedd (1039–63), Prince of Wales (1055–63) **1039, 1055, 1055–1063, 1070**

Gruffudd ap Llywelyn Fawr (d. 1244), father of Llywelyn II **1215, 1241, 1244, 1246**

Gruffudd ap Nicholas, sheriff of Carmarthenshire (1436–1456) and Deputy Justice of the South (1437–56) **1453, 1456**

Gruffudd ap Rhys, Prince of Deheubarth (1116–37) **1093, 1136**

Gruffudd de la Pole, 2nd Lord of Powis (1293–1309) **1286, 1309**

Gruffudd Llwyd (d. 1335), Lord of North Wales **1315–1318, 1322**

Gwenllian, Princess of Deheubarth (1116–37) and wife of Gruffudd ap Rhys **1136**

Gwenwynwyn ab Owain, Prince of Powys Wenwynwyn (1195–1216) **1198**

Hadrian, Roman emperor (117–38) **122**

Harold II Godwinson, King of England (1066) **1063, 1066**

Hengist and Horsa, Anglo-Saxon chieftains **449**

Henry Herbert, Earl of Pembroke (1570–1601), President of the Council of Wales and the Marches (1586–1601) **1595**

Henry I, King of England (1100–35) **1100–1135, 1105, 1135**

Henry II, King of England (1154–89) **1132–1160, 1154, 1157, 1162–1170, 1165, 1168, 1169–1171, 1173–1174, 1174, 1189**

Henry III, King of England (1216–72) **1216, 1220, 1227–1228, 1231–1234, 1240, 1247, 1264, 1267, 1267–1271, 1272**

Henry IV (born Henry of Bolingbroke), King of England (1399–1413) **1399, 1401, 1406**

Henry Percy, Earl of Northumberland (1377–1405), father of 'Hotspur' **1405**

Henry Percy ('Hotspur') (killed in 1403) **1403**

Henry V (born Henry of Monmouth), King of England (1413–22) **1413, 1415, 1422**

Henry VI, King of England (1422–61, 1470–1) **1422, 1429, 1431, 1450, 1469**

Henry VII Tudor, King of England (1485–1509) **1431, 1485, 1489–1502, 1505–1508**

Henry VIII, King of England (1509–47) **1504–1509, 1509, 1532–1540, 1536–1542**

Honorius, Emperor of the Western Roman Empire (395–423) **406, 410**

Hugh Despenser (younger), Lord of Glamorgan (1321–6) **1314, 1321–1322, 1326**

Hugh of Avranches, Earl of Chester (1071–1101) **1067–1099**

Hywel ab Owain Gwynedd, King of Gwynedd (1170) **1170**

Hywel ap Rhys, King of Glywysing (840–86) **840–886**

Hywel Dda, King of Deheubarth (909–50), Prince of Wales (942–50) **904–905, 928–935, 942, 945, 946, 950**

Ida, King of Bernicia (c.547–59) **547**

Idwal ab Anarawd (Idwal Foel), King of Gwynedd (916–42) **942, 950**

Ieuaf ab Idwal, King of Gwynedd (950–69) **950, 951, 952**

Iago ab Idwal, King of Gwynedd (950–79) **950, 951, 952**

Ina, King of Wessex (688–726) **690**

Isabella of France, Queen of England (1307–27) **1307, 1325, 1326, 1327–1330**

James VI and I, King of Scotland and England (1603–25) **1603, 1605**

James I, King of Scotland (1406–37) **1405**

James II, King of England (1685–8) **1678–1681, 1685, 1688, 1689**

Jasper Tudor, Earl of Pembroke (1452–61, 1485–95)

Joan, wife of Llywelyn Fawr and Princess of Wales (1203/04–37) **1205, 1216, 1229, 1431**

John I 'Lackland' or 'Softsword', King of England (1199–1216) **1173–1174, 1201, 1205, 1213–1214, 1215, 1216**

John II the Good, King of France (1350–64) **1356**

John IV of Montfort, Duke of Brittany (1341–5) **1342**

Julian the Apostate, Roman emperor (360–3) **361–363**

Julius Agricola, Roman Governor of Britain (78–84) **78–84, 83**

Julius Asclepiodotus, Praetorian prefect and consul (292) **296–305**

Julius Caesar (100 BC – 44 BC), Roman leader **1,400 BC, 100 BC, 58–50 BC, 55 BC, 52 BC, 27 BC**

Julius Frontinus, Roman Governor of Britain (74–8) **74**

Kynan Garwyn, King of Powys (c.550–600) **560–630, 616**

Leofric, Earl of Mercia (1017–57) **1039, 1055**

Licinius, ruler of the eastern empire (313–24) **293–311, 306–324**

Llywelyn ap Iowerth (Llywelyn I, known as Llywelyn Fawr), King of Gwynedd (1195–1240) and Prince of Wales (1216–40) **1195–1240, 1197, 1201, 1205, 1215, 1215–1217, 1216, 1218, 1227–1228, 1229, 1231–1234, 1240**

Llywelyn ap Merfyn, King of Powys (900–42) **942**

Llywelyn ap Seisyll, Prince of Powys and Deheubarth (1018–23) **1039**

Llywelyn Bren **1316–1317, 1326**

Llywelyn II 'the last', Prince of Wales (1246–82) **1246, 1247, 1255, 1257, 1267, 1274, 1275, 1277, 1278, 1282**

Louis VII, King of France (1137–80) **1168**

Louis XIII, King of France (1610–43) **1625**

Louis XIV, King of France (1661–1715) **1625**

Madog ap Gruffydd Maelor, Prince of Powys Fadog (1191–1236) **1201**

Madog ap Maredudd, Prince of Powys (1132–60) **1132–1160**

Maelgwn Gwynedd, King of Gwynedd (534–49) **490, 549–550**

Magnentius, Roman usurper (350–3) **350–353**

Magnus Maximus (Welsh: *Maxen Wledig*), Roman usurper (383–8) **383–388**

Marcus Roscius Coelius, Roman Governor of Britain (69) **68–69**

Marcus Trebellius Maximus, Roman Governor of Britain (63–9) **68–69**

Marcus Vettius Bolanus, Roman Governor of Britain (69–71) **68–69**

Maredudd ab Owain, Prince of Wales (986–99) **986–999, 989, 1039**

Maredudd ab Owain ab Edwin, King of Deheubarth (1063–72) **1072**

Mary I, Queen of England (1553–8) and Spain (1556–8) **1553**

Mary Stuart, Queen of Scotland (1542–67) and France (1559–60) **1586**

Matilda, Queen of England (1135–54) **1135, 1136**

Maximinus Daia, Roman *Caesar* (305–8) and *Augusti* (310–12) **293–311**

Maximus, Roman usurper of Hispania (409–11, 420–2) **406**

Merfyn Frych, King of Gwynedd (825–44) **825–844**

Morgan ab Athrwys, King of Glamorgan (d. 665) **665**

Morgan ab Owain, King of Morgannwg (or Glamorgan) (930–74) **942**

Nero, Roman emperor (54–68) **61**

Nerva, Roman emperor (96–8) **97**

Niall of the Nine Hostages, Irish king (5th century) **405**

Nicholas II, Russian emperor (1895–1917) **1837–1901, 1917**

Offa, king of Mercia (757–96) **757, 760, 776, 796**

Olaf III Guthfrithsson, King of Dublin, Ireland (934–41) and Northumbria (939–41) **937**

Oliver Cromwell, leader of Commonwealth (1649–58) **1649, 1658**

Osric, King of Deira (632/633–4) **632–633**

Ostorius Scapula, Roman Governor of Britain (47–52) **47–52, 48**

Oswald, King of Bernicia (634–42) **634, 642, 655**

Oswy, King of Bernicia (642–70) **635, 638, 655**

Otho, Roman emperor (January to April 69) **68–69**

Owain ap Gruffudd (d. 1282), brother of Llywelyn II and Dafydd III **1247**

Owain Gwynedd, King of Gwynedd (1137–70) **1136, 1154, 1157, 1162–1170, 1165, 1168, 1170**

Owain ap Hywel Dda, King of Deheubarth (950–87) **950, 951, 952, 960, 986–999**

Owain ap Maredudd (also known as Owain Tudor, d. 1461), grandfather of Henry Tudor **1431, 1461–1470**

Owain ap Urien Rheged, son of Urien Rheged **470–540**

Owain Cyfeiliog, Prince of Powys Wenwynwyn (1160–95) **1160–1195**

Owain de la Pole, 1st Lord of Powis (1286–93) **1286**

Owain Glyndŵr, leader of the revolt against England (1400–13) **1354, 1385, 1390, 1400, 1402, 1403, 1405, 1406, 1408**

Owain Lawgoch (born Owain ap Thomas ap Rhodri), pretender to the title of 'Prince of Gwynedd' **1337, 1360**

Owen I, King of Strathclyde (killed in 937) **937**

Penda, King of Mercia (killed in 655) **632–633, 642, 655**

Petilius Cerealis, Roman Governor of Britain (71–4) **71**

Philip II Augustus, King of France (1180–1223) **1213–1214, 1215, 1215–1217**

Philip II of Spain, King of England (1553–8) and Spain (1556–98) **1553**

Philip IV 'the fair', King of France (1285–1314) **1307**

Philippus II Severus, Roman emperor (237–49) **237**

Postumus, Roman usurper of the Gallic empire (259–74) **259–274**

Raedwald, King of East Anglia (600–24) **616**

Rhianfellt, wife of Oswy of Bernicia **635**

Rhiwallon ap Cynfyn, Prince of Powys and Gwynedd (1063–70) **1039, 1070**

Rhodri ap Hywel Dda, King of Deheubarth (950–3) **950, 951, 952**

Rhodri ab Owain Gwynedd, king of the western part of Gwynedd (1175–95) **1170–1195, 1175**

Rhodri Mawr, King of Gwynedd (844–78), Powys (855–78), and Seisyllwg (856–78) **844, 856, 872, 878**

Rhodri Molwynog, King of Gwynedd (until his death in 754) **705–709**

Rhun, son of Urien Rheged **626**

Rhydderch I Hael, king of Strathclyde (570-614) **573**

Rhys ab Owain, King of Deheubarth (1072–8) **1075, 1078**

Rhys ap Gruffudd ('Lord Rhys'), King of Deheubarth (1155–97) **1154, 1165, 1169–1171, 1176**

Rhys ap Maredudd, pretender to the throne of Deheubarth **1287–1288, 1292**

Rhys ap Tewdwr, King of Deheubarth (1078–93) **1081, 1093**

Richard Cromwell, son of Oliver Cromwell and leader of the Commonwealth (1658–9) **1659**

Richard de Clare, Earl of Pembroke ('Strongbow') **1169–1171**

Richard I 'Lionheart', King of England (1189–99) **1173–1174, 1189, 1199, 1202**

Richard II, King of England (1377–99) **1343–1376, 1377, 1389, 1399, 1400**

Richard III, King of England (1483–5) **1483, 1485**

Richard Marshal, Earl of Pembroke (1231–4) **1231–1234**

Riothamos, King of the Brythons **469**

Robert Fitzhamon, Lord of Gloucester **1093**

Robert I 'the Bruce', King of Scotland (1306–29) and brother of Edward Bruce **1315–1318**

Roger Mortimer of Wigmore, Baron Mortimer (1304–30) and Earl of March (1328–30) **1284, 1315–1318, 1321–1322, 1325, 1326, 1327–1330**

Roger Mortimer of Chirk **1284, 1315–1318, 1321–1322**

Roger of Montgomery, Earl of Shrewsbury (1071–94) **1067–1099**

Selyf ap Cynan, King of Powys (killed in 616), son of Kynan Garwyn **616**

Rory O'Connor, King of Connacht (1156–86), then High King of Ireland (1166–98)
   1169–1171

Septimus Severus, Roman emperor (193–211) **193–197, 211**

Severus, Emperor of Italy and Africa (306–7) **293–311**

Simon de Montfort, 6th Count of Leicester (1239–65) and 1st Earl of Chester (1264–5)
   1264–1267, 1265

Spencer, Lady Diana, Princess of Wales (1981–97) **1997**

Sophia of the Rhineland-Palatinate, mother of George I **1714**

Stephen Bauzan, Seneschal of Gascony (1255–7) **1257**

Stilicho, Roman General and Regent of Honorius (395–408) **399–408**

Suetonius Paulinus, Roman Governor of Britain (58–62) **61**

Tewdos ap Rhain, Irish King of Dyfed (until 710) **405**

Theodosius I, Emperor of eastern Roman empire (379-395) **367, 383–388**

Togodumnus (killed by the Romans in AD 43), son of Cunobelinus **AD 40**

Trahaearn ap Caradog, King of Gwynedd (1075–81) **1075–1081, 1081**

Urien Rheged, King of Rheged (Welsh: *Urbgen*, d. 593) **515–590, 570, 572–592, 593,
   626, 850**

Vercingetorix, leader of the Gaulish revolt against the Romans (58 BC – 52 BC) **52 BC**

Vespasian, Roman emperor (69–79) **68–69, 71**

Victoria, Queen of the United Kingdom (1839–1901) **1837–1901, 1862**

Vitellius, Roman emperor (April to December 69) **68–69**

Vortigern (Welsh: *Gwrtheyrn*) **420–450, 428, 449, 469, 1847**

Vortiporix, King of Dyfed (540–50) **549–550**

William de Braose, Lord of Brycheiniog (Breconshire), Abergavenny (Monmouthshire)
   and Builth Wells (Powys) **1229**

William Fitzosbern, Earl of Hereford (1067–71) **1067–1099**

William Herbert, Earl of Pembroke (1468–9) **1461–1470, 1469**

William I 'the conqueror', Duke of Normandy and first Anglo-Norman King of England
   (1066–87) **1066, 1067–1099, 1081**

William II, King of England (1087–1100) **1087**

William III of Orange, King of England (1688–1702) **1688, 1696**

Bibliography

Abalain, H., *Terre des Celtes: Histoire du Pays de Galles* (Editions Jean Paul Gisserot, 1991).

Abalain, H., 'Vers une nouvelle identité galloise?' in G. German, A. Hellegouarc'h and J.-Y. Le Disez (eds), *Pays de Galles: quelle(s) image(s)? What visibility for Wales?* (Brest, 2009), pp. 81–101.

Abels, R., *Alfred the Great: War, Kingship, and Culture in Anglo-Saxon England,* (Routledge, 2013).

Aitchinson, J. and H. Carter, *The Welsh Language, 1961–81: An Interpretative Atlas* (Cardiff, 1985).

Alcock, L., *Arthur's Britain* (Penguin Books, 1971, 1983).

Alinei, M., 'The Paleolithic Continuity Theory on Indo-European Origins: An Introduction', *Studi Celtici, An International Journal of History, Linguistics, and Cultural Anthropology*, Vol. II (Bologna, 2003).

Alinei, M. and F. Benozzo, 'Megalithism as a manifestation of an Atlantic Celtic Primacy in Meso-Neolithic Europe', *Studi Celtici: An International Journal of History, Linguistics, and Cultural Anthropology*, Vol. VII (Bologna, 2008–9), pp. 13–72.

Bala, I., 'Re:Imaging Wales. Wales-Art-World', in G. German, A. Hellegouarc'h and J.-Y. Le Disez (eds), *Pays de Galles: quelle(s) image(s)? What visibility for Wales?* (Brest, 2009), pp. 180–97.

Blake, N. F., *A History of the English Language* (London, 1996).

Bory, S., 2009, 'La politique environnementale de l'Assemblée: une vitrine pour le Pays de Galles?', in G. German, A. Hellegouarc'h, J.-Y. Le Disez (eds), *Pays de Galles: quelle(s) image(s)?-What visibility for Wales?* (Brest, 2009), pp. 113–27.

Bowen E. G. and C. A. Gresham, *History of Merioneth*, Volume 1 (Dolgellau, 1967).

Bowen, G., 'Roman Catholic Prose and its Background', in R. G. Gruffydd (ed.), *A Guide to Welsh Literature (c.1530–1700)*, Volume 3 (Cardiff, 1997), pp. 210–40.

Bromwich, R., *Trioedd Ynys Prydein* (Cardiff, 1978).

Camp-Pietrain, E., *La Dévolution: Ecosse, Pays de Galles* (2006).

Carr, A. D., 'Welshmen and the Hundred Years' War', *Welsh History Review*, Vol. 4 (1968), pp. 21–46.

Cavalli-Sforza, L. L. et al., 'The Genetic Legacy of Paleolithic Homo Sapiens in Extant Europeans: A Y Chromosome Perspective', *Science*, Vol. 290, No. 5494 (2000), pp. 1155–9.

Chadwick, N., *The Druids* (Llandybie, 1966).

Chadwick, N., *Early Brittany* (Cardiff, 1969).

Chadwick, N., *British Heroic Age* (Cardiff, 1976).

Charles-Edwards, T. M., *The Welsh Laws* (1989).

Charles-Edwards, T. M., *Wales and the Britons, 350–1064* (Oxford, 2013).

Chemereau, H., 'Quand le Port de Saint Nazaire vivait à l'Heure Galloise', in *Place Publique – Nantes/Saint Nazaire*, No. 25 (January–February 2011), pp. 69–73.

Cheyney, E., *Readings in English History* (1908, 1922).

Clavel, M. and P. Levêque, *Villes et Structures Urbaines dans L'occident Romain* (1971).

Cunliffe, B., *Europe between the Oceans, 9000 BC – AD 1000* (New Haven, 2008).

Davies, J., *The Welsh Language* (Cardiff, 1993).

Davies, J., *A History of Wales* (Penguin Books, 1994).

Davies, J. et al., *Gwyddoniadur Cymru* (Yr Academi Gymreig, 2008).

Davies, R. R. and G. Morgan, *Owain Glyn Dŵr, Prince of Wales* (Talybont, 2009).

Dillon, M. and N. K. Chadwick, *Les Royaumes Celtiques* (1979).

Dumville, D., *Britons and Anglo-Saxons in the Early Middle Ages* (1993).

Evans, G., *Land of My Fathers: 2000 Years of Welsh History* (John Penry Press, 1976).

Fischer, D. H., *Albion's Seed* (Oxford, 1989).

Fleuriot, L., *Les Origines de la Bretagne* (1980).

Foot, S., *Athelstan: The First King of England* (Yale, 2012).

Forster, P., 'Evolution of English basic vocabulary within the network of Germanic languages', in Peter Forster and Colin Renfrew (eds), *Phylogenetics Methods and the Prehistory of Languages* (Cambridge, 2006), pp. 131–7.

Freeman, P., 'Ancillary Study: Ancient References to Tartessos', in J. Koch and B. Cunliffe (eds), *Celtic from the West: Alternative Perspectives from Archaeology, Genetics, Language and Literature* (Oxford, 2010), pp. 303–34.

Garlick, R., *An Introduction to Anglo-Welsh Literature* (Cardiff, 1972).

Garlick, R. and R. Mathias, *Anglo-Welsh Poetry (1480–1980)* (Seren, 1982).

German, G., 'La triade des fléaux (n°36): quelques perspectives d'analyses', in H. Bouget and M. Coumert (eds), *Histoires des Bretagnes, Itinéraires et Confins* (Brest, 2011), pp. 19–35.

Gooden, P., *The Story of English: How the English Language Conquered the World* (Quercus, 2009).

Gray, T., *Poems: With a Selection of Letters and Essays* (Dent & Dutton, 1912, 1946).

Gruffudd, H., *Real Wales: A Guide* (Talybont, 1998, 2001).

Haycock, M., 'Problem der Frühmittelalterlichen Kymrischen Metrik', in H. L. C. Tristam, *Metrik und Medienwechsel / Metrics and Medias* (Tübingen, 1991).

Hays, R. W., 'Welsh Students at Oxford and Cambridge Universities in the Middle Ages', *Welsh History Review*, Vol. 4 (1969), pp. 325–61.

Hechter, M., *Internal Colonialism* (London, 1975).

Hunter, T. G., 'Contemporary Welsh Poetry, 1969–1996', in D. Johnston (ed.), *A Guide to Welsh Literature*, Volume 6 (Cardiff, 1998), pp. 117–58.

Isaac G., 'The Origins of the Celtic Languages, Language Spread from East to West' in J. T. Koch and B. Cunliffe, *Celtic from the West: Alternative Perspectives from Archaeology, Genetics, Language and Literature* (Oxford, 2010), pp. 153–67.

Jackson, K., *Language and History in Early Britain: A Chronological Survey of the Brittonic Languages, 1st to 12th c. A.D* (Edinburgh, 1953, 1963).

Jackson, K., *The Gododdin* (Edinburgh, 1969).

Jarman, A. O. H., *Aneirin y Gododdin* (Llandysul, 1990).

Jarman, A. O. H. and G. R. Hughes, *A Guide to Welsh Literature,* Volume 2 (Christopher Davies Editions, 1984).

Jenkins, G. H., *A Concise History of Wales* (Cambridge, 2007).

Johnston, D., *Iolo Goch Poems* (Llandysul, 1993).

Jones, F. M., *Welsh Ballads of the French Revolution, 1793–1815* (Cardiff, 2012).

Jones, M. and G. Leydier, *La Dévolution des Pouvoirs à l'Ecosse et au Pays de Galles* (2006, 2008).

Khleif, B., 'Ethnic Awakening in the First World: the Case of Wales,' in G. Williams (ed.), *Social and Cultural Change in Contemporary Wales* (London, 1978), pp. 102–19.

Koch, J. T. and J. Carey, *The Celtic Heroic Age: Literary Sources for Ancient Celtic Europe and Early Ireland and Wales* (2000).

Koch, J. T. (ed.), *The Gododdin of Aneirin: Text and Context from the Dark Ages North Britain* (Cardiff, 1997).

Koch, J. T., *Celtic Culture: A Historical Encyclopedia* (2006).

Koch, J. T. and B. Cunliffe, *Celtic from the West: Alternative Perspectives from Archaeology, Genetics, Language and Literature* (Oxford, 2010).

Laing, L., *Britain before the Conquest: Celtic Britain* (1986).

Lepelley, C., *Rome et l'intégration de l'empire: Tome 2 – Approches Régionales du Haut-Empire Romain* (1998).

Lewis, B., *Opening up the Archives of Welsh Poetry: Welshness and Englishness during the Hundred Years' War* (Aberystwyth, 2009)   Lewis, C. W., 'The Court Poets: Their Function, Status, and Craft', in A. O. H Jarman and G. R. Hughes (eds), *A Guide to Welsh Literature,* Volume 1 (Cardiff, 1992), pp. 123–56

Lewis, R. L., *Welsh Americans: A History of Assimilation in the Coalfields* (University of North Carolina Press, 2008).

Lloyd, N., 'Late Free-Metre Poetry', in R. G. Gruffydd (ed.), *A Guide to Welsh Literature c.1530–1700* (Cardiff, 1997), pp. 100–27.

Lord, P., 'Imaging the Nation', in G. German, A. Hellegouarc'h and J.-Y. Le Disez (eds), *Pays de Galles: quelle(s) image(s)? What visibility for Wales?* (Brest, 2009), pp. 199–217.

Mattingly, D., *An Imperial Possession: Britain in the Roman Empire* (Penguin Books, 2007).

May, J., *Reference Wales* (Cardiff, 1994).

Molinari, V., 2009, 'L'Assemblée Galloise: un modèle paritaire?', in G. German, A. Hellegouarc'h and J.-Y. Le Disez (eds), *Pays de Galles: quelle(s) image(s)? What visibility for Wales?* (Brest, 2009), pp. 129–47.

Morgan, K., *Wales in British Politics (1868–1922)* (Cardiff, 1963).

Nicholas, W. R., *The Folk Poets* (Cardiff, 1978).

Palgrave, Sir F., *History of the Anglo-Saxons* (1998).

Parry D., *A Survey of Anglo-Welsh Dialects, Volume 1, The South-East* (Swansea, 1977).

Parry D., *A Survey of Anglo-Welsh Dialects, Volume 2, The South-West* (Swansea, 1979).

Parry, T., *A History of Welsh Literature*, translated from the Welsh by H. Idris Bell (Oxford, 1955, 1970).

Parry, T., *The Oxford Book of Welsh Verse* (Oxford, 1962, 1981).

Persigout, J-P., *Dictionnaire de Mythologie Celtique* (2009).

Renfrew, C., *Archaeology and Language: The Puzzle of Indo-European Origins* (London, 1987).

Richards, M., *Welsh Administrative and Territorial Units* (Cardiff, 1969).

Roderick, A. J., *Wales through the Ages (From the earliest times to 1485)*, Volume 1 (Salesbury Press Ltd, 1959, 1975).

Roderick, A. J., *Wales through the Ages (From 1485 to the Beginning of the 20th Century)*, Volume 2 (Salesbury Press Ltd, 1959, 1975).

Rowlands, E. I., *Poems of the Cywyddwyr: A Selection of Cywyddau, 1375–1525* (1976).

Salway, P., *The Oxford Illustrated History of Roman Britain* (Oxford, 1993).

Schmidt, K. H., 'Insular P- and Q- Celtic', in M. Ball and J. Fife (eds), *The Celtic Languages* (London, 1993), pp. 64–100.

Scarre, C., *The Penguin Historical Atlas of Ancient Rome* (Penguin, 1995).

Stephens, M., *The New Companion to the Literature of Wales* (Cardiff, 1998).

Sykes, B., *Seven Daughters of Eve* (W. W. Norton & Company, 2001).

Sykes, B., *Saxons, Vikings and Celts: the Genetic Roots of Britain and Ireland* (Norton Paperbacks, 2007).

Vaughan-Thomas, W., *Wales: A History* (London, 1985).

Walter, H., *Honni soit qui mal y pense: l'incroyable histoire d'amour entre le français et l'anglais* (2001).

Warner, P., *Famous Welsh Battles* (1977).

Wells, S. and G. Taylor (eds), *The Complete Works* (1999).

Williams, D., *Cymru ac America (Wales and America)* (Cardiff, 1962).

Williams, G., *Welsh Poems, Sixth Century to 1600* (University of California Press, 1974).

Williams, I., *Canu Llywarch Hen* (Caerdydd, 1978).

Williams, I., *Armes Prydein: The Prophecy of Britain* (Dublin, 1972).

Williams, I., *The Poems of Taliesin* (Dublin, 1975).

Willis, D., 'Old and Middle Welsh', in M. Ball and N. Muller (eds), *The Celtic Languages* (London, 2009), pp. 117–60.

Williams, J. E. Caerwyn, *The Poets of the Welsh Princes* (Cardiff, 1978).

Websites

National Library of Wales: http://www.llgc.org.uk/

Welsh Biography Online: http://wbo.llgc.org.uk/en/index.html

National Museum of Wales: http://www.museumwales.ac.uk/en/home/

Glynn Vivian Art Gallery: http://www.swanseaheritage.net/museums/glynn.asp

Welsh Assembly Government: http://wales.gov.uk/

National Assembly of Wales: http://www.assemblywales.org/index.htm

http://www.britannia.com/wales/whist.html

http://www.eisteddfod.org.uk/english/

http://www.literaturewales.org/ty-newydd/ (Ty Newydd)

http://www.comisiynyddygymraeg.org/english/Pages/Home.aspx (Welsh Language Commissioner)

http://www.megalithic.co.uk/article.php?sid=2146412727 (about the Nannau Bucket)

http://www.museumwales.ac.uk/en/rhagor/article/1872/; http://www.museumwales.ac.uk/en/art/collections/williamswynn/ (on Watkins Williams-Wynn)

http://www.vam.ac.uk/moc/childrens_lives/education_creativity/education_england/index.html (Education Legislation in England since 1800 - Museum of Childhood)

http://history.powys.org.uk/history/common/educ3.html (Education in Wales)

http://digital.library.okstate.edu/encyclopedia/index.html (on Evan Jones)

http://www.llgc.org.uk/index.php?id=lettersformtheamericancivil (Letters from the American Civil War, John Griffith Jones)

First World War: http://www.1914-1918.net/

http://www.surgical-tutor.org.uk/default-home.htm?surgeons/owen_thomas.htm~right (on the Thomas Splint)

http://www.firstworldwar.com/battles/ypres3.htm

http://www.museumwales.ac.uk/en/art/collections/daviessisters/

http://ec.europa.eu/unitedkingdom/about_us/office_in_wales/index_en.htm (European Commission Office in Wales)

http://www.gardenofwales.org.uk/about-2/history-of-the-gardens/the-establishment-of-the-botanic-garden-at-middleton-hall/ (National Botanic Garden of Wales)

http://www.festival.si.edu/2009/wales/index.aspx; http://wales.gov.uk/newsroom/cultureandsport/2010/100702smithsonian/?lang=en (Smithsonian Folklife Festival, Washington DC)

http://www.cllc.org.uk/hafan-home?diablo.lang=eng (Welsh Books Council)

http://wales.gov.uk/about/cabinet/cabinetstatements/2011/110331one/?lang=en (about the One Wales Delivery Plan)

http://www.bbc.co.uk/news/uk-wales-politics-12648649 (Referendum, March 2011)

http://www.artcornwall.org/features/Iwan_Bala_Art_in_Wales.htm (article by Iwan Bala, *Art in Wales: Politics of Engagement or Engagement with Politics?*, 2010)